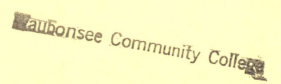

ANATOMY OF
GENIUS

ANATOMY OF GENIUS

SPLIT BRAINS AND GLOBAL MINDS

JAN EHRENWALD

Formerly Consulting Psychiatrist
Roosevelt Hospital
New York

 **HUMAN SCIENCES PRESS, INC.**
72 FIFTH AVENUE
NEW YORK, N.Y. 10011

Printed in the United States of America
0123456789

Library of Congress Cataloging in Publication Data

Ehrenwald, Jan
    Anatomy of genius.

    Includes index.
    1. Cerebral dominance.   2. Genius.   3. Split brain.
  4. Intellect.   I. Title.   [DNLM: 1.Creativeness.
2. Dominance, Cerebral.   3. Famous persons.   BF 412
E33a]
QP385.5.E37 1983   153.9'8   83-10704
ISBN 0-89885-148-3
ISBN 0-89885-292-7 paperback

CONTENTS

Foreword by Jules H. Masserman, M.D.   xi
Preface   xv
Acknowledgements   xix

I   INTRODUCTION   1

       1.   THE DIVIDED BRAIN   3

              Genius: More than IQ   5
              From Broca and Wernicke
                  to Split Brain Research   6
              Some Case Illustrations   11
              Horizontal Versus Vertical Organization   13
              Three R's Versus Three I's   14
              Lateralization and Two Cognitive Styles   18

II   GENIUS OBSERVED   21

       2.   BEETHOVEN: PORTRAIT OF A RIGHT
              HEMISPHERIC GENIUS   23

              Beethoven: Father and Son   25
              Hero, Antihero and the Existential Shift   30
              Right Hemispheric Dominance?   32

3.   NIETZSCHE: THUS SPAKE THE
RIGHT HEMISPHERE   36

Backward Child—Precocious Professor   37
Proto-Analyst Rather than Proto-Nazi   39
"Assaulted" by Zarathustra   41
"Inoculated" with Madness   45
Prophet of Own Doom   49

4.   LEONARDO DA VINCI: AMBIDEXTROUS
GENIUS   54

Science Versus Art   55
Existential Shift from Right to Left
Brain Dominance and Vice Versa   59
Homosexual? The Leonardo-
Salai Equation   62
Reconciliation of Opposites: How
Did He Do It?   68

5.   FREUD: SCIENCE VERSUS INTUITION   70

Scientist Versus Poet   71
Intuition or Aberration?   73
Freud and his Right-Brained Doubles   81
Freud against Oceanic Feeling: The
Hearing Cap and the Phylactery   83
Does the Left Hemisphere
Suppress the Right?   85

6.   JUNG'S SPLIT: A STUDY IN
COMPLEMENTARITY   88

Mystical Bent Versus Scientific
Aspiration   88
Spiritualistic Interludes   91
Collision and Break with Freud   94
Plunge into Psychosis or Shift
to Right Brain Dominance?   98
Self-Healing and Reconciliation of
Opposites   99

7.   MOZART, FATHER AND SON:
     TALENT VERSUS GENIUS   102

     Child Prodigy Who Throve on Closeness
        with Father   102
     Wolfgang Rebelling   105
     The Baesle Letters: Letting Go
        of Left Brain Controls   108
     Blending of Three I's and Three R's,
        Talent Exalted by Genius   112

8.   EINSTEIN: GENIUS EMERGING,
     TRIUMPHANT AND ECLIPSED   117

     Genius Who Will Never Amount
        to Anything   118
     Right Hemisphere and Genius
        Triumphant   121
     Rejects Quantum Theory: "God Does
        Not Play Dice"   125
     Genius Eclipsed: The Left Hemisphere in
        Ascendance. He Died from a Ruptured Aorta
        while God Was Apparently Playing Dice   128

9.   WHO WAS PABLO PICASSO? A CASE
     OF MULTIPLE IDENTITIES   131

     Picasso: Father and Son   132
     Pablo Rebellious   134
     Pablo Violent   137
     Multiple Personalities   140
     Who Was Pablo Picasso?   142
     Disowns Products of Own
        Right Hemisphere   144
     Both Child and Grandaddy of our Time   147

10. KAFKA'S CONFLICTS: THEME AND VARIATIONS   149

Psychoanalytic Perspectives   150
Existential Perspectives   154
Bi-Hemispheric Perspectives   155
Death from Starvation Foreseen by
   the Hunger Artist and the Saving Grace
   of Creativity   157

11. EILEEN GARRETT: FOUR VOICES
     OF A MEDIUM   161

Psychic, Author, Businesswoman   162
The Four Voices   163
The "Real" Eileen Garrett   166
"Psychic" Exploits and Personality Needs   169
"Psychics," "Holophrenics," and
   the Right Hemisphere   171

12. CORTES AND MONTEZUMA:
     A TALE OF TWO HEMISPHERES   174

Hernan Cortes   177
Montezuma   180
Meeting of Two Myths   186
Clash of Two Hemispheres   187

13. LEADERS, MIS-LEADERS
     AND THE REPTILIAN BRAIN:
     A DIGRESSION INTO PATHOLOGY   189

Leaders: Caesar, Napoleon,
   Churchill, et al.   189
Mis-Leaders: Hitler, Stalin, and
   the Reverend Jim Jones   191
Hitler: "Psychic," Shaman, or
   Paranoiac?   192
Mis-Leaders and the Reptilian Brain
   on the Rampage   198

III IMPLICATIONS   201

14. DEXTRAVERTS VERSUS SINISTRAVERTS: TWO
     VERSIONS OF BEING HUMAN?   203

     Two Psychological Types
        and Their Neural Matrix   203
     Lifecycle and Hemispheric Orientation   207
     How Can They Be Identified?   211
     The Importance of Being Bi-Hemispheric   213

15. RIGHT VERSUS LEFT HEMISPHERIC
     CYCLES IN HISTORY   216

     Right Hemispheric Ideologies   217
     Left Hemispheric Ideologies   219
     Right Versus Left Hemispheric
        Ideologies and the Generation Gap   220

16. NEUROSIS AND INTERHEMISPHERIC CONFLICT   225

     Clinical Vignettes   225
     Cursory Look at
        Shakespeare, Goethe et al.   232
     Can Analytic and Neurodynamic
        Readings Be Reconciled?   234
     "Repression" or Inhibition
        of Hemispheric Dominance?   237
     Some Diagnostic and Therapeutic
        Implicatons   239

17. WHAT GAIN HAS THE WORKER
     FROM HIS TOIL?   241

     Genius Restated   242
     The Cult of Education Versus the Cult
        of Illiteracy   244
     Toward a New Bi-Hemispheric
        Curriculum   248

18. LATERALIZATION AND THE FALL OF MAN 251

The Merits of Shifting Gears
and Linguistic Pluralism 252
Three Allegories of the Human
Condition: The Tree of Knowledge and
The Rise of the Left Hemisphere 254
Two Faces of Jesus and
the Wholeness of Man 257
Plato's Two Horses and
the Mysterious Charioteer 259

Epilogue 263
References 277
Glossary 287
Index 290

FOREWORD

Jan Ehrenwald, neurologist, psychiatrist, psychoanalyst, historian, philosopher and master of an erudite literary style, combines his talents in this intriguing book. Ehrenwald's principle themes are derived from observations by Sperry and Milner, Bear and Fedio, Desmet, Mandell and others who, by utilizing split-brain preparations, neo-plastic or other cerebral localizations and perceptual and cognitive studies, have demonstrated that in right-handed people the usually dominant left hemisphere "thinks" logically, categorically, syntactically and verbally, whereas the right hemisphere "feels" affectively and esthetically in mediating "intuition, imagination and inspiration." Ehrenwald holistically utilizes his own corpus callosum and anterior commissure to illuminate the lives of other "geniuses" who have delighted and elevated—or deluded and denigrated—mankind. Inadequate cinematic previews of attractions to come:

Ehrenwald attributes Beethoven's uncouth and often rude conduct and lifelong rebellion against Fate (equated with defiance of his cruel father) to a subdominant left brain, countered by a musically superb right hemisphere. Both influenced Beethoven's music, but the left brain dictated the precisely composed (and often harsh) odd numbered symphonies, and the right animated the more freely melodious and romantic even numbered ones. Beethoven devotees would add that this alternation is also apparent within many of his compositions; witness the unrelentingly mathematical introduction to his Third Rasoumoffsky string quartette, followed by the exquisite ethereality of the second movement, succeeded by the stereotyped pyrotechnics of the finale.

In the next chapter, Nietzsche, the ambiguous and syphilitic oracle of Zarathustra-Superman elevates (left) cerebral Apollo over dextrally unrestrained Dionysus—neglecting the circumstance that Apollo, Olympian god of science, was also the patron of art and music. Trying to maintain such dubious dichotomies may have helped drive Nietzsche mad.

Carl Jung, despite his preoccupations with intellectually unifying concepts such as "synchronicity" and a "Universal Unconscious," is portrayed by Ehrenwald as a predominantly right-hemispheric genius ridden by archetypal delusions of myths, spirits and magical mantras.

As in his discussion of Beethoven, Ehrenwald contrasts Mozart's dextrally irresponsible conduct and scatologic correspondence with the cerebrally sinistral elegance, purity, melody, harmony and counterpoint of his music. But even more interesting is Mozart's conjoint hemispheric resilience, as illustrated by an episode omitted by Ehrenwald: during the composer's courtship of the fickle Aloysia Weber, he wrote an exquisite love duet between viola (Mozart's favorite instrument) and violin (Aloysia) for his Symphonie Concertante. When she rejected him, no dirge followed; instead, he concluded the opus with a sprightly dance and married her younger sister Constanze.

Subsequent chapters elaborate Ehrenwald's concepts of other cerebral interactions. The ambidextrous savant-engineer/poet-artist Leonardo da Vinci is portrayed as history's most versatile genius, but with startling intellectual and esthetic failures when his hemispheres did not quite mesh. So also Freud, as purported scientist, outlined a well-reasoned "Project" for neuro-behavioral integration and decried "wild analysis," yet indulged in the latter in his biographies of Moses and Leonardo and in his essays on Totem and Taboo, and falterd sadly in his scotomatously sexual interpretation of the far more subtle, diverse and encompassing symbolisms of the Oedipus trilogy—to mention only *en passant* his excursions into the glories of cocaine and the cosmic significance of Fliess' numerology.

Similar themes, with appropriate Janusian variations in key and tempo, are developed in ensuing chapters on Einstein (dextrally inspired, left elaborated), Picasso (right artistic defiance to his tradition-oriented father; left catering to current tastes), Franz Kafka, Eileen Garrett, Hernan Cortes and Montezuma, with digressions to Goethe, Bach and Schuman. A spate of "leaders and misleaders" such as Caesar, Napoleon and Churchill *vs* Hitler, Stalin and Jim Jones are then cerebrally contrasted. Ehrenwald proposes that in the latter trio the dominant right hemisphere was also savaged by the lower "reptilian brain"—a Sherrington-Macleanian concept somewhat contrary to recent neuro-physiologic evidence that, while the so-called paleocortex may conceive primitive conations, the diencephalic centers mediate only the peripheral mimetics of affect and have little to do with either thought or motivation.

Reader, summon now all your erudition for the final section of the book. In Chapter 15 Ehrenwald ranges from tests of cerebral laterality to optimal child rearing, from social lags to historic "existential shifts," from rock and roll to the Shah of Iran, from sermons to skyscrapers and from Socrates to Khomeini—all with a wealth of cultural allusions and syncretically illuminating interpretations. As to Ehrenwald's thoughts on ideological cycles, the reader may recall that William James also described religious experiences that varied between left intellectual doubts and right luminescent transcendence. Chapter 16 follows with case vignettes to illustrate hemispheric dysharmony as a factor in neuroses. Chapter 17 proposes that you, too, can become a genius of sorts by cultivating cerebral synchrony. The terminal chapters and Epilogue explore ultimate pedagogic, social and philosophic controversies in which the reader is increasingly tempted to join.

Coda: The principal virtue of a book is its capacity to expand one's intellectual and esthetic horizons, as Anatomy of Genius did to mine. In previous writings I had proposed that the triune needs of mankind were, in brief, for (1) physical well being (2) social securities and (3) philosophic serenity. Yet after a day of largely left hemisphere research, teaching and clinical services which provided (1) a livelihood, (2) friends and (3) intellectual satisfactions, life still seemed incomplete until (1) I had returned home, (2) rejoined my wife and friends and (3) written some music and admired and/or played my Albani violin or viola. Manifestly, another more affectively and esthetically oriented cerebral hemisphere demanded equal expression. Right?

Jules H. Masserman, M.D.

AUTHOR'S PREFACE

Singing the praises of heroes and culture heroes has from time immemorial been a recurrent theme of legend and myth. Modern man is inclined to replace heroes and hero worship with analytic probing into the nature of genius, if not with his debunking and demythologizing. But he has also learned a sobering lesson: it is necessary to enlist genius in order to encompass the whole depth and width of genius.

However, we shall see that failing this, modern neuroscience, aided by psychoanalysis, Freudian, Jungian, or other, can at least provide a few clues about the mental machinery and the operation of the two sides of the brain that go into the making of genius. Chapter 1 will present a condensed survey of some of the facts and implications of contemporary splitbrain research. The Beethoven chapter will focus on the composer's life in terms of the dichotomy between hero and antihero, between the perfection of his art and the imperfections of his personality. The cleavage between the two will be correlated with the dichotomy of the right versus the left hemisphere.

Chapter 3 will present Nietzsche's genius as a tragic blend of all the inner conflicts and inconsistencies that threatened to rend apart the fabric of modern society, with Zarathustra serving as the mouthpiece—if not a ventriloquist's dummy—of the right hemisphere. The Freud and Jung chapters present the contrast and conflicting personalities of the two men as personifications of left versus right hemispheric preponderances. Chapter 4 focuses on Leonardo da Vinci's conflict between art and science, and its correlation to homosexuality and the two sides of the brain, with either Leonardo the artist or Leonardo the scientist in the driver's seat. The Mozart chapter focuses on the complementarity of the father's talent and the son's genius in left versus right hemispheric terms. The chapter on Einstein seeks to correlate the emergence, the triumph, and the eclipse of his genius with the changing patterns of right versus left hemispheric preponderance.

The Picasso chapter seeks to account for the many styles and periods of the master in terms of multiple personalities. A digression to Eileen Garrett, the gifted American trance medium, writer, and publisher, discusses the part played by the right side of the brain in the origin of mental dissociation and the emergence of secondary personalities. Franz Kafka's conflicts are discussed as variations on the same theme. The personalities of Cortes and Montezuma are viewed against the background of their preponderantly left versus right hemispheric orientation.

Chapter 13 is a digression into pathology: the miscarriage of leadership in Hitler, Stalin, & Jim Jones, and its attending neurodynamics.

The available evidence suggests that genius emerges from the ideal cooperation and integration of a favorable genetic endowment of the right, and the acquired discipline and cultural conditioning of the left cerebral hemisphere, fueled by lower centers. But even at the risk of circularity, we have to realize that anatomy is merely the instrument in the making of a genius. Like a Stradivarius without Beethoven, it is little more than an assemblage of a wooden box, soundholes, and varnish—or of neurons, myelin sheeths, and gila cells.

The concluding chapters present some of the broader implications of our inquiry. One implication follows from the observation that the two hemispheres do not always work together in unison or in the contrapuntal harmonies of two voices in a Bach cantata. They may inhibit or clash with one another. If so, they may mimic intrapsychic conflict in the psychodynamic sense. Indeed, they may be conducive to a picture of neurosis closely resembling the original Freudian prototype.

One more word about the organization of this book is in order at this point. Its goal is neither biography, psychoanalysis, or psychohistory, but neuropsychology of genius—in case a label is required. It proceeds along thematic, logical, not chronological lines, using men like Beethoven, Einstein, Leonardo da Vinci, or Picasso as its targets of opportunity, drawn from history and from the prodigious bounty of human experience. Each consecutive chapter brings into view a succession of specific aspects of the problem, supporting and reinforcing the argument pursued in the preceding chapters. It thus moves from hunches to hypotheses, from conjectures to tentative conclusions and generalizations about the characteristics, if not the nature, of genius.

Inevitably, a one-man symposium, cutting across diverse closely guarded boundaries of academic specialization cannot speak with the authority of an expert in each field. But it is the cumulative evidence, the concerted thrust, and the inner consistency of the assembled facts, coupled with the fascination of their subject matter, that should speak for itself and, it is hoped, carry conviction with the reader's right and left hemisphere alike.

J.E.

ACKNOWLEDGEMENTS

An early version of *Beethoven: Portrait of a Right Hemispheric Genius,* appeared in 1979, Volume 7, No. 1 of the Journal of the American Academy of Psychoanalysis. I am indebted to John Wiley & Sons, Inc., for permission to include it in this book. Thanks are also due to Harper & Row for permission to quote from *Picasso, Father and Son: Patterns of Contagion and Rebellion in Genius,* in *Neurosis in the Family and Patterns of Psychosocial Defense,* 1963. Also to the Parapsychology Foundation for quotes from *Hitler: Shaman Schizophrenic, Medium?* in *Parapsychology Review,* Vol. 6, No. 2, March-April, 1975.

I also wish to thank the anatomists Louis Bergmann for his suggestions concerning Table 1, and to Victor Millonzi for his meticulous artwork in Chapters 4 and 5. I am also grateful to the neurologist Elliott Ross of the University of Texas for discussing with me his work-in-progress concerning the part played by the right hemisphere in various speech disorders; to Professor Patricia Carpenter for enlightening conversations about Beethoven, Mozart, Schoenberg and others; to Dr. Eric Proskauer, for his invaluable aid in keeping me up to date about current developments in diverse scientific and humanistic disciplines; also to him and Mrs. Beatrix Van Tijn, the librarian of Barnard College, for their help in tracing Giovanni Papini's 1951 interview with Picasso. Thanks are due, furthermore, to the librarians of the New York Academy of Medicine, of the Morgan library and the Frick library for their help and cooperation.

Grateful acknowledgment is made for permission to quote from

the following sources: Nietzsche's *Gondola Song,* translated by
Walter Kaufman, in Vintage Books, Randon House Division;
from: Mozart's Letters, E. Blam (Ed.), Farrar and Rinehart; to D.
MacLean for permission to reproduce Fig. 1. in *New Dimensions in
Psychiatry,* S. Arieti and Chrzanowski (Eds.), John Wiley and
Sons; from: F. Kafka, Letter to His Father, Secker & Warburg and
Schocken Books; for Permission to reproduce David Levine's
drawing of Freud in the New York Review of Books.

I also wish to thank Miss Anita Furst of the Institute of New
Dimensions, for ferreting out, and to the publishers of Ten Speed
Press, Berkeley, Cal., for permission to use the engraving for the
jacket of this book. Special thanks are also due to Dr. Jules Masserman for his generous *Foreword*. It doubles as a welcome illustrative example of his congenial, left as well as right hemispheric, approach to genius.

Lastly, I wish to express my gratitude to my artist and scientist
patients for what I learned from them about the creative process,
and to my students for stimulating exchanges of ideas.

Jan Ehrenwald

I

INTRODUCTION

...each hemisphere seems to have its own separate and private sensations; its own perceptions; its own concepts; and its own impulses to act, with related volitional cognitive and learning experiences.

R.W. Sperry

1

THE DIVIDED BRAIN

Man has always been fascinated by encounter with the extremes of nature and human nature. Tempests, earthquakes, shooting stars, solar eclipses, filled people with awe or dread, but also with a wisp of exhilaration, provided that the attending danger remained only skin-deep. Extremes of human prowess, saintliness, heroism, or even the base cruelty of the "evil genius" are apt to call forth much the same response. The man of the street, in the pub in the agora, or the marketplace, derives vicarious pleasure from identifying with a hero, tragic or otherwise. We can share those triumphs and exaltations and may get an added thrill from the knowledge that we can do so with impunity, without the risks, frustrations, and agonies of genius.

In the eyes of the ancient Greeks, the hero's lofty aspirations risked incurring the wrath of the gods. We are told in Genesis that human beings fell from grace when they dared to reach out for the fruits of knowledge which were the privilege of God alone. In the

Middle Ages, the heretic, or religious reformer, had an equal chance of being beatified or burned at the stake. In the late 19th and early 20th century, the penalty the individual had to pay for genius was considerably lower: the stigma of mental illness. Genius and madness were supposed to be closely associated. This, at least, was the thesis proposed by such early students of human behavior as Galton, Lombroso, Moebius, Lange-Eichbaum, and many others.

In a more recent study the noted English neurologist, Russel Brain (1960) stresses the close association of genius with obsessive personality or with cyclothymia, that is, a predisposition to minor or major manic or depressive mood swings in the individual's life history. The psychologist Hans Eysenck (1961) found a close association of creativity with neuroticism.

Psychoanalysts, from Freud to the present day, have probed in countless essays, monographs, and symposia into the workshop of genius. Freud pointed to the artist's extraordinary ability to sublimate primitive impulses, and he noted that hysteria is derived from the same organic wellsprings as are found in the artist or genius. His followers, from Otto Rank, Ernest Kris, Lawrence Kubie, to Silvano Arieti or Kurt Eissler and many others, placed varying degrees of emphasis on its correlation with conflict and disturbances of sublimation. Eissler noted that the very addiction to creativy seen in genius is itself suggestive of psychopathology, at least "before the way has been opened for a productive breakthrough" (1961). He holds that an inadequate release of "phallic" energy and a high capacity for sublimation are the keys for the genius's creativity. This is certainly true for Beethoven, Leonardo, or Nietzsche, but the amatory exploits of Victor Hugo run counter to Eissler's thesis. Yet Hugo was a Frenchman and obviously unaware of the rules laid down by American or German psychoanalysts.

As far as pathological aspects are concerned, they have recently been called into question. Still, virtually all analysts agree that the fount and origin of genius has remained resistant to psychoanalytic inquiry. Freud himself noted that in Leonardo da Vinci's case an organic or biological factor—physical beauty and left-handedness—may have accounted for some aspects of his genius.

GENIUS: MORE THAN I.Q.

Some of the benefits—and limitations—of an essentially psycho-analytic approach, complemented by an inquiry into biological aspects, will be taken up in several chapters of this book. But it is needless to say that a purely organic viewpoint is apt to lead into a blind alley. This is illustrated by some older anatomists who tried to correlate intellectual prowess with the size of the brain, particularly of the brain hemispheres, and with the sheer quantity of neurons which they contain. The greater their numbers, they conjectured, the greater would be a person's intelligence. By the same token, genius was thought of largely in terms of an I.Q. skyrocketing into the uppermost regions of the Binet-Simon scale. We shall see in the next chapter that on this basis Beethoven would have scored on the dull-normal if not on the moronic level. Einstein, in the eyes of his high school principal, did not fare much better, and Edison was considered a moronic misfit as a child.

Such simplistic concepts of intelligence, creativity, and genius have long since been abandoned. Nor has the modern computer model of human intelligence; the intricacy of brain circuits; the quantity of arithmetical operations performed per second; or sheer facts of memory proved to be more helpful. Even the most accomplished computer is still far surpassed by human wisdom, inventiveness, and the creativity which went into its design and pro-gramming in the first place.

A more sophisticated neurological approach correlates intelligence with higher organizational principles. Russel Brain (1960) specifically stresses the superior integration of perceptual and motor skills in genius, coupled with a greater richness in brain "schemas," that is, organizations of neurons in the brain cortex. Professor J.Z. Young (1978), of the University of London, placed his main emphasis on heriditary sets of programs written in the genes on several levels of the brain.

Nobel Laureate Sir John Eccles and the philosopher Karl Popper (1977b, 1977) are focusing on a multitude of vertical *modules* or microcircuits in the cerebral cortex, each made up of a "complexity of organized assemblages of thousands of neurons."F.H.C. Crick, another Nobel Laureate, suggests the "parcellation" of the cortex into "more than 50 and less than 1000" areas.

The latest, perhaps revolutionary, theory of brain function proposed by Karl Pribram (1971, 1976) of Stanford University Medical School, is based on a holographic model. Holograms are mathematically definable wave and interference patterns derived from laser beams. They sweep over neurons and networks of neurons and form a three-dimensional pattern of coded information which remains "whole" even when big chunks of neural substance are destroyed. According to Charles Hampden-Turner (1981), Pribram's model is "the stuff of scientific revolution, resolving at a stroke the sterile dualism of mind and matter, humanities and sciences, existentialism and essentialism." It may hold the key to a better understanding of the global mind of genius. Yet another holistic model was proposed by Buckminster Fuller (1975) straddling neuroscience, architecture, and geodesics.

From Broca and Wernicke to Split Brain Research

However, these new developments in neuroscience do not invalidate some of the older concepts of neurological localization of diverse intellectual functions and sensory-motor skills in specific, contralateral projection areas of the brain. (See Fig. 1 and 2).

Among them are sensory and motor speech functions which are tied to Wernicke's and Broca's regions in the posterior and anterior parts respectively of the left hemisphere in the right handers. So are reading, writing, and arithmetics, and so are other specialized skills calling for manual dexterity, sensory discrimination and higher feats of comprehension. It should also be noted that, till the advent of modern split brain research, the functions of corresponding areas in the right hemisphere had been largely unknown.

A graphic illustration of the distinctive neurological functions of the two hemispheres was provided by the Wada test. For diagnostic purposes, a patient is given a sodium amytal injection into his left carotid artery. Since it supplies blood to the left side of the brain, the majority of right handers so treated lose their ability to write, to

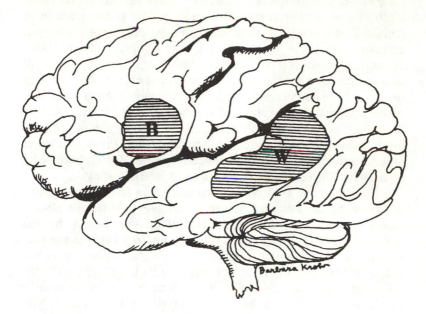

Fig. 1. Broca's and Wernicke's region in the left cerebral hemisphere. They control motor and sensory language functions respectively. According to some authorities, corresponding areas on the right side control prosody, that is, affective components of speech, including emotional gesturing and its understanding.

---

speak, or to comprehend language. The same injection applied to the right side leaves speech and consciousness unimpaired, showing once more the superiority of the dominant left hemisphere as far as higher intellectual functions are concerned.

Modern split-brain research, pioneered by CalTech psychologist R.W. Sperry, co-winner of the 1981 Nobel Prize (1969); J.E. and E.M. Bogen (1969); M. Gazzaniga (1970, 1978), and their associates, have introduced an entirely new model of brain functions into contemporary neuroscience. Their observations point to a far-reaching independence and division of labor between the two cerebral hemispheres. Their first subjects were epileptic patients whose seizures failed to respond to conservative treatment. A daring operation carried out by the neurosurgeon consisted of cutting the massive assemblage of fibers—the corpus callosum and a smaller set of fibers, the anterior commissure—which connect the two halves of the brain. The result of the operation was a dramatic cessation of the seizures with relatively little impairment of the patient's overt behavior. Yet, on closer scrutiny, a wide variety of psychological difficulties came to the fore. Owing to the intricacies of the wiring diagram of the brain, it was possible to set up conditions in which the experimenter **could send messages to, and elicit responses from, both sides separately. The technique is described as lateral testing.**

Typical of the hidden functional deficit in split-brain patients is one of the cases studied by the investigators. When the patient was shown an object in the left half of his visual field, he was unable to tell what he saw but he could point to a matching picture with the left hand. It is suggested that the right hemisphere, when left to its own resources, cannot verbalize its impressions. On the other hand, the right side of the brain is more competent in tasks involving spatial orientation, in the handling of so-called Koh cubes, in assembling patterns and recognizing faces and in gestalt perception in general.

The right hemisphere is also far better endowed with musical capacity. The Russian neuropsychologist, A.R. Luria (1973), described a composer who continued to be highly creative after suffering a massive stroke of the left hemisphere. J.E. Bogen (1969) observed gross impairment of a subject's ability to sing when the right carotid artery, supplying the right side of the brain, was injected with sodium amytal in the test. The composer Maurice Ravel suffered a massive stroke involving the left cerebral hemisphere. **He could no longer write music or recognize musical** scores. But his sense of rhythm, melody, and musical memory remained largely unimpaired.

Pioneering studies concerning the functions of the supposedly speechless right hemisphere have recently been carried out by E.D. Ross and his associates at the Neurological Department of the University of Texas in Dallas (Ross & Mesulam, 1979; Ross, 1981; and others). They found that lesions involving areas in the right hemisphere that correspond with Broca's and Wernicke's regions on the left side of the brain impaired the affective or emotional components of speech in a selective way. Such lesions blocked emotional gesturing, "the melodic line produced by the variations of speech, rhythm and stress of pronunciation"—what has been described as *prosody* of language. By the same token, patients of this group were unable to understand the meaning of the emotional components of the spoken word. They were not aphasic but *aprosodic*, as Ross put it. Thus, the right hemisphere provides the emotional ingredient, the background music, the *continuo*, the animation of verbal communication. Its failure to do so leaves his discourse flat, lifeless, robotlike; or else it leaves the patient at a loss to comprehend the emotional meaning of verbal or gestural messages. In effect, the *right hemisphere is dominant for nonverbal expression and comprehension of emotions*.

Earlier, Robert Ornstein and David Galin (1972) and others have noted that the right hemisphere, though verbally underendowed, has a particular knack for metaphorical expressions and puns. It speaks a language characteristic of dreams, slips of the tongue, symbolic allusions and poetic diction. Its mentality is closely related to what psychoanalysts have described as the primary process, by contrast to the secondary process which is the hallmark of rational, analytic discourse and, by indirection, of the left hemisphere.

Other authors describe the right hemisphere as the dreamer *par excellence*, as well as the source of hallucinations. Psychologist Roland Fisher (1974), commenting on the close relationship between dreams, hallucinations, and "ordinary" perceptions, notes that "perceptions may become transformed into what we moderns call 'hallucinations.' They are vivid visuospatial or audiospatial images and they can be accounted for by recent research findings which indicate that during hyper- (as well as hypo-) arousal, information processing is gradually shifted toward the nonverbal, visuospatial, or 'minor' brain hemisphere."

The different functional characteristics of the two hemispheres are also borne out by studies of the electric activity of the two sides of the brain. D. Galin and R. Ornstein (1972) found a greater tendency toward slow frequency, high amplitude alpha rhythms over the right hemisphere while the subject was engaged in verbal tasks; that is, in an activity involving the dominant left hemisphere. Vice versa, when the right side of the brain was kept busy with spatial-synthetic tasks, the EEG from the left hemisphere showed evidence of alpha rhythm; that is, of electrical inactivity. "During a verbal task the alpha rhythm in the right hemisphere increases relative to the left, and in a spatial task the alpha increases in the left hemisphere relative to the right," as Ornstein put it (1972, p. 62).

Of particular interest in the present context are reports by Bogen (1969), Galin (1979), Budzynski (1979), and others, that functional inhibition of the right hemisphere from the dominant left hemisphere has a dampening effect upon creativity and vice versa. This was further borne out by a recent study of three professional groups made by T.H. Budzynski (1979). Ingenious tests involving brain wave patterns showed a distinct prevalence of high amplitude alpha wave activity in the creative group; that is, among artists, dancers, and entertainers, as compared with a group of business men, lawyers, accountants, etc., under specifically designed test conditions. (Alpha activity is usually considered a sign of idling or rest of that side of the brain from which the EEG is obtained.) He concludes that, as a matter of basic principle, "alpha measurements show that the people from business, law, and accounting professions differ from individuals in creative professions in the way their hemispheres process cognitive tasks."

More recent parapsychological studies have thrown light on yet another potential of the right hemisphere. They have afforded growing evidence of its involvement in the processing of both experimental and spontaneous psi phenomena; that is, telepathy, clairvoyance, psychokinesis, and precognition. R.S. Broughton (1978) of the University of Edinburgh has found that ESP performance can be improved when the subject, using three-dimensional wooden targets instead of Rhine's familiar Zener cards, indicated his ESP target by *pointing* to it nonverbally with his *left* hand. At the same time, he was instructed to count backwards from 1000 by threes, fours, etc., thereby trying to neutralize left-hemispheric interference with the right hemisphere's involvement in the ESP task. The author concludes from this particular version of a major experimental series that "the right hemisphere is more successful at the accurate processing of some forms of paranormal information and that there may be an inhibiting mechanism connected with the operations of the left hemisphere which must be thwarted for the effect to show itself" (p. 16, Summary). Broughton's experimental findings are in need of further confirmation, but a large body of spontaneous observations point in the same direction.

SOME CASE ILLUSTRATIONS

In addition to these experimental findings, there is a great deal of clinical material showing the different ways in which the two hemispheres react to the stress of emotional conflict or to organic lesions of the brain. An observation of my own goes back to a case seen in 1939 at the beginning of Nazi persecution in Czechoslovakia. The patient was a healthy-looking young man of nineteen who had developed a hemianesthesia, that is, loss of sensation for touch and pain on the left side of his body. Otherwise, his neurological examination was negative. It transpired that he was the illegitimate son of a wealthy Jewish landowner and a Gentile mother. His father had just fled from Czechoslovakia, leaving his son behind. Meanwhile, his family secret leaked out to the rural community in which the patient lived and he became increasingly perturbed by the physical dangers of his situation and desertion by his father. Above all, he was ashamed of his half-Jewish origin and the stigma attached to it. This led to the compelling need to ignore, deny, or repress the Jewish "half" of his personality and to what amounted to his hysterical conversion symptom.

It should be emphasized that, in this case, the presenting symptom was not due to an organic lesion of the right side of the brain. It resulted from the existing psychological conflict which led through the power of the patient's imagination, as it were, to the mimicry of an organic neurological picture. Such cases are by no means unique. As far back as 1919, Sandor Ferenczi, one of Freud's close associates, has described several patients with so-called conversion hysteria exhibiting the same symptom.

Whatever be the *modus operandi* of conversion hysteria, my case brings the familiar symbolism of "right versus left," of "good versus bad" (or sinister), of "clean versus dirty"—if not "male versus female"—into sharper perspective. His symbolic denial of the reality of the left side of his body amounted to a metaphor come alive, conveyed by his repudiation of his half-Jewishness in typical right-hemispheric terms.

Observations of this order hark back to ancient Hebrew tradition according to which Eve was created from the left side of Adam's body. By the same token, Jewish folklore refers to a person's alter ego, the *Yezer Tov* representing his inclination towards goodness that stands on his *right* side, and the *Yezer-Ha-ra*, his inclination towards wickedness, standing on his *left* side. It is also closely related to the *shadow* in Jungian psychology.

Psychiatry is wont to draw a strict dividing line between organic and hysterical symptomatology. But clinical observations do not always stick to the traditional discrimination between the two. This is illustrated by a large number of cases in which a left-sided hemiplegia, that is, a combination of motor paralysis and anesthesia on the left side of the body, is associated with a denial or imperception of the existing defect. In clinical parlance, it is described as *anosognosia*. It is more frequent in men than in women and is usually confined to left-sided hemiplegia in right handers, while it is absent in right-sided stroke patients. In one respect, however, anosognosia duplicates the picture of conversion hysteria seen in my own or in Ferenczi's cases: the imperception of defect in hemiplegics closely resembles hysterical repression although it is originally due to gross organic pathology.

This is also illustrated by another case of my own: a fifty-nine-year-old male school teacher with a left-sided hemiplegia due to a major cerebrovascular accident. He became delirious and insisted on leaving the bed, stubbornly denying that he was paralyzed. He spoke incoherently to his wife, saying he had a nest of hands in his bed and that she should ask the doctor to cut them away. "I have always had a good hand, I want to throw that away. There is a dead hand and a dead foot in my bed," etc. Another male patient, aged sixty-four, lapsed into coma and became delirious following a similar cerebrovascular accident. On coming to, his head, eyes, and torso were maximally turned to the right side. Following this acute state, he developed motor paralysis of his left arm and leg. He insisted that the left hand was not his own, that it should be thrown into the garbage, and he blamed the nurse for her sloppiness in letting it lie around. Subsequently, he claimed that the whole left side of his body had changed. His limbs were prostheses that could be put on or taken off. In lieu of the left side of his chest, stomach, and belly, "they" had built in wooden boards and shelves. The contraption reached down to his anus with a hole in the middle. The patient was a right hander, was oriented in time and place, and showed no aphasia or other symptoms of intellectual impairment (Ehrenwald, 1931).

This patient is another illustration of the imperception of defect or anosognosia usually found in left-sided hemiplegia. They were published in older German, French, and English literature. Nevertheless, they are receiving scant attention in modern textbooks of psychiatry, and their interpretation is still controversial. We do not know whether their bizarre symptomatology is due to heightened imbalance between the left and what is left of the right hemisphere, to an excitation of still surviving right brain structures, or to what.

Horizontal Versus Vertical Organization

In any case, we have to realize that as a matter of basic principle the brain amounts to a slightly lopsided hierarchical organization in both the horizontal and the vertical. Figuratively speaking, the mind inhabits an edifice made up of a right and a left wing—the neomammalian brain—occupying the top floor, and several lower stories housing phylogenetically older structures including the limbic lobe and the reptilian brain. The top floor is reserved for the executive offices of the human enterprise including, presumably, the "Self," an inner sanctum catering to man's metaphysical need and what Tillich called his "ultimate concerns." The lower stories control the more or less automatic business of living, the drives, emotions, impulses, and diverse vegetative regulatory functions of the organism (see Table I).

There is general consensus among neuroanatomists, as well as

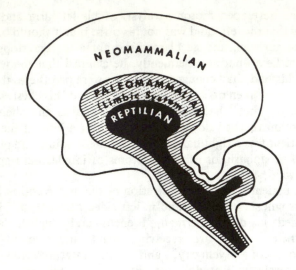

Fig. 2. Diagram of brain evolution according to Mclean, showing reptilian, paleomammalian and neomammalian developmental stages.

psychiatrists and psychoanalysts, that the lower centers play a crucial role in our mental organization. While our relatively recently acquired specialized skills and higher intellectual functions are located and "lateralized" in the left or right cerebral hemispheres respectively, the phylogenetically older functions are chiefly located in central portions of the brain and brainstem, of what the neuroanatomist McLean has described as the *triune* brain (1977). They are not subject to lateralization, to conscious awareness, or volitional control.

THREE R's VERSUS THREE I's

It is for this very reason that they continue to exert a powerful influence upon our emotional life, behavior, conduct, and decision making, as well as on our general outlook on the world, ideologies, beliefs, and value systems. In effect, they are the principal province of psychoanalytic inquiry into the unconscious, Freudian, Jungian, or otherwise. On the neuroanatomical level, they contribute a third major factor to an equation trying to do justice to minor or major upsets in the balance of left versus right hemispheric interactions.

If this is true, several puzzling features of the right hemisphere fall into place. As a result of the brain's division of labor, the right side lacks or lags behind in the development of such highly differentiated intellectual functions as reading, writing, and arithmetic. At the same time, it is closer to nature, as it were, and more open to the uprush of primitive, emotionally charged (or "cathected") drives, impulses, or other primary process material from subcortical structures—or the Freudian Id. On the other hand, damage to critical areas of the right hemisphere results in Ross' *aprosodias,* in alienation, derealization, and deperson-alization of the incapacitated left side of the body. In the cases described here, it amounted to an attitude of *revulsion* and disgust expressed by the patient's language or body language in no uncertain terms. It will be recalled that responses of this order do not occur in right hemiplegic patients.

On the basis of clinical evidence of this order, it can only be expected that arousal of an intact right hemisphere should be the source of a sustained emotional charge (or "hypercathexis") in the economy of our mental life. By the same token, an excessive degree of right hemispheric activity can be expected to produce the reverse of what happens in the case of its depression or destruction. This is, indeed, borne out by the whole cognitive style we have learned to attribute to the right hemisphere. Symbols, symbolic allusions, metaphors, poetic diction, and musical ability are all generated by, or processed with the assistance of, the right side of the brain. Hallucinations, and what in our culture is considered their delusional interpretation, likewise originate from the right rather than the left hemisphere. Wilder Penfield's (1975) celebrated experiments with electrical stimulation of the brain cortex suggest that it alone is merely conducive to more or less vivid imagery. The subject is fully aware of the artificial nature of his impressions.

All the more significant in the present context is the compelling sense of reality which the intact right hemisphere imparts on its

Table 1.

CORTICAL STRUCTURES

I Neomammalian

Hemisphere	Left	Right
Thinking	Abstract, linear, analytic	Concrete, holistic
Cognitive style	Rational, logical	Intuitive, artistic
Language	Rich vocabularly, good grammar and syntax; prose	no grammar, syntax; prosody, poor vocabulary metaphoric, verse
Executive capacity	Introspection, will, initiative, sense of self, focus on trees	Low sense of self, low initiative, focus on forest
Specialized functions	Reading, writing, arithmetic, sensory-motor skills; inhibits psi	Three I's, music, rich dream imagery, good face and gestalt recognition, open to psi
Time experience	Sequentially ordered, measured	"Lived" time, primitive time sense
Spatial orientation	Relatively poor	Superior, also for shapes, wire figures
Psychoanalytic aspects	Secondary process, ego functions, consciousness; superego?	Primary process, dreamwork, free assoc. hallucinations?
Ideal prototype	Aristotle, Apollonian mode, Marx, Freud Koestler's Commissar	Plato, Dionysian mode, Nietzsche, Jung Koestler's Yogi

SUBCORTICAL STRUCTURES

II Paleomammalian

Not lateralized,
e.g. limbic lobe, amygdala,
visceral brain, basal ganglia.
Controls emotion, appetite, aggression,
pleasure functions, copulation,
autonomic programs

III Reptilian (MacLean)

E.g. hypothalamus, brainstem, mostly medially
located,
reticular formation; controls arousal,
vigilance; such biological functions as
breathing, feeding, biorhythms.

Subcortical structures include:

II and III: Paleomammalian and reptilian-Limbic lobe, Corpus striatum, Amygdala, etc, Relay stations for incoming sensations and outgoing motor functions. On lower level: Hypothalamus, MacLean's Reptilian brain or R-complex. Also: Brainstem. Control autonomic functions, emotions, aggression, sexual behavior, feeding biorhythm, diverse vital functions I, II and III are also sites of chemoreceptors and neurotransmitters. Third level not lateralized.

Legend

Table I represents three successive steps on the evolutionary ladder; the cortical structures are symmetrical but lateralized, controlling diverse neurophysiological functions. The contrasting left versus right hemispheric functional types are ideal prototypes and rarely occur in real life. As a rule, the two sides of the brain work in tandem, or else diverse functions alternate or vie with each other. The lateralization of functions is more marked in men than in women. Children's brains are not yet strictly lateralized. Ideally, the higher and lower centers (I, II, III) cooperate in a synergistic way.

Some of the functions listed as distinctly right versus left hemispheric are still controversial. For instance the "localization" in the left brain of the sense of self, or of mathematical ability. Some authorities stress bilateral spread of language into the right hemisphere. Musical ability in the layman is right hemispheric but involves both hemispheres in professional musicians. Artistic drawing is controlled by the right hemisphere but technical drawings involve more the left side of the brain. Other authorities reject all attempts at cerebral localization and stress the part played by neurotransmitters and other chemical factors. Roger Sperry (1982), one of the pioneers of split brain research has cautioned that the "left-right dichotomy in cognitive mode is an idea which is very easy to run wild."

---

hallucinatory experiences, private perceptions, insights, and inspirations. More often than not, they carry the imprints of apodictic certainty for the individual. This is what the psychologist Julian Jaynes (1976) described as the hallucinatory voices of the gods, of departed kings, in preliterate cultures. We shall see in the chapters that follow that they are also powerful influences in the lives of the creative artist or intuitive scientist on the one hand, and of the religious fanatic, the crusader for paranoid causes, and full-fledged madman on the other.

By the same token, this heightened sense of reality of a person's world of inner experiences is the dialectical counterpart of the feeling of alienation, derealization, and depersonalization characteristic of patients with left-sided hemiplegia. It rounds out our picture of the part played by the right hemisphere in both health and disease. Put in a capsule, it could be stated that while the left side of the brain presides over the three R's, reading, writing, and arithmetic, the right side is concerned, among other things, with the three I's: Intuition, Inspiration, and Imagination—indeed, with the emotional and creative aspects of human existence.

LATERALIZATION AND TWO COGNITIVE STYLES

What does all this accumulated clinical and experimental evidence add up to? It has led to the emergence of two vastly different protagonists in the interplay of the two halves of the brain: the left hemisphere with its generally accepted intellectual and even moral superiority on the one hand and the right, or minor, hemisphere, once considered the dumbbell, with its dominance for nonverbal, intuitive performance and experience, on the other.

It may be as well to realize, however, that in real life neither one nor the other of the two fictitious characters is likely to hold center stage for any length of time. Much of the time, the hemispheres operate in tandem, or even in unison, tied together by millions of fibers and, perhaps, the proper mix of neurotransmitters. At other times, they may be in open conflict, with the dominant left hemisphere having a better chance to assert its superiority. Or else, they play a complementary role, with their performance orchestrated by the self, a mysterious conductor who has so far refused to give his address, to identify himself, or to take a bow in the orchestra pit.

Admittedly, such an extended repertoire of the right side of the brain is difficult to substantiate by reference to hard facts and figures obtained by the time-tested left-hemispheric methods of inquiry. But we shall see in the chapters that follow that they are supported by the concerted evidence of a combined right and left-hemispheric approach to genius. Indeed, it will be seen that such a study should throw added light into the workshop of genius and into the ways in which he succeeds in integrating his two cerebral hemispheres, or resolving the conflict between them.

Table I offers a summary of the contrasting cognitive styles, or fictitious personality profiles, described in the literature. It will be noted, however, that the Table extends its frame of reference from the currently fashionable horizontal, "lateralized" model of the brain into the vertical so as to include more archaic, subcortical levels. At the same time, it makes allowance for developmental aspects and for the hierarchical organization of the central nervous system. For better or for worse, it is these lower, phylogenetically older, prehuman, premammalian structures which are the reservoir for man's raw instinctual drives. It is they who breathe life into the more civilized "secondary" process transactions of the two cerebral hemispheres.

Still, it goes without saying that the mind in action is not compartmentalized. Like the contrapuntal organization of a symphonic piece or the final image of a three-color print, it is a synergistic whole. Its constituent parts, or the seams of its fabric, are only brought into the open by the scrutiny of a left-hemispheric observer.

II

GENIUS OBSERVED

Before Genius the psychoanalyst
has to lay down his arms...

Freud

But the neuropsychologist can
point to the existential conflict
between the intuitive right, and
the analytic left side of the
brain—and its creative
resolution.

J.E.

2

Beethoven
Hero and Antihero
Portrait of a
Right Hemispheric Genius

Why does Beethoven occupy the pride of place among the geniuses included in this series? One reason is that throughout my life, I have been deeply stirred by the beauty and grandeur of his music. Secondly, ever since his death in 1827, generations of music lovers have acclaimed him as the ideal prototype of genius, a heroic figure at the keyboard and in the concert hall, in stark contrast to the dismal failure of his private and social life. But a more immediate reason is wholly incidental. Long before becoming familiar with the findings of modern split brain research, I had come across a striking misspelling and slip of Beethoven's pen which put me on the track of the part played by the right or "nondominant" cerebral hemisphere in his mental organization.

Yet before going into these aspects, a few words on some of the earlier Beethoven studies and on his personal history will be in order. Some 200 years after his birth, the literature on Beethoven has filled countless shelves in libraries all over the world. It ranges from awestruck hagiography to straight accounts, of his life, musicological tracts, symposia. More recent additions to the list are several psychoanalystic contributions following in the footsteps of Freud or Erikson.

Scholarly studies along these lines though aiming, by definition as it were, at an objective, dispassionate attitude, often leaned over backward to avoid the reproach of hero worship. Yet in so doing they ran the risk of projecting the author's own preconceived ideas—if not complexes—upon the subject of their inquiry. In the extreme case, such an approach may be more in the nature of a Rorschach response than of what the analyst has originally set out to do.

Critics have noted that even Freud's trail blazing study of Leonardo da Vinci (1910) has not altogether succeeded in avoiding such pitfalls. Eric Erikson's psychohistories of Martin Luther or Ghandi have apparently been more successful in doing so. The straight psychoanalytic study: *Beethoven and his Nephew* (1954) by Edith and Richard Sterba, has both the virtues and the flaws of such an approach. They concluded that Beethoven was a latent homosexual with an all-pervasive resentment of women and especially mother figures. This, they hold, is borne out, among other things, by his inordinate attachment to his nephew Karl, by his hatred of Karl's mother Johanna, and his inability to form a wholesome relationship with any one of his female admirers. His alleged paranoid delusions and ultimate psychotic breakdown should indeed be in keeping with such an interpretation.

Maynard Solomon's (1977) scholarly study, *Beethoven,* is a more timely and more evenly balanced birthday offering. It adds another wrinkle to the vast Beethoven literature, psychoanalytic and otherwise. Solomon points to Beethoven's "family romance," as described by Freud, Rank, and others, as the crucial factor in the composer's personality development. He describes his fantasies of being of royal birth: Beethoven had persuaded himself that he was the offspring of his mother's extramarital affair with one of the kings of Prussia, seemingly unconcerned that he was thereby impugning her marital fidelity. Another mechanism of defense noted by Solomon is Beethoven's attempt at restoring the family triad by becoming his nephew's "bodily" father and mother at the same time, though he was unable to "take the step that would have united the three as a cooperative family unit." Solomon also points to Beethoven's gradual mental deterioration and delusional trend in his declining years.

There can be little doubt about the validity of both the Sterbas' and Solomon's analytic evaluations, even though they focus on two widely divergent aspects of Beethoven's psychohistory. Yet, oddly, both tend to gloss over two no less significant factors in Beethoven's personality development: one pertaining to family dynamics, notably his disturbed relationship with his father; the other to striking flaws in his neurophysiological organization. I propose to show that these two factors were responsible for a deep cleavage in his personality makeup, for its noble and heroic, versus its less noble and antiheroic aspects. It is a cleavage which ever since his meteoric rise to greatness has puzzled both his admirers and detractors.

I submit that the salient feature of Beethoven's psychohistory is his abiding conflict with a tyrannical father—a conflict elevated and personified to a relentless struggle with implacable *Fate,* writ large. I also propose to show that it is the heroic, if not mythological, dimension of this struggle which lent grandeur to his music, while the image of the antihero is brought home to us by some of Beethoven's glaring shortcomings and characterological deficiencies. Thus both his admirers and detractors happened to be at least partly correct in their appraisal of Beethoven the Artist and Beethoven the Man. However, they failed to do justice to the "other" side of his personality. We shall see that the two sides were, in effect, geared to a striking imbalance of his right versus left cerebral hemispheres.

BEETHOVEN: FATHER AND SON

I hinted that the outstanding feature in Beethoven's psychohistory is the heroic struggle of a mere mortal with a cruel, impersonal, yet personified Fate; but I also noted that in Beethoven's case, Fate stood for the brutal, tyrannical, exploitative father. Some of his biographers tend to belittle the fateful impact of the elder Beethoven on his son. However, there can be no doubt that Ludwig's early experience, real or imaginary, of such a man, was a decisive factor in his future development. We are told by Thayer (1964), his early biographer, that Johannes Beethoven had repeatedly locked the boy in a dark cellar or had beaten him for minor misdemeanors. Indeed, Ludwig may well have been what is today described as a battered child. There are reports from neighbors who saw the child standing on a stool weeping while he practiced scales at the piano. We are also told that the elder Beethoven, coming home late at night with one of his drinking companions, would rouse little Ludwig from sleep and force him to practice until the wee hours of the morning. Such experiences may well account for Beethoven's cruelty to his servants, brothers, in laws, and even his beloved nephew Karl.

Ludwig showed his knack for improvisation early. His father, a court singer and mediocre musician in Bonn, sternly reprimanded him: "You first learn to play your instrument and leave composing for later." Eking out a meager living at the princely court of Bonn, he was determined to exploit Ludwig's precocious talents and to turn him into a child prodigy like Wolfgang Amadeus Mozart. Unfortunately, Johannes van Beethoven was sorely lacking the accomplished musicianship and pedagogic know-how Leopold Mozart had been able to provide for his son in his comfortable home in Salzburg.

We shall see in Chapter 7 that the elder Mozart rightly stressed his "untiring diligence who as a real father availed himself of his children's (and especially of his 'Wolfgangerl's') talent." As a result, Wolfgang Amadeus became a direct linear extension and continuation of his father and of the heritage handed down to him by his forebears, the culmination on an exalted plane of the classical tradition that had preceded him.

Yet Beethoven's unequal struggle with his father also carried its own rewards. One was his delight in improvisation in the circle of his friends and in the concert hall. It seems to be a direct derivative of his early defiance of his father's insistence on the dreary routine of practicing the scales and of his squelching the little boy's attempts at spontaneous self-expression. We know today that it was this irrepressible urge that led him to the dizzying heights of creative innovations in virtually all forms of the musical idiom.

Thus, Ludwig van Beethoven's genius grew and came to flowering rather despite than by the aid of father. Whatever support he had in his early years came from his mother, Maria Magdalena. The daughter of a cook from a village near Bonn, she tried hard to make ends meet and kept the family together as best she could. She is described as a long-suffering, overworked, pathetic woman who, like the lady in the TV commercial, was never seen to smile. Still, she gave Ludwig, the oldest son, as much love and attention as she had to spare. His relations with women in later life still reflected his unremitting search for the full measure of maternal love he had lacked in his childhood.

She died in 1787 when Ludwig was sixteen years old. There is reason to believe that her loss gave rise to Beethoven's lifelong longing for an idealized mother figure to satisfy his oedipal strivings. It also reinforced his fears of implacable Fate: of a cruel father, punishing him for his incestuous fantasies. Speculations abound regarding Beethoven's actual relationships with women. He seemed to fall in love with nearly every unattainable woman who came his way—or to make her unattainable as soon as she seemed to respond to his advances. The celebrated letter to the anonymous *Immortal Beloved* has puzzled his biographers ever since it was discovered among his personal effects after his death in 1827. Marek (1969) lists nine possible candidates and finally opts for Dorothea von Ertmann, a married woman and accomplished pianist, as its intended recipient. Solomon adduces strong presumptive evidence pointing to another married woman, Antonia Brentano, as Beethoven's secret lady-love. But despite Marek's or Solomon's painstaking researches to lift the veil of the Immortal Beloved, Beethoven's letter leaves her shrouded in mystery: generic woman, devoid of personal identity, standing midway between the imaginary companions of a lonely child, and the image of an idealized Maria Magdalena giving her undivided attention to Ludwig as her *only* son. In any case, his letter to the Immortal Beloved is more an anguished cry for maternal love, for emotional sustenance, than an expression of a consummated and fulfilling give-and-take relationship between lovers. No evidence has emerged from the voluminous diaries, Conversation Books, or even contemporary hearsay that would point to any ongoing liaison with Dorothea, Antonia, or any other of his woman friends.

All this tends to cast doubt on the existence of the Immortal Beloved as a real personage. Even if she was real, she may merely have been the main protagonist in a scenario rooted in Beethoven's fertile imagination. Such an interpretation is in keeping with his tendency to indulge in such daydreams and fantasies as his family romance, his royal birth, and, last but not least, his delusion of being the "bodily"father (*der leibliche Vater*) of his nephew Karl. The fictional character of the Immortal Beloved is further supported by the fact that Beethoven's letter was never delivered. It does not look like an undelivered draft of the original: it does not carry the hallmarks of the corrections, cancellations, and erasures characteristic of Beethoven's musical scores. Another curious feature is the writer's addressing the letter to his *immortal*—not "Eternally"—beloved. Was it meant to suggest that Beethoven's very devotion to his beloved would bestow the reflected glory of his immortality on her too? A more likely explanation is that the adjective was a misnomer due to his unconscious attempt to deny Maria Magdalena's death and to replace her with an unlosable, abiding, and undying mother surrogate.

Beethoven's desperate fight for the sole possession of his nephew Karl may in turn have been due to more than a "mere" homosexual attachment. Here, again, a strong narcissistic factor may have colored the picture. His excessive devotion to and possessiveness of the boy indicates that he considered him as his alter ego—a reincarnation of his own emotionally deprived childhood self. He put himself into Karl's shoes and showered him with all the love he did not obtain from his unloving, tyrannical father.

I submit that such a reading of Beethoven's psychohistory is more to the point than the Sterbas' homosexual interpretation, although a latent homosexual trend underlying his relationship with Karl, the musician Amenda, and other male companions does lend support to their thesis. The part played by his family romance emphasized by Solomon is likewise unmistakable. Here too, the evidence is at hand but its relevance to the overall development of the composer's personality remains conjectural. On balance, it is his masochistic love-hate relationship with his father that brings into sharper focus one of the salient features of his personal history: his ceaseless struggle with his *Schicksal*—with Fate.

I have hinted that the dark, menacing power of Fate is in effect a personification—if not a mythological elaboration and magnification—of the inexorable and unpredictable father figure, facing the helpless puny little boy of four or five. I could quote many remarks and letters to his friends in which Beethoven vowed that he would "take Fate by its throat" and never give in to its domination. It was Fate that had overtaken him on his hurried trip from Vienna to his mother's deathbed in Bonn. It was Fate that made him awkward, ungainly, and clumsy with women. It was Fate that meted out his deafness, the cruellest punishment that could befall a composer and master performer on the keyboard. Over and over again, he raged against the Creator who exposes his creatures to the hazards of undeserved and accidental afflictions. Indeed, to Ludwig it was the very irrational punishment which the loss of hearing had meant to him that must have recalled the memories of his father's irrational, unpredictable outbursts of temper.

We are told that when Beethoven was lying on his deathbed, a sudden bolt of lightning and clap of thunder roused the dying man from his coma. He rose once more in his bed and lifted his clenched fist against the sky. It was the last defiant gesture of the stricken giant directed against his implacable enemy, the real or introjected father of his early years. Like the chains dragged behind by the prisoners in Pizarro's dungeons, Ludwig was weighted down by his father to the end of his life.

At the same time, his stubborn defiance of authority and his refusal to acknowledge defeat had become the mainstay in his struggle for self-expression. Doggedly and indefatigably he followed the dictates of his intuition. When growing deafness drove him into increasing isolation, he kept on denying his affliction. Despite his need for closeness and intimacy, he recoiled from the women he professed to love. But for a few fleeting episodes with prostitutes, he apparently remained celibate. He scoffed at the pious counsel of relying on God's help. Among his favorite dictums were "Man, help yourself," or "Strength is the morality of those who distinguish themselves." Nevertheless, he was far from enthusiastic when he learned that Napoleon, following the maxim, had crowned himself emperor in 1804. He flew into a rage: "So he is no more than an ordinary mortal," he shouted, "and from now on he will trample on the rights of man and further only his own ambitions." Unfortunately, Beethoven the "antihero," did much the same thing with his servants, the housekeeper, his brothers, their wives, and even his nephew Karl.

Analytically speaking, he identified with his father (more than with his mother, as suggested by Sterba and Sterba) and introjected him into his personality structure. At the same time, he used a more ominous, paranoid mechanism of defence: he projected his own repudiated hostile-destructive impulses into the outside world—on his enemies and rivals, even his patrons, friends, and associates. We shall see on a later page that the tendency to projection and externalization became the nucleus for the emergence of the "other" Beethoven personality.

The Eroica is generally considered Beethoven's most sublime artistic accomplishment, a turning point in his career and in the history of music at large. Sullivan (1960) called it a "miraculously realized expression of an important experience," a major milestone in his spiritual development: "Never before has so important, manifold and completely coherent expression been communicated" (p. 77).

But the same power of expression runs through the whole of Beethoven's work, from the youthful charm of his early Trios to his nine symphonies and the grandeur of his late string quartets. It was obviously his ability to express in the musical idiom his rhapsodic mood swings—in what Arieti (1977) described as the *tertiary process*—that saved him from mental deterioration and ultimate breakdown throughout his creative period. It deflected inner turmoil from physical manifestations, and helped to drown out the vicissitudes of the other, antiheroic, side of his personality. It was a magnificent alternative to diverse somatic and psychosomatic ailments. Creativity, in Beethoven's case, had a distinctly self-healing quality.

HERO, ANTI-HERO AND THE EXISTENTIAL SHIFT

We have seen that the "other" Beethoven personality was never completely in abeyance. His heroic struggle with Fate, with Father, with the Demon Illness and presumably with alcohol, was not without setbacks. At times it led to masochistic surrender to his father, or else to identifying with the Enemy: the dissolute court singer Johannes Beethoven. Indeed, Ludwig had the propensity for both the hero and the antihero in his personality makeup. His music delved into "new depth of human consciousness never before explored by a creative artist," as Sullivan put it. Sullivan did not try to put Beethoven on the analyst's couch and focused mainly on positive aspects. But he added: "He had more levels of existence at his command than any ordinary man. He (was) dealing with borderland states of consciousness" (p. 81).

This intuitive appraisal has a decidedly modern ring. It anticipates contemporary concepts of altered states of consciousness, and their extension to what I have described as the *Existential Shift* (1978). The Existential Shift is a person's ability to switch his perceptual orientation, his motor and psychomotor responses and his whole behavioral repertoire from one mode or level of existence to another. Indeed, the Beethoven of the charm and gaiety of the finale of the Eroica, of the majesty of the Missa Solemnis, seems to be a wholly different person from the misanthropic, irascible eccentric who haggled with the servants about their daily allotment of coffee or bread; who cut corners dealing (and double-dealing) with his publishers, and shocked occasional visitors with the sight of unemptied chamber pots, or of garbage strewn on the floor. There are many stories about his neglected personal grooming. On one occasion, he was picked up by the police who had mistaken him for a vagabond. Street urchins mocked him on his lonely walks during his years in Heiligenstadt, and his nephew complained to his friends about the eccentricities of the "old fool." An English visitor, Lord John Russel, who called on the aged composer in 1821, described an ill-tempered, unkempt, dissolute Beethoven, "full of rude energy;" but he added: "The moment he was seated at the piano, he is evidently unconscious that there is anything in existence but himself and his instrument" (Marek, p. 566). This is indeed a graphic illustration of an abrupt transition from one state of consciousness to another, or rather of the global existential shift.

But the cleavage between two opposing existential positions—between the "main" and the "other" Beethoven personality—is by no means confined to a few dramatic incidents. The same dichotomy, though in a lower key, runs through his whole personal history. Beethoven, the composer, whose self-expression in his musical idiom had encompassed the entire range and depth of human experience, from the heights of elation to the depths of despair, from the urgency of passion to masochistic surrender; from thundering rages against Fate to the ineffable bliss of accepting the inevitable, was at the same time notorious as a man completely at the mercy of his uncontrollable tempers and instinctual drives. We are told that he was lacking all social graces, awkward in his movements, had poor muscular coordination, and never learned to dance. He was tongue-tied with women, painfully aware of his inability to match the eloquence of his music with the spoken or written word. His letters, written in the stilted prose of his time, fell flat compared with the standards of his more literate contemporaries. His *Heiligenstadt Testament* is a touching human document but shows his faltering attempts to spell out his emotional predicaments in words. In one of his letters, he noted: "When I wish to write down (my thoughts) I usually throw the pen away because I cannot write as I feel."

RIGHT HEMISPHERIC DOMINANCE?

This was by no means his only handicap. We learn from his biographers that he had never mastered the elements of arithmetic beyond addition and subtraction. A thirteen-year old boy whom he had befriended tried unsuccessfully to teach him simple multiplication and division. His handwriting was atrocious and nearly illegible when under stress, with letters leaning haphazardly from left to right and from right to left. Some words show omissions of letters, like "Allego" instead of *Allegro*.

Even his name is sometimes spelled as "Ludwig Beehoven" with the "van" showing some inappropriate curlicues (see Fig. 3). He scrambles letters in the word *empfehlen,* spelling it "empehlen." He describes himself as an "esteniker" instead of *astheniker;* "gleichtgultig" instead of *gleichgultig;* "upetit" for *Apetit,* "Mahogni" instead of *Mahogony,* he misspells *Haydn* as "Haidn" or his first violinist Schupanizigh as "Schupnanzig."

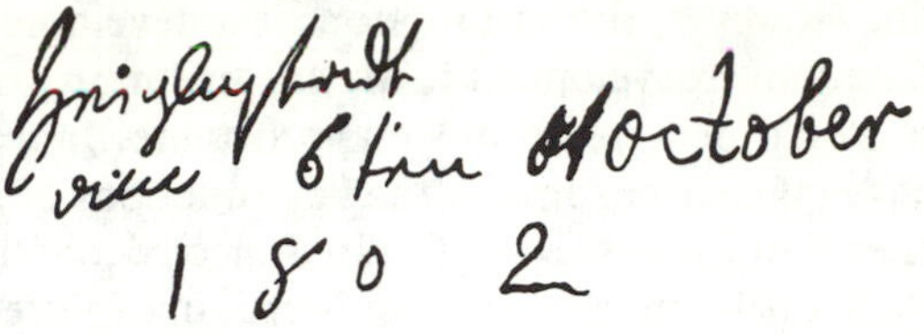

Figure 3. The word *Heiligenstadt* is misspelled, showing omissions, displacement, and reversal of letters.

Max Unger (1926) who devoted a monograph to Beethoven's handwriting points to a number of such spelling, if not agraphic errors, in his autographs. They include such subtle mistakes as displacement of the umlaut sign in *Fräulein* or *Säue,* shifting it one space from left to right: *"Fräulein"* or *"Säue."* Yet the most striking scrambling of letters occurred in the Heiligenstadt Testament, Testament, spelling it "Heiglnstadt" (see Fig. 3). Such a tendency is familiar in children with dyslexia which is at times associated with minimal brain damage. Indeed, it was this finding that put me on the trail of Beethoven's right hemispheric dominance. Some of his mistakes may admittedly be due to passing situational stresses rather than to a real structural deficit. On the other hand, it may well be that his frequently illegible scrawls had served to camouflage his precarious control over his spelling and writing skills. By contrast his original musical scores show no such disturbances.

His troubles with the three R's were compounded by difficulties in performing such elementary tasks as sharpening his pencils or cutting his quills. He needed the services of his friends to help him do so. His biographers repeatedly note his lack of manual dexterity and general clumsiness. "Food spilled, dishes broke, glasses tumbled to the floor when Beethoven took hold of them" (Marek, p. 176).

An irreverent neurologist may well be tempted to attribute such a picture to minimal brain damage to the left parieto occipital region of the brain. However, the assumption of a developmental deficit and associated overdevelopment, if not triumph, of the right hemisphere would perhaps be more appropriate. Indeed the latter may well have taken over some of the key functions of the left side.

What, then, do these seemingly disconnected observations add up to? They open up a novel, hitherto unexplored aspect of Beethoven's personality makeup. In the light of modern split-brain research, they suggest that he was one of those individuals in whose mental organization the right hemisphere of the brain played the dominant role, and that all functions residing in the usually dominant left hemisphere were relatively inferior. We have seen in Chapter 1 that in the right-handed individual, the left side of the brain presides over the three R's: reading, writing, and arithmetic. It is in charge of linear, analytic, intellectual functions. By contrast, the right side of the brain is the poet, the dreamer, the maker of metaphors. It is responsible for our hunches and intuitions and, specifically, for our musical abilities as shown by Sperry (1964), Gazzaniga (1967), Geschwind and his associates, and many others.

In effect, Beethoven's genuis was presided over by his preponderant right hemisphere, while his shortcomings in the three R's were due to the left side of his brain lagging behind the right side in his intellectual functions. Yet there can be no doubt that transcribing the flow and beat of musical sound and the ready response by the vocal or instrumental performer to the printed score is one of the spectacular feats of the musically trained left cerebral hemisphere. Paradoxically, this state of affairs might have earned one of the greatest minds of his century a disconcertingly low IQ. Yet we have learned from several studies of creativity that genius is by no means positively related to a high IQ. Nevertheless, we have to realize that a more narrowly endowed but specially skilled left hemisphere had an equally important hand in the organization and elaboration of Beethoven's musical output.

We know today that with advanced musical training and experience more and more of the native musical skills "migrate" from the right to the left hemisphere (Howard Gardner, 1982). An earlier largely intuitive formulation by Ernest Kris (1952) points in the same direction. He noted that as a matter of basic principle, creativity is predicated on the combination of inspiration, elaboration, and communication. If so, it is reasonable to assume that the latter two ingredients are contributed by the artist's left hemispheric potential. In the last analysis, creativity may be a function of what Arieti described as the "tertiary process" superimposed on Freud's primary and secondary process. It amounts to an exalted ability to sublimation and in turn requires a process of higher integration, blending the intuitions of the right side of the brain with the skill, know-how and discipline of the left. The ideal outcome is then an accomplished work of art, a scientific discovery, a philosophical insight. On the other hand, it may well be that the cleavage between the hero and antihero—between the fumbler and the genius—that ran through Beethoven's personality for most of his life, was largely due to the existing tension between the two sides of the brain. Admittedly, neurological speculations along these lines are premature at this point of our argument. They cannot readily account for his assorted personality quirks: his misanthropy, his temper tantrums, paranoid ideation and bouts of depression. But there can be little doubt that the stellar hours of stilled inter-hemispheric conflict, and their attending raptures of artistic self-expression—the bliss of turning suffering into surcease, turmoil into harmony—more than made up for the agonies that went into their making.

3

NIETZSCHE

Thus Spake the Right Hemisphere

Western civilization has been generous in bestowing the accolade of genius on men as diverse as Beethoven, Mohammed, Napoleon, or Goethe. It did not pause to probe into its right or left hemispheric origins and was satisfied that geniuses, towering head and shoulders over their fellow beings, were just "there." It measured the height of mountain peaks regardless of whether they resulted from volcanic eruptions or from geological upheavals in the earth's crust. Friedrich Nietzsche, the son of a Lutheran parson, self-styled crusader against Christian values, philosopher of the Will to Power, one of the trailblazers of Existential philosophy, past master of German prose and paragon of Stefan George's or Rilke's poetry, was one of those peaks.

He predicted, in his characteristic visionary, epigrammatic style that, though neglected in his lifetime, his greatness would be recognized by generations to come. But he would have certainly deplored that he was also to become accessible to hordes of tourists carried up to his summit by cable car.

This chapter is not an attempt to join the select group of Nietzsche scholars or academic specialists crowding the well-trodden paths of philosophical or psychological exegesis. It merely aims at re-examining his life and literary output in the light of modern neuroscience, particularly what light it can throw on the part played by the two cerebral hemispheres in his mental organization. Nietzsche would have certainly scoffed at such an undertaking as a fruitless attempt to grasp the beauty of a painted masterpiece by chemical analysis of the paint it is made of.

BACKWARD CHILD—PRECOCIOUS PROFESSOR

Still, on trying to trace the origins of Nietzsche's genius to his childhood years, we see less evidence of pathology or family conflict than of apparent conflict between the right and the left side of his brain. His biographers describe him as a precocious child, yet like Edison, Einstein, or Hermann Hesse, he was late in learning to speak. Indeed, his family became concerned that he was retarded. On being pressed to name objects at two and a half years, the first word little Friedrich was able to utter was "Omama" in order to ask for the picture of his grandmother. The psychoanalyst J. E. Gedo (1978) who has unearthed this biographic detail rightly notes at this point the "discrepancy between the lack of verbalization and the complexity of thought implicit in recognizing a pictorial gestalt" (p. 89). It was evidently due to a relative developmental lag of the left hemisphere, as compared with the relative developmental advantage of the more holistically oriented right side of the brain.

Another more conjectural pointer in the same direction is a dream which, according to a diary note made at the age of fourteen, Friedrich had dreamed as a child of five. It occurred about one year after the untimely death of his father: "To the accompaniment of funeral music, the father's grave opened, the dead man climbed out, entered the church and returned with *a child under his arm* (the italics are mine). He then descended again into the grave, which closed over him as the dreamer awakened (Gedo, p. 87). Gedo, who draws attention to this dream also correctly interprets it in terms of the child's wish for reunion and identification with his deceased father. Yet the fact is that Friedrich had a baby brother who had died immediately *after* Friedrich's nightmare. Rightly or wrongly, Nietzsche, as well as his family, considered the dream precognitive. This may in effect have been the reason why it had become part of the family lore.

In any case, the young Friedrich soon got over his initial speech impediment. He turned into a well-behaved, serious-minded boy, nicknamed the "Little Pastor" by his friends. He, too, became aware early of his superior talents—of the "long secret operation and artistry of my instincts" as he put it in his autobiography, *Ecce Homo,* (Messer Ed., Vol. II, 1930, p. 271). At twelve years of age he had a vision: he had seen "God in his glory." A few years later, at seventeen, he addressed him in a poem:

I want to know thee, thou Unknown One
Thee, touching deeply in my soul
Thou, unfathomable one but Kindred to me
I want to know Thee, serving Thee...

(My trans.).

His higher guardianship was, he asserted, so strong "that I never even suspected what was growing in me; so much so that one day my faculties seemed to spring from my being in their full perfection...I lack any memory of ever having troubled to seek them—it is not my nature to struggle...For instance, I found myself established as a Professor at the University (of Basel). Never did I even remotely think of such a possibility, for I was only twenty-four" *Ecce Homo,* (my trans.).

In another passage of *Ecce Homo* he pays similar tribute to his intuitions: "I am possessed of a consummate, uncanny hypersensitivity and responsiveness of instinct for cleanliness. As a result, I can sense physiologically the proximity—nay, the very innards, of a human soul. I can smell it. My psychological antennae are responsive to every secret: to feel it, to lay hands on it. I can fathom the hidden filth at the rock bottom of a person—perhaps as a part of his blood heritage, even though it be camouflaged by his education. it becomes clear to me at our first contact" (p. 258).

PROTO-ANALYST RATHER THAN PROTO-NAZI

It is intuitions of this order that made him a forerunner of psychoanalysis. He knew much about the unconscious and its powers over the intellect; about the machinery of instincts and their virtually indestructible energies. He described the mechanism of repression, though he used the term inhibition for it. It was Nietzsche who coined the term and conceived the concept of sublimation. Above all, he specifically pointed to the fusion in the Dionysian spirit of creativity and destruction, of *Eros* and *Thanatos*—of Freud's still controversial life and death instincts. Some 50 years before Freud, he anticipated his *Civilization and its Discontents,* and Alfred Adler's thesis of the quest for power as one of man's fundamental motivations.

Freud stated in his autobiography that he had not been familiar with Nietzsche's work till late in his career. But critics have rightly pointed to the philosopher's impact upon intellectuals of the late 19th and early 20th century (Henri Ellenberger, 1970). There can be little doubt, therefore, that it had reached Freud second or third hand, as it were. At the same time, it is equally apparent that Nietzsche's aphoristic, metaphorical utterances fell far short of a concise, systematic presentation. It was for the laborious, clinical work of Freud and his followers to develop the theory and practice of psychoanalysis as it is known today.

Nevertheless, there are crucial differences between the Freudian and Nietzchean position. Had Nietzsche survived a decade or two beyond his untimely death in 1900, he might well have ranked among Freud's major dissenters. And it is another matter that Nietzsche's philosophy of Christianity as the morality of slaves; of the Superman; of the Blond Beast lording it over the weak, the worthless and the expendable, had become some of the most destructive themes of the Nazi creed. It is partly due to his very oracular, methaphorical, right-hemispheric style which eminently lent itself to many and varied—and often conflicting—interpretations. Yet to make matters worse, the tragic misinterpretation of his message was greatly furthered by his younger sister, Elizabeth Foerster-Nietzsche, the editor and often falsifier of his literary heritage. In this she was aided and abetted by a growing circle of proto-Nazis who had gathered around her. (Kaufman, 1974). On the other hand, such critics as the Israeli writer Eran Laor (1962) have rightly noted that Nietzsche had in many ways misunderstood himself, as well as the potentially disastrous impact of his message.

Nietzsche himself had always abhorred systems, even though he did so at his own peril. Philosophical systems, he stated, amount to a "one-sided demand to see things just so, and not otherwise" (Kaufman, p. 76). Kaufman specifically contrasts Nietzsche's aphoristic style with the rigor of Hegel's or Kant's presentations of their philosophical systems. If Kant aimed at offering his readers an "experiment in pure reason," at spelling out to them an entire world view, Nietzsche's aphorisms were like raindrops reflecting all the colors of the rainbow in a microcosm, or in Kaufman's phrase they were "monadologic wholes," self-sufficient, yet throwing light on almost any other aphorism.

Clearly, Nietzsche's style is worlds apart from the pedestrian plodding language of his academic forerunners. On the other end of the spectrum, modern symbolic logic, the latest disembodied version of philosophy, has its propositions boiled down to abstract mathematical formulae, no longer open to conflicting interpretation. Nietzsche's language is at the other extreme of the scale. It is the poetic diction of the right, as opposed to the businesslike, no-nonsense discourse of the left side of the brain.

Metaphors, in their passage from the scriptures, to Leibnitz, to Nietzsche, or to Walter Kaufman—seem to be contagious. Taking a leaf out of Nietzsche's prose, it could be stated that the richest and most dazzling array of his sun-catching "monadological" raindrops are contained in his *magnum opus, Thus Spake Zarathustra*. Zarathustra was the legendary Persian sage who served in this book as Nietzsche's mouthpiece or alter ego. Addressing the sun, Zarathustra asks: "What would be your happiness, you stellar giant, without those whom you illuminate?" And he goes on to say: "Like you, I must go down, as men put it—men to whom I will descend... And thus began Zarathustra's *Untergang*—or downfall." A few pages later Nietzsche comes to the very heart of his message: "I am teaching you the superman. Man is that which has to be overcome. So far all creatures have created something in which they transcended themselves: yet you want to be the ebb of this great tide, you want to go back to the animals instead of over-coming man? What is the ape to man? A laughingstock or a painful shame. And this precisely should man be for the superman: a laughingstock and a painful shame."

From the beginning to the end of the book's four parts, there is a similar outpouring of incandescent imagery conveying several levels of densely packed meaning, if not a virtually endless regress of meaning lining up in its wake. In one and a half pages of Part One I counted 46 metaphors, each section ending with the refrain: "Thus spake Zarathustra" (Messer ed., Vol. I, p. 313–315, my trans.). It is significant that his early work *The Birth of the Tragedy from the Spirit of Music*, the first fruit of his academic career, lacks the stylistic cornucopia of his Zarathustra phase. Still, Nietzsche's main thesis of the polarity between the Dionysian and Apollonian spirit already prefigures in a capsule his seminal ideas. In his later work the metaphors tend to be increasingly condensed, abstruse, if not bizarre, foreshadowing his ultimate mental disorganization.

But despite the lack of overall structure, he keeps pursuing his ideas in ceaseless thematic variations to the end: Man must tran-scend himself, regardless of consequences; his traditional values must be thrown overboard and replaced by a radically revised system of values; truth is in the eye of the beholder, subject to what Vaihinger later described as the principle of *as-if*; civilization in its contemporary form is doomed, it is suffering from the iniquities of the intellect; god is dead; we must face up to a philosophy of European nihilism; our only option is a Spinozan *amor fati*, combined with man's artistic endeavors. This may culminate in the advent of the superman who faces the reality of both life and death with composure, even with zest. The world itself is not knowable but subject to eternal recurrence—including the advent and downfall of superman. Hence every living being, and especially superman, has to be keenly aware of what Henri Ellenberger called "the awful majesty of every human act," even in the face of our inability to forestall the tragic outcome.

"ASSAULTED" BY ZARATHUSTRA

As noted earlier, this is not the place to try to give more than a cursory inventory of Nietzsche's principal message. Like the foregoing Beethoven chapter, it focuses on the *modus operandi* of genius; on the wellsprings of Nietzsche's creativeness and the prophetic vision of himself and of the fate of western man. In Nietzsche's words "The first Zarathustra occurred to me on my walks on the Italian Riviera," or, rather, Zarathustra "assaulted" him there. He had overtaken him like an inspiration; he made him feel more like a medium, an incarnation of overwhelming external powers, than his ordinary self. The fact is that he wrote down the first part in a ten days' frenzy of creative inspiration. Parts Two and Three followed, taking no more than the same time for their completion. The fourth part was finished a year or two later, with several interruptions.

Thus we have Nietzsche's own account of what today would be described as an "altered state of consciousness" from which his Zarathustra experience had sprung. Its poetic, if not musical qualities—so close to Nietzsche's heart—are borne out by a dithyrambic, almost ecstatic language, far removed from the ordinary level of discourse. Its archaic grammar and syntax are reminiscent of the Old and New Testaments; of the songs of the Psalmist: it still carries the stamp of the religious instruction the "Little Pastor" had received in his father's parsonage. Yet it does so despite the fact that Nietzsche had long since lost the faith of his childhood years and in effect repudiated everything Christian— or that had even remotely been touched by the Christian "contagion."

Still, even the basic plan of Zarathustra seems to duplicate the four Gospels, with Nietzsche the self-styled Anti-Christ donning the mantle of the four Evangelists and proclaiming his own advent. There is thus a deep cleavage between form and content running through the work. It mixes two different cognitive styles. It straddles two millennia: from Christ to Anti-Christ, from the simple faith of his childhood to the philosophy of radical nihilism, barely relieved by Zarathustra's Yes-saying to his own destiny.

Paradoxically, this concatenation of the old and the new, of a ruthless confrontation with the decadence of his time, and baleful anticipation of an inescapable doom, has only deepened Nietzsche's impact on his contemporaries and perhaps even more so on generations to come. The fact is that not unlike the Old and

New Testaments, *Zarathustra* resounds with visions and ambiguous prophecies of things to come. They foretell Nietzsche's own ascent to future, posthumous greatness, mingled with dark admonitions to his disciples: "Die at the right time," "I praise my death that comes when I will it to come."

There are more ominous forebodings of threatening calamities: "Not only the wisdom of the millennia—their madness too breaks in on us. It is perilous to be an heir." In another passage he berates his followers, asking: "Where is the lightening to lick you with his tongue? Where is the madness with which you should be inoculated? Behold, I teach you the superman: He is the lightening; he is this insanity" (Messer ed. p.295). And again: "What is great in man is that he is a bridge, not an end in himself, what is lovable in man is that he is an *Untergang*—a downfall . . . I love the one who wills his downfall."

Another ominous passage is found in Part Three of *Zarathustra* (p. 478–479). After declaring that he had turned his innermost soul inside out and laid it open to the light of day, he is overcome by disgust and a sense of woe. "Barely did Zarathustra utter these words, he fell down like a dead man and stayed a long time as if he were dead. When he came to, he was pale and atremble and did not want to drink nor eat. This (condition) lasted for seven days." Today we would describe it as a seizure, followed by a semistuporous state. For Nietzsche it was yet another premonition of Zarathustra's ultimate descent into the abyss which was to engulf him in 1889.

I noted that it is the essence of metaphors to be loaded with multiple meanings. The psychiatrist and Existential philosopher Karl Jaspers specifically stressed the ambiguity of Nietzsche's aphoristic style (1965), and Kaufman remarks that ambiguity, *Vieldeutigkeit*, or multiple meanings, were a basic feature of Nietzsche's philosophy. No doubt the predicted downfall of the race has to be taken in a largely symbolic fashion. So was Nietzsche's reference to the "inoculation" with madness. But the question is whether or not such passages inadvertently touched upon Nietzsche's personal destiny: upon the motif of his plunge into insanity 6 or 7 years *ahead* of time. He writes in a letter to his friend Gast in 1881: "Alas, my friend, at times a premonition passes through my head that I actually live a most perilous life, for I belong to those machines which are apt to explode...." Two years later he adds: "The thought occurred to me that I am probably going to die from such an explosion of feelings" (Bertram, 1937, p. 290).

Some 5 years thereafter, on November 20, 1888, after finishing his *Ecce Homo*, he writes to Georg Brandes, the Danish literary critic: "It (*Ecce Homo*) is an *Attentat* against the Crucified One that is certainly going to be world-shaking... It ends with lightning and thunder claps. I am Christendom's first psychologist and I can marshal heavy equipment against it... which no one in Christianity had even dreamt about... I am swearing to you that in 2 years time we shall have the whole earth in convulsions... I am a *Verhangnis* (a doom and a bringer of doom)."

The letter reflects his incipient trend toward disorganization and delusions of grandeur. It also amounts to a gigantic overstatement and distortion of things to come: it was not the earth, but Nietzsche himself who was to suffer an "earthshaking" attack of convulsions. Nor was the time of its onset 2 years away. Two or three weeks later he had a mental breakdown in a street of Turin. As he was passing a horse that was being flogged by the coachman, he threw his arms around it and apparently went into an epileptic seizure. It was the first clinical symptom of his fatal illness: general paresis of the insane. The attack was followed by a stuporous condition lasting some 2 days.

When a friend was called to his lodgings in Turin, he found Nietzsche confused and strangely elated. They boarded a train to Basel where the patient was admitted to an asylum. On the train he sang his *Gondola Song* from *Ecce Homo*:

> At the bridge I started
> Lately in the brown night,
> From afar came a song:
> As a golden drop it welled.
> Over the quivering surface
> Gondolas, lights, and music
> Drunken it swam out into the twilight
> My soul, a string instrument,
> Sang to itself, invisibly touched
> A secret gondola song,
> Quivering with irridescent happiness.
> ——Did anyone listen to it?[1]
>   translated by W. Kaufman

The psychoanalyst C.P.Ellerman (1970), commenting on Nietzsche's singing of the *Gondola Song*, rightly sees in Nietzsche's crossing of the bridge his passage from man to superman. It was to serve at the same time as a consolation for his "going under" or *Untergang*. The symbolism is, of course, a recurrent theme in Nietzsche's writings. The rest of Ellerman's argument is too involved to be repeated here. More relevant in the present context seems to be the clinical aspect of Nietzsche's breakdown. A middle-aged, mustachioed German university professor is abruptly shedding all conventional mores and inhibitions and passes into a full-fledged manic phase. Psychoanalytically speaking, it amounts to an emphatic denial of the tragic aspects of his *Untergang*. Several exultant but confused letters written shortly after the attack reflect the same euphoria, grandiosity, and confusion.

In one letter, dated Turin, 5 January 1889, addressed to Jakob Burckhardt, the famous historian, he writes: "In the end I would prefer to be a Professor in Basel instead of being God; but I did not have to carry my private egotism so far as to avoid for its sake the creation of the world." He signed his letters as *Dionysos*, or the *Crucified One*. Fig. 4b shows the deterioration of his handwriting 3 years later, in 1891. It is tremulous, jerky, erratic. The word *herzlich* shows condensation of the letters L and H in the first capital. This is in striking contrast to his once impeccable, refined penmanship (4a) and it reflects the ravages of the organic brain damage due to the syphilitic process. Still, the ecstatic mood of some of the post-Turin letters seems to celebrate the fulfillment of a wish expressed some 8 years prior to his downfall: "Oh ye heavenly powers, may you grant me madness. Madness that I at long last may believe in myself" (The Dawn of Day, 1881).

"Inoculated" with Madness:
Gift of the Tarantula

Where, then, does Nietzsche's obsessive preoccupation with madness come from? Did he carry, unbeknown to himself, the seeds of his malady in his innermost soul—or, to be more specific—in his genetic makeup? The question has been widely dis-

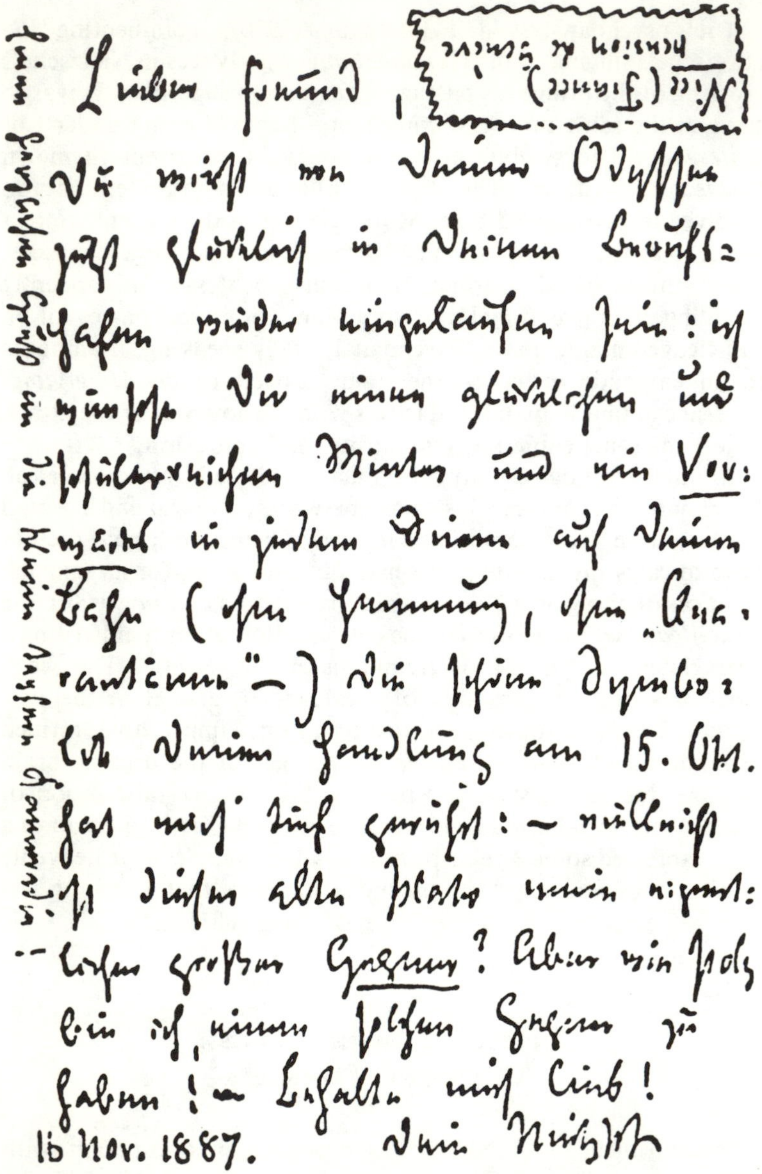

Fig. 3a: Nietzsche's handwriting in 1887 before his breakdown.

cussed by his biographers. The hypothesis of heredity is now being answered in the negative. Alternately: did his illness amount to his unconscious "project," as proposed by such Existentialists as Camus or Ortega y Gasset, or, as I discovered, in Picasso's childhood memory of the *Thousand Doves* (Ehrenwald, 1963). In short, has madness been a self-fulfilling prophecy in which Nietzsche both foresaw, and helped to bring about, its realization? Lastly, was his genius indeed capable of steering his life towards the tragic consummation of his own choosing? Was it the handiwork of a Freudian *death instinct*, several decades before Freud?

If we could "factor out" Nietzsche's syphilitic infection—his "inoculation" with madness—from his argument, the answer would be in the affirmative. But his recent biographers agree that Friedrich had in his student days in fact contracted the disease in a brothel, and much has been made of his apparent failure to undergo a full course of antisyphilitic treatment. True or not, no cure of the cerebral sequelae of the infection was available at his time. Some suggest that Nietzsche had not even been consciously aware of his illness, or had denied its reality to himself.

In either case, viewed against the history of his syphilitic infection, his reference to an "inoculation with madness" has a prophetic ring. It is a macabre counterpart to his nightmare at the age of five, presaging the death of his little brother Joseph. Significantly, Nietzsche himself seemed to be aware of his oracular propensities...In his *Will to Power* (p. 316 Messer ed.) he describes himself as a "Soothsayer spirit who is *looking back* when he narrates what is coming *in the future*" (my italics).

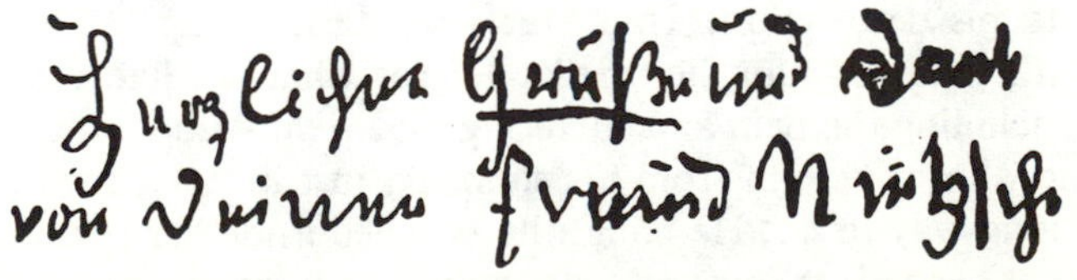

Fig. 3b: Nietzsche's handwriting in 1901 after his breakdown.

This is also illustrated by what seem to be more specific references to his syphilitic infection. They are symbolized by the bite of the adder and the tarantula in *Zarathustra I*. "Zarathustra fell asleep under a fig tree. Lo, there came an adder and bit him on the neck so as to make him cry out in pain. And he beheld the snake, she recognized his eye, turned around clumsily and wanted to be gone. Not yet, spake Zarathustra. You did not receive my thanks as yet; you did wake me in time; my journey is long." "This journey is short," sadly replied the adder; "my poison kills." Zarathustra smiled. "When, if ever, did a dragon die from the poison of the snake?" he asked. "Still, take back your venom, you are not rich enough to bestow it on me." At that the adder threw herself again around his neck and licked his wound. (Was the adder the unknown girl he had met in a house of ill-repute when Nietzsche was nineteen years old? Was it she who happened to inoculate him with madness?)

In another passage, he enters the tarantula's cave and cries out, "Woe, there the tarantula bit me, my old enemy. Divinely sure and beautiful, she bit me in the finger...there should be justice and punishment—this is what she thinks. Not for nothing should he (Zarathustra), in honor of friendship, sing his song." (Zarathustra II. Messer ed. p. 374). The passage is obscure, but the symbolism of the cave (the womb of the female); of the bite of the tarantula (*die Tarantel*, inflicting the poisonous infection); and of the finger (as a phallic symbol) is apparent.

The adder allegory is more involved. In her case (*die Schlange* in German is feminine) the presumed precognitive element is concealed in several layers of a metaphor. Zarathustra receives and acknowledges her poisonous bite as a gift (incidentally, *gift* in German, means poison) because it is the superman's destiny to go down to his destruction. Thus, far from begrudging the woman who inflicted it on him, he thanks her for what she had done for him—including the pain and suffering that went with it. Indeed, it was she who woke him from his slumber, just in time, for he still had a long way to go. He haughtily brushed aside her remonstrations that her poison is *deadly*, as though he were talking of a test of strength between man and woman. Was it not Nietzsche after all who had said: "You go to the woman, don't forget the whip." The scene ends with the adder—the *femme fatale*—trying to make up for the harm she had done by licking (i.e., sucking) the poison from his wound.

Such a rather orthodox Freudian interpretation of the adder and tarantula incidents is all the more suggestive since it is applied to material going back some 2 decades before the advent of Freud, leaving Nietzsche himself in the dark as to its hidden meaning. There is, however, one more, rival, interpretation of the adder and tarantula theme in his *Zarathustra*. Kaufman notes that Nietzsche, while engaged in the writing of the book, had been involved in a stirring but frustrating relationship with a real *femme fatale*, Lou Andreas-Salome, aged twenty-one, just embarking on her literary and, later, psychoanalytic career in the course of which she captivated such famous men as Rilke and Freud himself, but, who, according to her biographers, was still a virgin at that time. The relationship ended on a discordant note and had obviously hurt Nietzsche to the quick.

There is no need to play out one interpretation against the other. In Nietzsche's eyes the adder and the tarantula were Jungian archetypes: generic woman, encompassing mother figures, like Cosima, the wife of his fatherly friend, Richard Wagner; his sister Elisabeth; the temptress Lou Salome of Sils Maria; and last but not least, the girl in the brothel in Leipzig. Either way, the snake and tarantula symbolism is evidently overdetermined. We have to be satisfied with an ambiguous, essentially right-hemispheric reading of the case, and neither one nor the other is amenable to scientific proof. All that can be asserted with a reasonable degree of certainty is that Nietzsche had created Zarathustra as his *double*, or secondary personality, and that his "trance" productions had all the hallmarks of repressed material reappearing in a suitable disguise in his stream of consciousness or artistic expression.

PROPHET OF OWN DOOM

What, then, was the impact of madness on Nietzsche's genius? We are still groping in the dark about the nature of genius, but we know a little more about his illness. Historically, the polemic over its nature ranges from a veritable "ascent into the mystical" (Bertram, 1933) to psychopathy; despair over having been misunderstood by his contemporaries; to "senile" degeneration of his brain; to a clearcut case of general paresis of the insane (Lange-Eichbaum, 1946, Erich Podach, 1931, and others). The weight of the evidence available today clearly tips the balance in favor of the latter diagnosis. It is also supported by the specimen of his handwriting from 1901 (see Fig. 4b).

General paresis of the insane is one of the late sequelae of the syphilitic infection. It is due to an invasion of the central nervous system, and especially the brain by spirochetes after years of incubation. There are no symptoms after the "primary affect" and diverse skin eruptions have receded, and there is no reason to believe that the ensuing incubation period in any way affected Nietzsche's physical well-being.

The young man's brooding over having been contaminated by the disease is another matter. It must have left him with a profound feeling of guilt and shame, and he may have had a hard time convincing himself of the folly of such a reaction. From this to attitudes of denial, reaction formation, and repression was only one step. Guilt and shame, he stated in his *Re-evaluation of All Values*, is itself merely the result of contamination with conventional Christian (read *societal*) value judgments. Significantly, the word contamination or infection repeatedly recurs in his writings. Besides, the visible wound inflicted on him was to become a challenge, to overcome its fearsome consequences in a heroic struggle with destiny, or in case of need, by stoic surrender to the ineviatble, as exemplified by Spinoza's *Amor Fati*. For him, overcoming the frailties and iniquities of being human was the supreme goal of man—in effect, the goal of growing into *superman*. Such a defiance and denial of his own limitations, of the perils attendant to his superhuman or Dionysian mission may perhaps be regarded as unrealistic or irrational, but did not Zarathustra proclaim: "There is always madness in love"? (did he mean sexual abandon?) and "method in madness"?

Still, Nietzsche was bound to live with the stigma of his affliction and its dreaded consequences. It was at the time when venereal disease was virtually incurable and when a crown-prince, heir to the Austrian empire, took his own and his mistress' life in a suicide pact because they saw no other way out of their predicament.

Countless lesser victims of venereal disease had chosen the same path. Yet young Nietzsche chose to live—to live perilously, to deny his plight, while at the same time asserting that he was grateful to the snake under the fig tree for her "gift" of the poison. Thus Nietzsche, the tragic hero, succeeded in the end in extracting a creative response even from the bite of the snake, the sting of the tarantula, and was ready to pay for his hubris with his self-proclaimed *Untergang*. This was his existential response to the confrontation with the abyss.

Alas, the "earth-shaking convulsion" that was to overtake him at the age of fifty-five in a street in Turin, was to push him over the edge. We know today that the acute phase of general paresis may be ushered in by epileptic seizures, transient strokes, manic or depressive mood swings or bizarre psychotic behavior and deterioration of habits. Most of this syndrome can be found in Nietzsche's case history. We also know that the prognosis is better in preponderantly manic patients, and worse in the dull, inert, depressive types. This is also borne out by Nietzsche's stubborn survival for close to 10 years in various mental hospitals, and at times under the care of a hapless aged mother and an unloving, domineering sister.

Initially, Nietzsche seemed still to be functioning with the momentum provided by the sudden release of neural inhibitions. Whether or not this was due to excitation of the right hemisphere, the frontal lobes, or to the eclipse of left hemispheric controls is a moot question. The letters preserved from this time still persist in what by now had turned into frank delusions of grandeur and wholly undisguised identification with *Dionysos* or the *Crucified One*. In one of his letters to Cosima Wagner, now widowed, he addresses her by her nickname *Ariadne*, "Ariadne, I love you." It is an open and undisguised confession of his oedipal attachment to an idealized mother figure. The organic brain process had torn the last cover of repression from his unconscious, laying it bare for everyone to see, like the ruins of a magnificent Greek Temple.

Evidently there is little that can be learned from this condensed case history about the way Nietzsche's insanity affected his genius. Still, some light can be thrown on the way genius may affect the operation of *its* brain. (The stress on *its* goes back to Eccles' and Popper's trailblazing book, *The Mind and Its Brain*, 1977). We must realize, however, that illness is more, much more, than a bunch of spirochetes or other microbes being thrown into a Petri dish filled with agar-agar or chicken broth. It amounts to a human being—or his brain—meeting with a noxious agent, or with an indifferent, if not frankly hostile, universe.

We have seen Nietzsche's first encounter with the demon illness. It affected his outlook on the world, his tragic, in effect nihilistic, philosophy of life, with its ultimate triumphant affirmation, despite the built-in suffering, horror, and despair, in his enunciation of the *Superman.* I have hinted that it was his "irrationally" elated, hypomanic state of mind that had helped him, for close to 10 years, to keep alive, while others usually succumbed to the process in a year or two.

Some of his medical biographers suggest that Nietzsche's luetic brain affection had anteceded the full-fledged clinical picture by several years. In any case, it appears that in the wake of his "inoculation" and silent incubation with insanity he had reached new heights of creativeness: *Ecce Home,* in 1888; *Genealogy of Morals,* 1887; the fourth and third *Zarathustra,* 1884-85; *the Twilight of the Idols,* 1889 (Kaufman, p. 484). Viewed in this light, his reactions; to the "bite of the snake" can be compared with that of some modern users of hashish, LSD, or psylocibin: the spectacular uprush of creative energies, real or imaginary. Though threatened by the gathering clouds of confusion, loss of reality-testing, and the insidious onset of delusions of grandeur—they were in Nietzsche's case still founded on solid grounds of a flawed genius.

Still, the boost to the activity of the right hemisphere is perhaps the limit of what the mind can do "for its brain." It succeeded in using the deadly toxin of the spirochetes—the venom of the tarantula—as a stimulant and source of inspiration, of Dionysian raptures and ecstasies, in much the same way as some experimental subjects may use psilocybin or peyotl for enchantment and uplift to religious or mystical experiences; while others may merely go into a bizarre but otherwise sterile "altered state" of consciousness—or plain stupor.

I have also hinted that it is premature to speculate whether or not Nietzsche's premonitions and diverse prophetic utterances, as they are recorded in *Zarathustra,* in his *Ecce Homo,* and elsewhere, were mere flukes, or valid though symbolically disguised precognitive hunches. We know today that psychedelic drugs cannot, by themselves, inject genius or paranormal faculties into personalities lacking their basic prerequisites in the first place. But I noted in the introductory chapter that there is growing evidence of the right cerebral hemisphere being involved, one way or another, in their processing. This is particularly relevant to Nietzsche's personality, to his idiosyncratic cognitive style, to his glowing metaphorical language, to the poetic cadence and musical quality of his diction: he had composed music long before he was writing his aphorisms and essays. In ancient Greece he would have perhaps sung and danced—not just recited his message. In his first major work, he traced the origin of poetry, and the arts in general, to the "Spirit of Music." This is reflected in virtually all his subsequent literary and poetic writings. It also echoes Richard Wagner's profound influence on the young classical scholar, and tends to obscure the customary cleavage between two levels of discourse: prose and poetry.

The philosoper Ernst Cassirer (1946) has placed great emphasis on the distinction between the two. He contrasts "primitive" metaphorical thinking with the ordinary, linear level of discourse. Metaphorical thinking is the source of myth and poetry. Many consider it superior to literal language, the latter being concerned with empirical truth, the former with transempirical, intuitive truth.

More recently, Julian Jaynes (1976) has taken a similar position. Poetry, he suggests, conveys "divine knowledge" (p. 363). Above all, poetry was originally *sung*. Drawing on the results of modern split brain research, he too reaches the conclusion that song, in contrast to speech, is primarily a function of the right hemisphere and as such closely akin to Plato's "divine madness."

Alas, we have Nietzsche's word for it that the gods are dead or, according to Jaynes, banished to the wax museum of the "bicameral" mind. Contemporary critics are more likely to consider Nietzsche's illness of venereal rather than divine origin. But this should not detract from the greatness of his genius. It rather confers the sparks of the divine—of the Dionysian spirit, even on the venom—on the "Gift"—of the tarantula's sting and on the innate potentials of the right cerebral hemisphere.

4

LEONARDO DA VINCI
Ambidextrous Genius

There is no facet in Leonardo da Vinci's life history, no stroke of his pen, chisel, or brush, no wrinkle of his prodigious output as a painter, artist, writer, composer, or engineer that has remained unexplored by biographers, art historians, writers of doctoral theses, or psychoanalysts. Why then yet another attempt at going over familiar territory, at digging up layers that have already been thoroughly worked through by such authorities as Sigmund Freud, Kurt Eissler, Paul Valéry, Bernard Berenson, Meyer Shapiro, Kenneth Clark, or Martin Kemp (1981) to mention only a few most familiar to the general reader?

The reason is that here, again, focus on the vicissitudes of conflict versus cooperation between the two cerebral hemispheres should throw new light on the inner workings of this ambidextrous genius. To be more specific, three dichotomies can be seen running through his life: (1) the dichotomy of artist versus scientist; (2) the polarity of right versus left hemispheric dominance; and (3) the cleavage between male versus female, of activity versus passivity, in his sexual orientation.

SCIENCE VERSUS ART

Leonardo's first dichotomy, that between art and science, had already struck some of his contemporaries. In April 1501, the friar Pietro de Lovella reported to the Marchesa Isabella d'Este that Leonardo had flatly rejected her commission for a major painting. He was so deeply immersed in the study of mathematics that he neglected painting altogether "and the sight of the brush put him out of temper." Again, from 1504 to 1505, the study of Euclid and Archimedes occupied most of Leonardo's time. On St. Andrew's Night, 1504, he was greatly elated when he thought he had found the solution of the quadrature of the circle. He was in error, but continued to pursue the problem in several pages of the *Codex Atlanticus*. It was a period when painting and other artistic pre-occupations were pushed completely into the background. This was followed by his artistically most productive "third Florentine" period.

His biographers, especially Freud (1910) and Kurt Eissler (1966), rightly note that Leonardo had used mathematics as an outright escape from painting to meet deep-seated emotional needs of his own. Of course it is difficult to pinpoint the dates of Leonardo's recurrent changes of heart. We know that in the same years he had also been busy with work on the Mona Lisa and on the cartoons for the Battle of Anghiari. Yet apart from minor fluctuations, his notebooks show that major cycles of ebb and flow were characteristic features of his career. They appear on nearly every page of the Codices that have come down to us. They also show his disconcerting habit of adding, seemingly out of context and haphazardly, new entries, drawings, or pencil sketches whenever he found blank spaces on a given page, making attempts at their dating virtually impossible. Nevertheless, the cleavage between art and science in Leonardo's mental organization and psychohistory is unmistakable. It consitutes his first dichotomy.

As a left hander, Leonardo wrote most of his notebooks from

right to left. But he also showed a tendency to shift the writing of figures either from right to left or from left to right. A typical example is his meticulous copy of a multiplication table taken from the book *Summa Arithmetica* of his mentor Luca Pacioli. He copied the table in the conventional way, but added in the left margin his own summary—in mirror writing. On the other hand, he wrote down the musical score as well as the words of the song *Love gives me pleasure* with his right hand, left to right. Even more striking is a passage in MacCurdy's classical edition of Leonardo's *Notebooks* (1959, p. 1123) which shows his tendency to *reverse letters of a whole word*. For instance: "Find Ligny and tell him you will wait for him in *Rome*." MacCurdy notes that in the original, *Ligny* stands for *Ingil* and "in Rome" is transposed to "a morra." The same tendency can be found in *La Panna* for "in Naples" or in "*e no igano dal*" for donation. MacCurdy speculates that such reversals may have been due to Leonardo's need for secrecy. But they also reflect his ability to switch, playfully, and with apparent ease, the directional impulse of either the right or the left hemisphere from one side to the other. It will be noted that occasional reversals of this order, though on a smaller scale, can frequently be seen in dyslectic children of our time.

Born out of wedlock, Leonardo was apprenticed to the workshop of Verrocchio at the age of ten. He was largely self-taught in the sciences and humanities of his time. Yet despite his efforts and considerable accomplishments in mathematics, he was at times careless, if not ineffectual, at simple calculations. On reporting the death of his father, he mixes up his correct age. In an inventory of 48 of his books, he falls short of 2 in his addition. The *Codex Atlanticus* contains a page with drawings illustrating an ingenious mathematical-geometric game. Yet a simple error in figuring mars the outcome of his elaborate calculations. Elsewhere he tries to figure out the cube root of 128. Yet, according to Augusto Marinoni (1974), he gives his answer "in the words of an artist, not a mathematician." That is, he arrives at "5 and a certain inexpressible fraction, which is easy to make but hard to say" (p. 73).

According to George Santillana (1966) who was an authority on Leonardo's writings in his own right, Leonardo's spelling was atrocious. Though all his diaries were written "in the neat and sure hand of a notary's son, his spelling proves to be pure chaos, one that far exceeds the irregularities of the day." And Santillana goes on to say: "the words are severed and broken, and also amalgamated...the spelling is that of a servant girl or the recruit..." (p. 191). In short, Leonardo would have received poor marks in the three R's from a schoolmaster of our day. It will be recalled that in this respect his shortcomings resemble those of Ludwig van Beethoven described in an earlier chapter or of Einstein whose occasional trivial errors in calculation had been a source of much merriment among his admirers.

Leonardo himself frankly admitted that he was "unlettered," as compared to some of his more scholarly contemporaries. But he was also fully aware of the merits of his own spectacular artistic and intuitive approach: "the poet may surpass the painter in representing the works of nature...But how much more difficult it is to understand the works of nature than the book of the poet." In his *Treatise on Painting* he tries to elaborate the point with a story. A poet had brought a poem to King Mathias of Hungary to celebrate the birthday of the king's beloved. The poet's rival was a painter who brought the king a portrait of the lady. "The king greatly admired the painting but quickly closed (i.e., rejected) the poet's book. Thereupon the poet "very indignantly said: Oh king, read, but read, and you will learn matters of far weightier substance than a mute picture." Then the king, resenting the reproach that he was admiring mute things said: "Silence; you do not know what you are saying; this picture serves a nobler sense than your work . . . Give me something that I can see and touch and not only hear, and I do not blame my choice when I put your book under my arm (i.e., set it aside) and am holding the painting with both hands before my eyes to enjoy; because my hands chose of their own accord to serve the nobler sense and not just the sense of hearing."

The story serves to underscore a point frequently made by Leonardo: painting is the highest of all arts and sciences. He, Leonardo, may not be able to master to the full the flowery language of his contemporary rivals for princely favors. He knows he cannot express himself in words as he would like to. But it is for the painter to study "the divine book of nature every day, interpreting and reproducing directly the words of the supreme master." Indeed, in so doing he comes closest to the Creator himself.

Marinoni who made a special study of Leonardo's literary record stresses that throughout his work "figurative discourse alternates with oral (i.e. literal) discourse. "The subordination and underestimation of the latter," he holds, "is one of the main causes of the fragmentation of his thought into thousands of disconnected and unrelated notes." It will be recalled that the same could be said of Nietzsche's aphoristic, metaphorical style. Leonardo's prose has an uneven, rambling quality. "It proceeds in fits and starts and rarely covers more than a half or a whole page at a time." A wealth of ideas is thrown forth here and there, but soon abandoned without further elaboration. "Tears come from the heart, not from the brain," he notes in the middle of a passage on anatomy. At other times, his figurative discourse attains rare poetic beauty. It has "a changeable musical rhythm that binds and exalts Leonardo's phrasing in his better moments." At times it suggests "the reverberations of rhythm and of sound (and their culmination) in veritable stanzas" (p. 82).

The fact is that a notable musical ability was an added facet of his genius. He had invented or re-invented, the *lyra* and it is said his playing it, accompanying his singing, had enchanted audiences at the court of Lodovico il Moro in Milan.

Countless mechanical inventions prefiguring the bicycle, the flying machine, the armored car, or the submarine, are further testimonies to his creative if not prophetic capacity for innovation. So are his occasional flashes of intuition scattered haphazardly on the pages of his diaries. There is his casual remark *Il sole non se muove*—the sun does not move—some 100 years before Galileo. There are his reports and descriptions of experimental procedures long before the advent of the scientific revolution. And there is his radical condemnation of wars as *bestialissima pazzia*—the most bestial madness.

Such feats seem to duplicate nature's capacity for innovation and mutation in the evolutionary process itself. And here again we have to assume that it is the brain cortex—more specifically the nondominant, as yet not specialized or lateralized right hemisphere—which has served as the cutting edge of change.

What does this concatenation of surpassing creative abilities in both science and the humanities add up to? It is suggestive of an optimal integration and orchestration of the two cerebral hemispheres, fueled by powerful motivations from lower subcortical centers in an *Uomo Universale*—a Renaissance man. At the same time, it is not surprising that his passions, raw instinctual drives, both sexual and aggressive, had literally been relegated to the back burner in his mental organization. Nevertheless, the conflict between cortical and subcortical centers in the vertical, as well as between his right and left hemispheres in the horizontal, had been very much in evidence throughout Leonardo's life. It is reflected in the trivial errors in spelling or figuring discovered by his thoroughly left hemispheric biographers. It may have also been conducive to his painful disability to finish some of his artistic and scientific projects. "O Leonardo," he asked in his diary, "why do you labor so hard?" Maybe it was to try to cope with both his conflicts and his embarrassment of riches. We have seen how he tried to do so by his occasional escapes from art to science, and from science back to art again. It constitutes Leonardo's second dichotomy: the dichotomy of right versus left hemispheric dominance.

Existential Shift From Right to Left Brain Dominance and Vice Versa

Elsewhere I have described abrupt changes of this order as existential shifts, that is, global alterations of a person's conscious experience and behavioral repertoire that may affect his whole mode of existence or "being in the world." I also noted the close association of such shifts with the pendulum swings of right versus left hemispheric preponderance. A typical example is Beethoven changing gears from inspired composer to a social misfit or tortured misanthrope.

Leonardo's personal history is punctuated by minor and major shifts of this order. They can be seen in the abrupt changes of his topic from fact to phantasy; from experience to imagination, as Kenneth Clark put it (1966). In his notebooks he changed his level of discourse, style of presentation, and even direction of handwriting from page to page, from paragraph to paragraph. Yet I have also stressed the major tidal changes of his output over the years. For weeks or months he would chain himself to his easel and canvas. Suddenly he would drop his brush to embark on the study of the flight of birds in the Tuscan hills. Or else he would spend night after night in the hospital mortuary to dissect bodies, to draw every bone, muscle, blood vessel, and nerve to lay the foundation of human anatomy some 50 years before Vesalius. He immersed himself in the study of Latin at the age of forty-two, or built canons, fortifications, and battering rams for Lodovico il Moro in Milan—to say nothing of the pageants and other spectaculars he staged at his court.

Much has been said about Leonardo's inability to finish any one of his masterpieces to his own satisfaction. Apparently the conflicting demands of his two masters, art and science, if not of the right and left hemispheres, made it impossible for him to do so. He planned, but was never able to write, a definite *Treatise of Anatomy,* and one on the art and science of painting; still less could he present a systematic statement of his philosophy. Here again the **similarity with Nietzsche's fragmented, "monodological" style is unmistakable.**

Still, he had come as close to integrating the two conflicting principles in his work as any man, and to making his cerebral hemispheres operate in tandem. There can be little doubt that it was his explorations of nature at first hand that imparted to his drawings the loving and informed perfection which he sought. Conversely, it was in his penetrating with the painter's eye every nook and cranny of the "divine book of nature"—from cloud formations to blades of grass, from hunchbacks to dancing maidens—that he acquired the intimate knowledge of their **"essences" that no objective scientific observer would attain.**

Ladislao Reti, the art historian, commenting on Leonardo's drawings of the flight of birds in the *Madrid Codex* (1974), notes that they show "a steady progression from art to the abstractions of science." In a like vein, it is his studies in hydraulics that opened his eyes to the similarity of braided hair or his own beard to ocean waves. The same "progression" is true of the dazzling array of his last drawings, the swirling waters of the *Deluge* which Kenneth

Clark compares with the greatness of Beethoven's late string quartets.

Still, with all his accomplishments, Leonardo was left with the painful feeling that all along he had fallen short of perfection. Over and over again, he asked in his diaries: *"Has ever anything been done?"* And he prayed for God's forgiveness for having left so much unfinished. Yet it was perhaps his very need for perfection that made him seek escape from the flaws of an unfinished masterpiece to the austere certainties of mathematics—and back to his paintings again. Giorgio Vasari, his none too reliable biographer, claims that he was seen to tremble when embarking on a new project. This may well have been due to his fear of confronting the matchless perfection of his inner vision with the realities of the slowly and laboriously evolving painting on the canvas. But we are also told that once the work had started, he found it as difficult to tear himself away from it as Michelangelo from the Sistine ceiling, Beethoven from his piano, or Nietzsche from his *Zarathustra*.

Nevertheless, in his heart of hearts he owed his first allegiance to painting as man's closest approximation to the Creator himself. Whether or not the ultimate key to his dedication to art lies in its freedom from left hemispheric constraints, that is, from a stern paternal superego, as opposed to a more gentle and permissive maternal superego figure, is another matter.

It should also be noted that Freud in his classical though still controversial monograph *Leonardo da Vinci, a Study in psychosexuality* (1910), approaches the problem from an altogether different angle. He interprets Leonardo's conflict between art and science in purely psychodynamic terms: it was due to the vicissitudes of repression versus sublimation in his psychosexual development. Freud suggests that Leonardo, owing to his early chidlhood conditioning, channelled his sexual drive into a thirst for knowledge—or else into artistic ability. At the same time, Freud suggests that his overall sexual orientation was that of a latent if not overt homosexual.

Yet Freud qualifies this statement by granting that such organic factors as Leonardo's left handedness, and even his physical beauty, may have contributed to the ultimate outcome. Even so he places his main emphasis on what is here described as Leonardo's third dichotomy: the cleavage between masculine versus feminine orientation, or between heterosexuality versus homosexuality.

HOMOSEXUAL? THE LEONARDO-SALAI EQUATION

What are the facts? As an illegitimate child, Leonardo spent the first few years of his life in his father's house in Vinci, some 30 to 40 miles from Florence. He was taken care of by his grandfather and two successive stepmothers. At about ten Ser Piero, a successful notary, placed him as an apprentice in the workshop of the famous painter and sculptor Andrea Verrocchio in Florence. From then on Ser Piero may have been at best an absentee father to Leonardo, siring a dozen or so "legitimate" half-brothers and sisters with three successive wives, some 20 years his junior.

Leonardo, living above Verrocchio's workshop on the Via del Agnolo in Florence, must have been exposed to a completely new mode of life in the big city. At twenty-one, he and four other youths were accused of homosexual acts with a male model of ill repute. They were acquitted; were accused again; and acquited a second time. But rumors persisted after the incident. In 1560 the painter Gian Paolo Lomazzo, in a Renaissance equivalent of a gossip column, wrote an imaginary dialogue between the sculptor Phidias and Leonardo da Vinci. Referring to his youthful apprentice and house servant, Salai, Leonardo declares: "I loved him more than all the others, and there were several!!!" Whereupon Phidias asks him: "Did you perhaps play with him the game in the behind?" Needless to say, Lomazzo has Leonardo answer in the affirmative: "And how many times? Have in mind that he was a most beautiful young man, especially at fifteen."

Lomazzo's story must be taken with a grain of salt. But the fact is that at thirty-eight Leonardo adopted and took into his household a ten year old boy called Giacomo or Salai as an apprentice and house servant. In his notebooks he describes him dryly as "thievish, liar, obstinate, glutton..." Nevertheless, he kept him in his household, took him on his travels wherever he went and shared with him part of his exile in France. Ultimately, he made Salai, together with his faithful friend Gionvanni Melzi, the beneficiary of his will. His diaries also list such recurrent gifts for Salai as expensive garments, necklaces, rings and monetary gratuities. At the same time he repeatedly complains about the "little rogue." One of Leonardo's favorite models, Salai appears time and again in his paintings and drawings. The master was obviously delighted with the charm and vivacity of his protegé.

Like many other great figures of the Renaissance, including Verrocchio, Leonardo remained a bachelor. There is no record of his ever having been involved with a woman. Nor have any letters come down to us suggesting such an involvement. However, I have hinted that one of the strongest arguments for Leonardo's homosexuality is based on indirect, psychoanalytic evidence. It was suggested by Freud's analysis of a childhood memory of Leonardo's when he was still lying in his crib. According to Leonardo, a vulture came down to him, and with his tail, opened his lips and struck him repeatedly in the mouth. It is not necessary to go into the details of Freud's argument that led him to interpret this memory as a fellatio fantasy, indicative of Leonardo's passive-feminine identification; of attributing the possession of a penis to his mother, and confusing the penis with mother's nipples.

Not surprisingly, Freud's theory was vehemently attacked by art historians, philosophers, and writers, from Meyer Shapiro (1956) to Brian Farrel (1966) and Robert Payne (1978). They either refuted his evidence or objected to the glory of a great man being sullied. However, Freud, Kurt Eissler, and other analysts have adduced further evidence to support their thesis. Kurt Eissler, especially, in a monumental labor of love (1966) took issue with Freud's critics and went to painstaking lengths to confirm most of his interpretations. At the same time he threw more light on Leonardo's feminine identification, including his castration anxiety and deficient integration of the penis with his body image. On analyzing his anatomical drawings, he arrives at the startling conclusion that he must have been suffering from "urethral fixation," if not spermatorrhea.

However, speculation aside, conclusive evidence of Leonardo's sexual behavior, homosexual or otherwise, is conspicuously absent. The meaning of the mysterious backward spelling of a few key words in his diary, mentioned earlier is anybody's guess. It may well refer to an assignation of the aging Leonardo with a certain *Ligny* ("Ingil"), in *Rome* ("a morra") or in Naples ("a panna"), including the reference to a *donation* ("*e no igano dal*"). Be that as it may, his double secrecy (mirror writing as well as backward spelling) would be reasonably attributable to Leonardo's painful memories of the homosexual trials in his youth.

It goes without saying that both art historians and psychoanalysts have paid considerable attention to the sexual aspects of his pictorial output. They have noted Leonardo's marked intuitive ability in the presentation of the female figure. They emphasize the enigmatic, yet nonetheless bisexual, hermaphroditic quality of his last major painting of John the Baptist; to say nothing of their interminable speculations about the smile of Mona Lisa, with its purported connotations of intrigue, if not the demonic.

Even more to the point is Leonardo's drawing known as *Pain and Pleasure,* or the *Oxford Allegory* (see Fig. 5a). It represents a youth and an older man, both standing in the nude, their backs seemingly fused like those of Siamese twins, while their heads, torsos, and arms are those of two separate persons. The older man, dominating the picture, is bearded; his penis is in full frontal view, while his hands are spread wide apart, as though (according to Eissler) he wanted to avoid masturbation. The younger man, apparently in his late teens, has been identified as Salai, while the older man is supposed to represent the aging Leonardo.

According to Leonardo, *Pain and Pleasure* are represented as twins as though they were joined together, "for there is never the one without the other; and they turn their backs because they are contrary to each other. If you should choose pleasure, know that he has behind him one who will deal out to you tribulations and repentance..." (MaCurdy, 1959, p. 1097).

What Leonardo failed to note is another aspect of the drawing. The appealing curly head and profile of the youthful Salai shows a striking resemblance to a charming head of David in the famous sculpture made by his teacher Verrocchio when Leonardo was about Salai's age (see Fig. 5b).

The suggestion comes to mind that in the drawing under review the aging Leonardo had identified with his youthful companion. It

Figure 5a
Leonardo da Vinci
Pain and Pleasure
(*the Oxford Allegory*)

Figure 5b
Leonardo da Vinci
Virtue and Envy

will be recalled that Leonardo too had been placed in Verrocchio's
workshop when he was ten years old. He may well have developed
an erotic attachment to his teacher, prefiguring or duplicating in
reverse his infatuation with his apprentice Salai. This may have
been the reason for his forebearance and indeed angelic patience

with the boy. In turn, Salai's ingratitude and impudent behavior with his master had been his way of retaliating for his emotional (or sexual) exploitation by Leonardo. If so, the apparent incongruity of the subject and title of the drawing becomes readily understandable: the older man's sexual involvement with a child is apt to be both pleasurable and painful in more ways than one.

On the other hand, it appears that Leonardo's dependent needs on his disciples—including the Florentine nobleman Francisco Melzi, his youthful friend and more deserving love object, duplicated an earlier pattern of dependence which can be discerned throughout Leonardo's formative years, and which stayed with him well into his maturity: his searching for a succession of benevolent father figures, from Verrocchio to Lorenzo il Magnifico or Lodovico il Moro, from Cesare Borgia to Pope Leo X, or to King Francis and the Cardinal Luigi of Aragon in France. The fusion of the two figures in his drawing lends support for both interpretaions along these lines. It symbolizes the blissful but potentially dangerous union with the lost love object.

Indeed for Leonardo the sexual acting out and consummation of his homosexual impulses—if it occurred at all—has been of little more than nuisance value. In one of his diary notes he was frankly dismayed over his inability to control the involuntary movements of his penis. Far more important than sexual-outlet was the finding of an idealized, affectionate and dependable father surrogate to replace Ser Piero who had deserted him when he was in need of his protection and guidance. Leonardo expresses his aversion, if not disgust, for the sexual act in no uncertain terms, and he wonders how any one in his right mind would find the sight, the feel, and the touch of genital organs attractive. In one of his otherwise wholly realistic anatomical drawings, he represents the female genitals as a yawning abyss, indicating his intense fear of woman. On the other hand, Eissler has brought together persuasive evidence of shame, guilt, and anxiety which, in Leonardo's mind had been associated with masturbation. More than that: he developed various defenses or reaction formations against the sexual impulse. "Intellectual passion drives out sensuality" he noted in his diary.

By the same token, Leonardo repudiated violence in all its manifestations. He was gentle and considerate with his fellows, but withheld confidence even from friends. His real confidant was his diary. It is said that the Cabots of Boston talked only to the Lodges, and that the Lodges talked only to God. In a similar vein, it appears that Leonardo talked frankly only to his diaries. He was a vegetarian and his compassion for birds caught by the peasants and put up for sale on the market place was legendary. He bought them up and released them from their cages. His diaries contain a long recital of the wrongdoings of a certain German craftsman who for a time shared his workshop. Giovanni the mirrormaker spent his time shooting birds in the countryside instead of attending to his commission in the workshop. It may well be that in Leonardo's eyes Giovanni represented the dark, sadistic aspects of the father figure, reactivating his still smouldering resentment against Ser Piero with his assorted youthful wives.

Yet by contrast with Salai's open show of rebellion against his master, Leonardo's was a resentment which he had always been at pains to keep under control. Occasional evidence of what Freud called the return of the repressed, for instance his readiness to build war machines and fortifications for his princely sponsors, or his eagerness to cut up human bodies in the mortuary, is by no means incompatible with such a reading. They were thinly disguised derivatives of his own violent impulses. Thus Leonardo's third dichotomy was made up of his wavering between feminine and masculine identification, including the derivatives of masochistic versus sadistic tendencies. It too may have well been tied to his right versus left hemispheric orientation.

It is interesting to note that recent studies in such organic conditions as patients suffering from temporal lobe epilepsy (Laura Schenk & David Bear, 1981) abrupt changes of handedness, (from right to left or from left to right) were occasionally observed. They went together with the dramatic emergence of secondary or multiple personalities and at times included fleeting episodes of changed sexual preference. Such cases are of course worlds apart from Leonardo's dichotomies, but they tend to bear out the conjectures about their underlying neurodynamics presented here.

Fig. 5b, a companion piece to the *Oxford Allegory* of *Pleasure and Pain* is another illustration of Leonardo's male versus female dichotomy. Described as *Virtue and Envy,* it represents two bodies

facing each other and growing out of one pair of legs. The male figure has an androgynous quality and has been compared with traditional representation of Apollo. *Envy* is a somewhat emaciated
female, half squatting on the torso of her companion, sapping his
strength. She tries to poison *Virtue's* face with her tongue striking
like a snake, and to set his hair afire. Eissler suggests that the
deeper meaning of the drawing is a hostile sexual encounter: all
good is in the male, and all evil in the female.

Leonardo himself remarked of *Invidia* "She is shown lean and
wizened because she is always wasting away with perpetual desire...
She holds a vase in her hand full of flowers, with serpents and toads
and other venomous things lying below it. She rides on Death, for
Invidia never dies and has lordship (even) over him ..."

RECONCILIATION OF OPPOSITES: HOW DID HE DO IT?

Thus both the drawings and Leonardo's comments show once
more the extremes of his male versus female dichotomy. Yet at the
same time they dramatize his groping for reconciliation of the
opposites in both his artistic and scientific expression. Whether or
not they also express a deep-seated confusion about his sexual identity must remain a matter of speculation. So is the question of a
habitual or on-again off-again association between his superbly disciplined, masculine, "scientific" orientation, coupled with his left
cerebral hemisphere on the one hand; and with his tender minded,
artistic, feminine identity, and his right cerebral hemisphere on the
other. In any case, such a hypothetical link between the right side
of the brain and male homosexuality suggests a reasonable explanation for the frequent association between homosexuality with creativity and high artistic achievement.

Be that as it may, Leonardo was at his best at coping with the
vicissitudes and contradictions of the first two of his three dichotomies. I believe that the reconciliation of what he felt were conflicting elements in human nature was the quintessence of "Leo-
nardesque" science. By contrast, the growing specialization of the
arts and science in the ensuing 16th and 17th centuries have only
deepened the cleavage. It is still running through the fabric of our

contemporary society.* Yet while Leonardo asked questions—and provided answers—long before they were raised by generations to come, he left us at a loss as to how he succeded in bringing about the magic synthesis of his "two cultures." Did it involve a miraculous fine-tuning and coordination of his right and left hemispheres whenever he was engaged in either a scientific or artistic project, with either side of the brain bringing its best to bear on the task at hand? Was it due to the lightning speed of his sensory-motor reflexes and of his cerebral computer effecting its cortical, trans-cortical, and transcallosal transactions in a harmonious way? Was it his ability to synthesize mental functions far transcending the routine of right versus left hemispheric specialization?

Neither his *Treaties on Painting* nor the close to 10 thousand pages of his diary notes give us an answer. Obviously, he himself could not tell. But the legacy of his work is an object lesson showing that it is humanly possible, after all, for the two hemispheres to work together both in conflict and harmony like Bach's Well-Tempered Klavier. Yet it also suggests that such a consummation need not be the exclusive privilege of an ambidextrous genius of Leonardo's stature. It is a goal for all ordinary men, women, and children to strive for. Above all, Leonardo's example should caution both left hemispheric traditional educators and right hemispheric counterculture enthusiasts against trying to poise human existence on the precarious balance of just one half of the brain.

---

* A classical 17th century example is Isaac Newton: *Scientist and Magician* (Ehrenwald, in press).

5

FREUD

Science Versus Intuition

Freud was perhaps one of those whose
bent towards speculative abstractions
is so powerful that he is afraid of
being mastered by it and feels it
necessary to counter it by studying
concrete scientific data.

Franz Wittels

Among the many facets of Freud's personality, the image of
the austere, uncompromising scientist stands out. More than three-
quarters of a century's accumulated scientific reputation and
popular acclaim, aided by hero worship, have joined to sculpt his
features like one of the presidential heads on the Rushmore moun-
tainside. Flanked by the portrait of Jung, he gazes at us through the
mist, a semimythological figure, though his living memory still
lingers in some of his surviving disciples.

Yet in the 1960s and 70s an up-and-coming generation of post-
Freudian dissenters and detractors has been busy chipping away at
the monument and, in the end, boring into its core. It is the same
generation that a few years back had demythologized the Bible,
declared war on authority in general, and turned loveless sex into a
social, if not antisocial, parlor game.

Freud's commanding position in our culture was particularly apt
to elicit such an attack. It made his assailants forget that he himself

70

had once decried *Civilization and its Discontents.* But for the new oedipal revolutionaries the discovery that, *horribile dictu,* the master has a sex life of his own, bordering on either the heterosexual or the homosexual, seemed to be a dirty secret calling for newspaper headlines or an un-cover story in a popular magazin *Newsweek,* Nov. 30, 1981).

Even the shadowy figure of his father, Jacob Freud, could not escape severe posthumus censure of his alleged philandering and other youthful peccadillos. In turn, Sigmund Freud's hobby of hunting mushrooms and collecting statuettes has been interpreted as evidence of latent cannibalistic urges aimed at gobbling up sylvan representations of the paternal phallus. At the same time, we are told that collecting stone statues was a tell-tale sign of Freud's identification with Don Giovanni who invited the funereal statue of the Commendatore, his slain oedipal adversary, to dinner at his house. This, at least, is the reading offered by the French psychoanalyst Marie Balmary (1981). That in such a view, half the population of Europe which is likewise given to mushroom hunting (as well as a small elite given to collecting stone statues) would be harboring cannibalistic, "phallophagic" impulses, perhaps combined with a Don Giovanni complex, is another matter. In either case, such recent samples of rather arbitrary interpretations suggest that Freud's warnings against what he called "wild analysis" had a distinctly prophetic quality—even though he could not anticipate that ultimately he himself would become its victim.

Scientist Versus Poet

Still, apart from what it reveals about some overgrown adolescents peeking through the keyhole of parental bedrooms, very little was gained from such an exercise. What is relevant in the present context is not Freud's dilemma of marital fidelity versus infidelity or purported homosexual undercurrents, but the cleavage between his avowed "strictly scientific" objectives, versus his lingering intuitive, creative, if not artistic, inclinations. The fact is that while the dichotomy between Leonardo da Vinci's art and his scientific pursuits was apparent to everyone, and the cleavage between

Nietzsche, the classical scholar and philologist, and his brain child *Thus Spake Zarathustra,* was obvious even to Nietzsche himself, Freud's right hemispheric alter ego or *Doppelganger* eluded the notice of the naive observer and of some of his closest associates alike.

Freud's public, professorial self was the product of the 19th century spirit of materialistic inquiry, as represented by Helmhotz, Du Bois-Reymond, or Ernst Haeckel in the German cultural orbit, or by Darwin, T. H. Huxley, Robert Spencer, or Hughlings Jackson in the English tradition. Equipped with a brilliant mind, a splendid memory, and a gift for languages, Sigmund Freud early decided that the surest way to satisfy his aspirations for a successful career, for fame and for power, was through education and knowledge. Yet soon the thirst for knowledge, the satisfaction of his boundless curiosity, became a goal in itself. Studying for a medical degree was incidental toward this goal. He was never sure that the medical profession was his true calling. Still, he attained the highest credits in all medical disciplines, engaged in painstaking and, in some areas, pioneering research in histology, neuroanatomy, and neuropathology, and was among the first to discover the analgesic and psychoactive properties of cocaine.

Despite his poverty and the stigma of Jewishness operating against him, Freud sufficiently impressed the luminaries of the faculty to appoint him a docent—a lecturer—at the University of Vienna. He was also given a travelling fellowship to Paris where he studied with the great Jean-Martin Charcot. Back in Vienna he established himself as a specialist for nervous and mental diseases in 1886 to make a living for himself and his family. However, his medical practice too was to serve him largely as a new laboratory for the methodical exploration of the human mind, with hypnosis, and later the technique of free association and dream interpretation as his research tools.

Psychoanalysis as a theory and practice of treatment was the fruit of some 50 years of monumental effort. It was based on the insight gained from Freud's self-analysis, on clinical observations of thousands of patients, of candidates undergoing training analysis, on studies of art, literature, mythology, and anthropology. Yet, invariably, they were based on premises of the scientific method.

Mental processes, Freud held, are subject to the same laws of cause and effect as apply to physical or biological processes: they are strictly determined. People are usually unaware of the deeper roots of their behavior; it is derived from the unconscious. Nevertheless, it too is causally determined. The psychic energies involved are mutually interchangeable, subject to the laws formulated by Robert Meyer or Rudolf Boltzmann. They manifest themselves as instinctual drives; conflict between them and the ego is conducive to neuroses. Cure can be effected by analytic inquiry into the causes of the conflict, that is, by interpretation and insight, coupled with re-education and "working through"—a technique akin to modern behavior therapy.

Freudian analysis, supplemented by a set of highly speculative propositions—so-called metapsychology—is an internally consistent, well-nigh self-sealing system of thought. Yet it claims that all its data are based on empirical findings in many fields of human affairs. It claims, furthermore, that their validity is also borne out by its therapeutic efficacy, especially in the psychoneuroses for which it was originally designed.

Freud laid great stress on the pragmatic origins of psychoanalysis. He distrusted specualtion both in himself and in others. In any case, he sought to put the brake on his own speculative bent. On the face of it, he was on bad terms with his intuitions, his imagination. He disclaimed any interest in mysticism and frowned at what he described as "oceanic feeling," picking up the phrase from Romain Rolland, the friend he quotes in *Civilization and Its Discontents*.

INTUITION OR ABERRATION?

Yet here, too, there is ample evidence that under the cloak of strictly left hemispheric discipline and academic respectability, an unmistakeable element of right hemispheric intuition, inspiration, and imagination was at work. In 1895, in the wake of the breakdown of his collaboration with Dr. Joseph Breuer, a fatherly friend and respected medical authority, he engaged in a spirited correspondence and exchange of ideas with a younger friend, the flamboyant, imaginative Dr. Wilhelm Fliess of Berlin. It was Fliess to whom he confided his plans for a new research venture, known today as Freud's *Project,* an attempt at formulating a neurophysiological theory of the mind. Freud introduced it under the heading: *Project for a scientific psychology,* announcing: "The intention of this project is to furnish us with a psychology which shall be a natural science: its aim, that is, to represent psychical processes as quantitatively determined states of specifiable material particles and so to make it plain and void of contradictions...." (1954, p. 355).

It was a bold but desultory attempt at a definitive, strictly scientific approach, based on all the available evidence about physics, neurophysiology, anatomy, and histology of the day. Ingenious theories about three types of neurons, about their presumed points of contact, about quantitative and qualitative aspects of their interactions are prominently featured. Karl Pribram, the noted neuropsychologist and his co-worker, Morton Gill (1976) rightly describe it as a seminal work prefiguring most of the fundamental propositions of psychoanalysis which Freud, then thirty-nine years old, was to develop over the ensuing decades. There is the clear distinction between conscious and unconscious mental processes, between primary and secondary process functioning; there are references to the pain-versus-pleasure principle; to the dynamics of repression; to the part played by wish fulfillment in dreams; to the ego as an organ of perception, as a facilitator or inhibitor of excess stimulation or action; there are allusions to the constancy and preservation of energy, to physiological regulatory processes, anticipating Freud's Nirvana principle.

More than that: Pribram notes that some of Freud's electrophysiological formulations anticipate more recent insights based on brand-new developments in the field of cybernetics, computer technology, and particularly Pribram's own theories of holography as an optical information gathering and coding system operating in the brain. Indeed it can well be stated that Freud's *Project* represents a spectacular intuitive quantum jump or existential shift from the neurophysiology of his time to proto-cybernetics, to classical psychoanalysis and modern information theory.

Freud's elation and feverish excitement over his discovery is reflected in his letter to Fliess of October 20, 1895:

....Now listen to this. One strenuous night last week, when I was in a stage of painful discomfort in which my brain works best, the barrier suddenly lifted, the veils dropped, and it was possible to see from the details of neurosis all the way to the very conditioning of consciousness. Everything fell into place. The cogs meshed, the thing really seemed to be a machine which in a moment would run of itself. The three systems of neurons, the "free" and "bound" states of quantity, the primary and secondary processes, the main trend and the compromise trend of the central nervous system, the two biological rules of attention and defense, the indication of quality, reality, and thought, the state of the psycho-sexual group, the sexual determination of repression, and finally the factors determining consciousness as a perceptual function—the whole thing held together, and it still does. I can naturally hardly contain myself with delight (p. 129).

The message is loud and clear. What Freud described in his letter is a typical *heureka* experience. Despite his unconditional commitment to the primacy of reason, to the virtues of linear, analytic, left-hemispheric thinking, he had the feeling that the whole thing was indeed like a machine which "in a moment would run of itself." He was quite apparently under the sway of his right hemispheric intuitions, much the same as Nietzsche when he felt "assaulted" by his *Zarathustra* personality. It is no coincidence that Freud, in a more detached mood, had described his *Project* as a tyrant whose domination he was glad to escape.

He dispatched his manuscript to Fliess on October 8, 1895. Yet on October 29, he seems to have completely dissociated himself from its spell: "Dear Wilhelm....I am in top working form, 9 to 11 hours hard work, 6 to 8 analytical cases a day—most beautiful things, all sorts of new material, for original work I am entirely lost...I no longer understand the state of mind in which I concocted the Psychology. I cannot conceive how I came to inflict it on you. I think you are too polite; it seems to me to have been a kind of *Aberration*" (my italics). The fact is that Freud had soon lost all interest in the *Project*. He abandoned it altogether and never asked for its return. The manuscript was found after Fliess's death among his effects and only saved from oblivion by his son, Robert Fliess, and Freud's disciple, Marie Bonaparte, who smuggled it out of

Nazi-occupied terrirory during the Second World War. But for this, Freud, the Spartan father, had thrown his hapless brain child down the Taigetos.

Ernest Jones describes the *Project* as one of the turning points in Freud's career, marking his progress from the "dogged worker to the imaginative thinker." Yet on a deeper level Freud seemed to have known all along how to let "the machine" (his internal computer), "run of itself." This is indeed one of the characteristics of intuition: the unconscious processing of information and automatic decision making, without recourse to planned or deliberate volition. The combination of such essentially right hemispheric impulses with his prevailing left hemispheric control was in effect the hallmark of Freud's genius.

His later discovery of free association as one of the major tools of psychoanalysis is another case in point. Yet it is one of the paradoxes in his life that despite his preponderantly left hemispheric orientation, his new technique opened the door for the intrusion of essentially right hemispheric "irrational" elements into his universe of discourse. The procedure is familiar. The patient is instructed to relax on the couch, to tell what comes into his mind and to relinquish all attempts at censoring or controlling his associations. In effect, the exclusion of "all selective conceptual goals of the ego," as Fenichel put it, was to become the basic rule of psychoanalysis.

Freud was led to this procedure when he and Josef Breuer realized that their use of hypnosis or "hypnoidal" states had taken them into a blind alley. Their therapeutic effects were skin-deep and transient. Moreover, Freud himself had become increasingly wary of the magic implication of hypnosis. Free association, by contrast, seemed to be best suited to reveal the patient's innermost secrets; it laid bare his unconscious complexes; it often resulted in cathartic release of tensions and set in motion a process of personality reconstruction.

Post-Freudian critics are less sanguine about the unique therapeutic value of the process. This should not, however, detract from its importance as a means to bring about altered states of consciousness, or what I described as an existential shift. The patient, stretched out on the couch, insulated from his workaday environment, focusing on his inner experience, is removed from the control of his customary, goal-directed, utilitarian way of thinking. He lays himself open to the influx of seemingly nonsensical, inchoate material, that is, of influences which for all intents and purposes fall into the domain of the right hemisphere. Free associations are in effect the closest approximation to bringing about a state of mind inimical to a person's prevailing left hemispheric dominance.

Thus the new technique, like his disowned and discarded *Project,* is indeed a joint product of insight and intuition. Yet in Freud's case, intuition had an added slant, transcending his own intentions. It anticipated, though inadvertently, the therapeutic applications of the relaxation response in meditation; of "letting go"; of the emancipation of the self from the tyranny of the ego advocated by diverse esoteric cults from Zen to Sufism and the counterculture of our day.

It is these wider implications of the new technique, compounded by prudery, that explain the violent reaction of early academic and establishment critics to the purported irrationality of psychoanalysis. Despite his socialist leanings, the same factors account for Alfred Adler's defection from the Freudian fold: his was an exclusively rational, if not rationalistic, approach to psychotherapy, and he could not accept a therapeutic procedure that tried to do away with the patient's left hemispheric controls, supposed to be the mainstay of the treatment process.

Yet it is precisely such a procedure that proved best suited for the treatment of obsessive-compulsive personalities. They are patients most in need of relief from excessive superego controls and an overactive left hemisphere. Not surprisingly, Freud considered himself a member of this "club"—which in turn suggests that he may have intuitively hit upon free association as a remedy tailored for his own neurosis.

At the other end of the scale are schizophrenics and borderline patients with brittle egos who are from the outset more open to influences emanating from the unconscious, and, presumably, from the right hemisphere. They have turned out to be poor risks for the technique of free association and had to be excluded from orthodox psychoanalytic treatment. And here again it is no coincidence that Jung, despite his pioneering researches with the word-association test, ultimately rejected free association as a treatment of his choice. We shall see on a later page that Jung was a typical right hemispheric personality and often plagued by hallucinatory voices and other intrusions from what he called the collective unconscious. Had the vocabulary of his native Schwitzer Dütch included such an idiom, he may well have decided that he needed free association like a hole in the head. In this respect too his was the diametrical opposite of Freud's personality makeup.

Freud's most significant contribution to right hemispheric psychology is, however, his *magnum opus,* the *Interpretation of Dreams* (1900). There he had undertaken to listen intently to what Erich Fromm later called the "forgotten language" of dreams—those of his patients as well as of his own. At the same time he subjected them to the first truly scientific exploration in history.

Yet here too Freud made sure to dissociate himself from their message, pleading insanity, as it were as a defense against their irrational, oedipal, pregenital or otherwise morally repugnant implications. Paradoxically, his early critics and detractors nevertheless accused him of permitting the intrusion of bizarre, irrational, unscientific material—of "old wives' tales"—into his universe of discourse. This may have been an added reason for the avowedly uncompromising left hemispheric stance in his public statements. Nor was he aware at that time of the unexpected therapeutic potential of the very existential shift involved in turning both the patient's and the therapist's attention from habitual left hemispheric pursuits to such right hemispheric subjects as dreams or free association.

Freud's vacillation between accepting and rejecting the validity of the hunches and intuitions emanating from the right, purportedly intellectually underprivileged, side of the brain, is also reflected in his changing attitude towards psychical research or parapsychology. In 1922 he published a much quoted article on *Dream and Telepathy*—his own and some of his associates' misgivings not withstanding. It offered an ingenious psychoanalytic interpretation of several such incidents reported to him by his patients. But he closed the article with the caveat: "Have I given you the impression that I am secretly inclined to support the reality of tele-pathy in the occult sense? If so, I should very much regret that it is so difficult to avoid giving such an impression. In reality, however, I was anxious to be strictly impartial. I have every reason to be so, for I have no opinion. I know nothing about it."

A few years later, in 1925, he notes, "When such things as tele-pathic messages do exist, we cannot rule out the possibility that they reach the sleeper and may be grasped by him. Nay, judging from the analogy with such other materials as sensory impressions and thought processes, we must assume that telepathic messages, received in the waking state, might be registered in the succeeding night." Yet in 1933 he writes: "I am convinced you will be rather dissatisfied with my attitude towards this problem: not fully con-vinced yet ready to be convinced. Maybe you will say to yourself: There you have another instance of a man who after a life's work as a respectable scientist is becoming demented or gullible in his ripe old age."

His wariness of the irrational, the mystical, or oceanic feeling—even of the religious experience—reflects the same atti-tude. It expresses his commitment to pragmatism, to the scientific method as the ultimate arbiter of truth. I have hinted that it was his distrust of magic, of the belief in the omnipotence of thought, which was one of the reasons for his abandoning hypnosis early in his career. By the same token, he cautioned his disciples of the dan-gers of the analyst's countertransference to his patients. Such an attitude may well have resulted in dampening his own therapeutic zeal. Insight, and insight alone, he stated, should help to "make the unconscious conscious," and to give the ego whatever power it could muster to shape its own destiny. At times he was puzzled over his charismatic impact on his patients. Like one of the medieval English kings credited with the Royal Touch, he was taken aback by his patient's occassional unexpectedly rapid improvement. Psychoanalysis for him had to remain a science, not an arcane, esoteric ritual.

Even his approach to the arts was that of the analytically detached observer. In his study of Michelangelo's *Moses*, he con-fessed that he was wholly unresponsive to music since he found nothing in it that came within his intellectual grasp. He was a connoisseur of artists rather than of art. On contemplating a sculpture or a painting, his enjoyment was derived more from the decoding and intellectual understanding of the artist's message than from the masterpiece itself. His penetrating studies of Sophocles' *Oedipus* cycle; of Leonardo da Vinci's childhood memory, or of some of Shakespeare's characters, have become cornerstones of psychoanalytic theory and models of analytic psychohistory. But all this did not turn Freud into a recognized art critic. Willing surrender to the musical, the religious, the mystical, or even the ESP experience, was apparently too threatening to him. Weary of the Oceanic feelings, he embarked on the chemical analysis of sea water instead. His abiding loyalty was to his demanding superego and to the discipline of the left cerebral hemisphere.

Yet despite his defensive posture, Freud has shown throughout his life a strong affinity for the artistic temperament—in others. Invariably, they were personalities diametrically opposite to his own. The flamboyant, extroverted Wilhelm Fliess, 2 years his junior, belonged into his class. So did, as will be seen in the chapter that follows, his great adversary, the more sedate but romantically, if not mystically, inclined, Dr. Carl Gustav Jung. So did Sandor Ferenczi, his brilliant, imaginative but ultimately emotionally imbalanced protege. So did Otto Rank, and a few lesser figures in his entourage.

Still, Freud's fascination was not confined to living protagonists of this type. It extended to what the psychoanalyst Mark Kanzer aptly described as his *Literary Doubles* (1976). Freud felt drawn to the literary output of such contemporary writers as Arthur Schnitzler, Romain Rolland, or Thomas Mann. Arthur Schnitzler, a graduate of the Vienna medical school, playwright and successful novelist, 6 years his junior, was particularly close to his heart. In 1906 he noted that Schnitzler knew "by intuition what Freud had learned from laborious work with other people over the years" (Kanzer, 1976, p. 234). Freud admired Romain Rolland for the freshness of his writings and for the comfort he could afford his readers. In a similar vein, he listed himself as one of Mann's earliest readers and admirers. He envied the creative writer for his ability to arrive through pure intuition at what he himself had to arrive at by painstaking scientific investigations. "You create illusions but I destroy them" he wrote to Romain Rolland.

But the fact is that Freud himself had been a master of German prose in his own right. Some of his case histories read like short stories by an accomplished novelist. It was an achievement for which he felt he had to apologize to his confrères. He considered his literary talents for which he was awarded the coveted Goethe prize as mere means towards an end.

FREUD AND HIS RIGHT-BRAINED DOUBLES

What, then, is behind Freud's ambivalence toward his own artistic bent and intuitive abilities? Why did he stifle these gifts as aberrations in himself, while paying such generous tribute to them in others? Kanzer's interpretation hews to the orthodox psychoanalytic line. He suggests that Freud permitted "his creative imagination to receive recognition only indirectly through projection onto writers and artists towards whom he experienced a sense of Doubles." He saw them as extended parts of his own personality who functioned vicariously in his behalf. According to Kanzer, such an attitude is in the nature of a neurotic defense against accepting responsibility for creative inspiration which, in Freud's case, was associated with an oedipal taboo. In the last analysis, it was dictated by a harsh superego with which he failed to come to grips in his self-analysis. This is why he had to turn to his Doubles in order to savor, by proxy, as it were, the forbidden fruits of oedipal fulfillment. Dr. Kanzer's argument is certainly persuasive and is supported by further psychoanalytic considerations.

Starting from different premises, the New York psychoanalyst Max Stern (1980) arrived at similar conclusions. He notes that almost all biographers regarded as a main trait of Freud's character the deep conflict between an overpowering trend to speculation and the need to control it (p. 2). But Stern emphasizes that Freud's conflict was not between instinctual drives and their repression. He holds that the "culprit" was the intuitive process which, in his view, is "an archaic mechanism" and one of man's basic defenses against death." In effect, he attributes Freud's dilemma to an evolutionary or "teleonomic pressure" derived from the need for survival.

There is, however, a third interpretation of Freud's dilemma, closely akin to Leonardo's dichotomy between art and science discussed in an earlier chapter. It is the dilemma between Freud's pragmatic, uncompromising, essentially left hemispheric orientation, and his yearning to give free rein to his creative imagination, intuitions, and inspirations issuing from the right cerebral hemisphere. Thus the present focus is not so much on Freud's "Doubles" as proposed by Dr. Kanzer, as on his right hemispheric alter ego—on the double within.

If this is true, it leads to an intriguing conclusion. We have to assume that the Freudian superego is itself operationally connected with, if not "localized" in, the left hemisphere; that is to say, that the left side of the brain is in effect the executive organ of the superego and, by indirection, of diverse ego functions as well. Such a conclusion is indeed in good keeping with the daring thesis put forward by Sir John Eccles and Karl Popper (1977) that the left hemisphere is the side of what they call the *self-conscious* mind.

By the same token, the concept of Freudian repression would have to be expanded to include not only such essentially biological processes as instinctual drives, emanating from the Id, but also those right hemispheric influences which have fallen victim to modern man's culturally determined left hemispheric dominance. However, this should not detract from the fact that a primitive, pre-literate precursor of mature superego functions is prefigured in what Julian Jaynes had called the hallucinatory voices of gods. They originate from the intuitive right side of the brain, as anonymous forerunners of the named and numbered Ten Commandments or ethical imperatives of modern man.

We have seen that Freud's conscious attitude towards his intuitions has been one of suspicion, if not dismay. He relegated them to a *salon des refusés* of the early French Impressionists. Still, despite their habitual repression, hunches and intuitions seemed to provide a steady—though barely audible—*continuo* in the orchestration of his creative output. At the same time he envied his literary Doubles for their freedom to indulge in them to their heart's desire.

Freud against Oceanic Feeling: The Hearing Cap and the Phylactery

Yet if his attitude towards intuition was ambivalent at best, it was wholly negative about religion, particularly its formal paraphernalia. He attended no services, insisted on a civilian ceremony for his wedding and at one time considered relinquishing his ties with Judaism. Religion, he held, was an illusion without a future. Nevertheless, his metapsychology, with its tripartite picture of personality structure, seems to hark back to a tripartite organization of the Christian universe, with the Superego representing Heaven, the Ego standing in for Earth and the Id for Hell. By the same token, on studying his diagrammatic picture of the "mental apparatus" (1925) I discovered striking evidence of what can be described as the return of religion as the left hemispherically repressed. In the diagram the Superego is represented as an

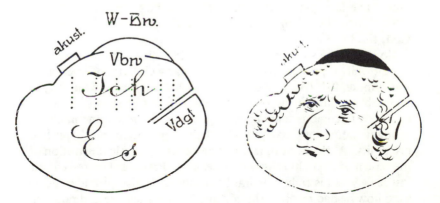

Fig. 6 A represents the "mental apparatus" according to Freud, consisting of Ego, Id, and Superego. *Vbw* stands for *Vorbewusst* or preconscious. Freud described the little box on the top left as the *hoerkappe* or hearing cap. It is a diagrammatic picture of Wernicke's area in the left brain cortex, concerned with receptive speech functions. Fig B transforms the diagram into the head of rabbinical student with the skull cap: the forlorn image of his religious indoctrination in early childhood.

outgrowth from the main body of the personality structure (see Figure 6a, 6b).To its left is a *box-shaped* attachment. Paradoxically, Freud describes it as the *Hoer Kappe* or *Hearing Cap,* representing that area of the left hemisphere which is concerned with the hearing of words and the formation of concepts; but he leaves the cubic shape of the "cap" unaccounted for.

It will be noted that the diagram shows a striking resemblance to the head of a rabbinical student wearing a yarmulke or skull cap. It should also be noted that the pious Jew must wear his yarmulke all day long—except when in his bed or in the bathroom, that is, precisely the places where the shedding of superego restraints is likewise deemed permissible.

To make the resemblance even more intriguing, the hearing cap looks very much like the replica of a little box—the main part of the phylactery—which the faithful has to put on his forehead when reciting his morning prayers. It is a ritual Freud must have witnessed in his parental home over and over again as a child. He must have also been aware that the little box contained, among other things, the solemn invocation *"Hear*, oh Israel: the Lord our God, the Lord is One..."

No doubt the similarity between Freud's diagram and forgotten or culturally repressed images from his early childhood experiences was unintended. (As a paterfamilias he had banned the lighting of Sabbath candles in his own household.) But it shows the close affinity of religious and superego commands in his unconscious, brought home to us by both their conceptual and spiritual proximity. At the same time, the diagram is a graphic illustration of the return of the culturally (not necessarily Freudian) repressed: the lost legacy of his right cerebral hemisphere. It also provides a clue as to how he had resolved the conflict between science and religion: by readmitting the disowned God into the realm of the superego.

Such a reading brings out Freud's ideological, left- versus right-hemispheric conflict in a minor key only. We shall see in the chapter that follows that a similar conflict threatening the return of the culturally repressed—though compounded with psychosexual factors—may assume more ominous proportions. It may have been at the root of at least three dramatic incidents in Freud's life which have puzzled his biographers ever since. They occured in his stormy relationship with two of his closest associates: with Wilhelm Fliess, his erstwhile soul mate, and with Carl Gustav Jung, his heir apparent, turned rival and adversary.

DOES THE LEFT HEMISPHERE SUPPRESS THE RIGHT?

But the significance of Freud's conflict about oceanic feelings as part of the culturally repressed goes far beyond its purely private, biographical implications. We shall see in Part III that it is a recurrent theme in the lives of both geniuses and ordinary people. It both encompasses and transcends the psychoanalytic frame of reference: it is compatible with Freudian psychodynamics but at the same time it shifts the emphasis from such basically disparate meta-psychological constructs as instinct versus reason, of ego versus

Fig. 7

In this cartoon by David Levine, Freud seems to be caught in the dilemna between the shades of the two cerebral hemispheres. Did the artist intuitively presage the argument presented in this chapter?

superego or id, to an unalloyed unitary category of events. In so doing, the new approach prefigures a radical departure from outmoded Aristotelian or Cartesian views of the human mind. It provides a blueprint that makes it possible to calibrate such Freudian concepts as repression, the conscious, the unconscious, the ego, the superego, or the id against well-defined neurophysiological functions or processes. To be more specific, it suggests a close association of the ego and the superego with the perceptual or executive functions of the left hemisphere; it postulates a similar connection between the preverbal or nonverbal information processing in the right hemisphere, and it bears out once more the long-suspected relationship between the Freudian id and deeper subcortical structures. By the same token, we have seen that repression, as it is conceived here, is in effect an ongoing (or intermittent) process of pitting one cerebral hemisphere against the other, or of both hemispheres joining forces in warding off potentially disruptive impulses welling up from the limbic lobe, the reticular formation or from MacLean's reptilian brain.

On the other hand, it may well be argued that free association as well as dreams and dream interpretation—Freud's royal road to analytic insight and resolution of conflict—are not merely means towards an end, but close approximations of the goals of therapy themselves. They bring about an existential shift from linear, verbal, left hemispheric communication to a free-wheeling, metaphorical, right hemispheric pattern. Free association, coupled with the descent to the twilight world of dreams, liberates both patient and therapist from the tyranny of the left hemisphere (from which the trouble may have started in the first place) and helps the right hemisphere to spring to life. It will be noted that both the language of dreams and the flow of free associations have all the hallmarks of right hemispheric functioning: from the vagaries of the dream scenario to the seemingly aimless ''psychobabble'' of the patient on the couch. This is what psychoanalysts describe as regression in the service of the treatment. It is in effect a corollary of the temporary *abeyance or blocking of left hemispheric control, and of the ascendancy of the right hemisphere.*

It goes without saying, however, that such attempts at translating nebulous psychological terms into the more precise language of modern neuroscience are still in their infancy. At this writing, they engage the talents of a number of up-and-coming investigators in this country and abroad. Whether or not they will ultimately fulfill the promise held out by Freud's *Project* will be for the future to tell. In the meantime the basic dichotomy between the rational and the irrational; between the conscious and the unconscious—between right versus left hemispheric dominance—is likely to endure as a testimony to his scientific acumen—and a tribute to his unerring intuition. (See Fig 7) The Levine cartoon seems to be a fitting illustration of his dilemma.

6

Jung's Split

A Study in
Complementarity

In May 1967 I gave a Freud Memorial Lecture to the Israeli
Psychoanalytic Society in Jerusalem. It was titled: *Freud versus
Jung, the Mythophobic versus the Mythophilic Temper in
Psychotherapy*. Not surprisingly, the juxtaposition of the two men
drew some flak from the audience. Could Freud's greatness as a
new Copernicus or Darwin of the human mind brook comparison
with the imaginative Seer, the Haunted Prophet of the Zurich
Lake? Did not Jung's short-lived love affair with the Nazi
philosophy disqualify him from assuming a place alongside Freud
in the pantheon of 20th century psychiatry?

Mystical Bent Versus Scientific Aspiration

Yet personal value judgments aside, their juxtaposition was
meant—and is now meant—to be a case study in two contrasting

temperaments, cognitive styles, and the fluctuations of their respective left versus right hemispheric orientation. Early on, in his *Memories, Dreams, Reflections* (1962), Jung sets the stage for such an inquiry. To begin with, he stresses that he cannot experience himself as "a scientific problem," as one which can be described "in the language of science." He is merely anxious to "tell stories," to present his "personal myth." In one such recollection, at seven or eight years of age, he was sitting on a stone, wondering whether he himself had been the stone on which "he" (meaning somebody else) was sitting: "Whether it was I or I was *it*." (p. 20).

It was a frankly mystical experience, coupled with the feeling of "disunity of the self," and it was to occur to him in many variations in years to come. It also gave rise to an imaginative childish game with a wooden mannikin he had carved for himself. He used it as a playmate and secret projection of his own personality, as a miniature alter ego, that was always at his beck and call.

At twelve, he had another experience of splitting: "Suddenly I came upon myself... previously I had existed too, but everything had merely happened to me. Now I happened to myself... previously I have willed to do this or that, now I willed." John Eccles and Carl Popper, in their book *The Mind and Its Brain* (1977), could not have asked for a better characterization of what they described as the passive, nonreflexive, well-nigh automatic set of responses originating from the right hemisphere, versus the capacity for deliberate volition and for generating the "self-conscious mind" attributed to the left cerebral hemisphere.

At about the same age, following an undeserved chastisement by a bullying grownup, Jung felt for the first time "quite clearly" that he was actually two different persons: "One of them was the schoolboy who could not grasp algebra and was far from sure of himself, the other was important, a high authority, a man not to be trifled with, as powerful and influential" as the man who had bullied him. The other personality was "an old man who had lived in the 18th century, wore buckled shoes"—and was in effect a famous 18th century Basel physician whose history had appealed to the youngster's imagination and with whom he identified himself in his daydreams.

Phantasies of this order were interspersed with a spate of obsessive-compulsive ruminations, anxieties, and grandiose ideas. They made him feel that he was both "blessed or accursed." He also experienced a series of fainting fits which were wrongly diagnosed as epileptic seizures and kept him out of school for several months.

Gradually his two identities crystallized into two distinct personalities: "Somewhere deep in the background I always knew that I was two persons. . . One was the son of my parents, who went to school, was less intelligent, attentive, hardworking, decent, and cleaner than many other boys. The other was grownup—old in fact—skeptical, mistrustful, remote from the world of men, but close to nature, the earth, the sun, the moon, the weather, all living creatures and above all, close to the night, to dreams and to whatever 'god' worked directly in him." Yet Jung was quick to add that the play and counterplay between personalities "No. 1" and "No. 2" which has run through his whole life, "had nothing to do with a 'split' or dissociation in the ordinary medical sense. On the contrary, it is played out in every individual" (p. 44).

This is not the place to engage in a posthumous disputation about the nature of Jung's personality split with the greatest authority on Jung, Jung himself. His remark that the same split can be found in "every individual" has the ring of truth. Nor is there reason to believe that, in Jung's case, the split had been of schizophrenic origin. What is debatable is his esoteric, typically Jungian interpretation. It has to be weighed against the available evidence reviewed here suggesting that Jung's No. 1 and No. 2 personalities showed all the hallmarks of a recurrent conflict between his right versus his left hemispheric orientation.

His *Memoirs* are replete with references to his sense of destiny, to his apodictic certainty derived from dreams, visions, and intuitions: "I did not have this certainty, *it* had me. . . Often I had the feeling that in decisive matters I am no longer alone, but was alone with God. . . I was Outside time, I belonged to the centuries." And he declares: "These talks with the 'Other' (side of his personality) were my profoundest experiences; on the one hand a bloody struggle, on the other supreme ecstasies." He extols his insight based on instinct or *participation mystique* with others. It is as if the "eyes of the background do the seeing in an impersonal act of perception" (p. 50). And he notes: "It was the same with my mother. She did not know what she was saying, it was like a voice wielding absolute authority, which said exactly what fitted the situation."

In a similar vein, he reports that in the course of his life it often happened to him that he suddenly "knew something" which he really could not have known at all. In some instances it had all the hallmarks of a telepathic response. As a practicing physician, he was one night awakened by a feeling of dull pain, "as though something had struck my forehead and then the back of my skull." The following day he received a telegram saying that a depressed patient of his who was told to get in touch with Jung when "his spirit was sinking," had shot and killed himself.

Jung later learned that the bullet had lodged in the back of the man's skull (p. 138).

Another case along these lines is described in his monograph on *Synchronicity* published jointly with Wolfgang Pauli, the theoretical physicist and Nobel Laureate (1951). A highly educated woman patient, a rationalistic "Cartesian mind," was unable to make any progress in her psychotherapy. Jung hoped against hope that something ultimately would come up to jolt her out of her detached posture. She related that she had had a dream the night before, a dream in which she was given a golden scarab—"a costly piece of jewelry...While she was still telling me the dream, I heard something behind me gently tapping on the window...it was a fairly large flying insect...I caught it in the air as it flew in (through the window he had opened). It was a scarabeid beetle, or common rose-chafer (*Cetonia aurata*) whose gold-green color most nearly resembles that of a golden scarab." And he adds: "This experience punctured the desired hole in her rationalism and broke the ice of her intellectual resistance."

Spiritualistic Interludes

Jung's interest in synchronicity goes back to his early preoccupation with spiritualism which was in turn another outgrowth of what he called his No. 2 personality. A fifteen-year old cousin, Helene Preiswerk, had developed striking mediumistic abilities. She went into trances and produced such physical and mental manifestations as table tilting, the emergence of diverse secondary personalities or "spirit controls," among them a medieval knight called *Ulrich von Gerbenstein*, a girl called *Ivenes*, and so on. Jung participated in the seances and ultimately made the medium the subject of a pioneering study of the psychology of trance mediumship. Helene's trance personalities, he suggested, were derived from her own unconscious "complexes" and served to meet her repressed personality needs.

Some of Helene's productions turned out to be fraudulent. Nevertheless, Jung's early forays into the occult had a decisive influence upon his further development: he himself was to encounter several purportedly spiritualist manifestations. One day, while studying for his exams, he was jolted by a loud report, "like a pistol shot," issuing from a seventy-year-old walnut table in the dining room. The table top had a split from the rim to beyond the center. His mother and the maid were witnesses to the event. Two weeks later, in the presence of his mother and fourteen-year-old sister, a bread knife had "exploded" in the sideboard with a deafening report. The blade had split into four fragments, leaving the handle intact.

Jung was puzzled and dismayed by these firsthand encounters on his home ground with the occult. He kept the broken pieces in a strongbox ever after and sent a snapshot of them to Dr. Rhine at Duke University. He wondered whether it was Helene, the medium, who had a hand in the mysterious occurrences. At the back of his mind he even thought of the possibility that he himself was possessed with the potential for mediumistic powers.

Yet he did not permit his No. 2 personality to drown out or override completely his here-and-now oriented No. 1 personality. He was a gifted and precocious child, and his father, a Lutheran pastor, taught him Latin at the age of six. He was a diligent and ambitious student, brilliant in humanistic subjects; but he had a poor number sense, hated mathematics, and found algebra far beyond him. In addition to his spells of fainting, he suffered from recurrent childhood ailments and diverse phobias. Yet he claims he overcame them by sheer acts of will. In the end, after vacillating between theology, philosophy, and archeology, he chose medicine as his career: the No. 1 personality, with its commitment to science, was to take the upper hand.

Soon thereafter Jung decided that psychiatry would be the specialty closest to his heart. Once immersed in the field, he discovered that Freud's psychoanalysis was the approach most congenial to him. The history of Jung's and Freud's ensuing correspondence, followed by the vicissitudes of their love-hate relationship, need not be told here. In effect, it was a replay and projection into social reality of Jung's own inner conflict between science and what was to become his personal myth. Freud was to be the guardian of his dedication to science and sober reality testing. At the same time he hoped to enlist Freud's aid in coming to terms with his secret commitment to another, esoteric, ineffable psychic reality.

That Freud perceived their relationship in an altogether different light is another matter. For him Jung held the promise of an ally, a welcome fellow campaigner, an up-and-coming leader in the field of psychoanalysis. He wanted to groom him as his crown prince and heir apparent who would help to remove the stigma of a "Jewish science" from his brain child. Secretly, he reached out to Jung as a replacement for his lost soul mate and alter ego, Wilhelm Fliess. It is not surprising that their association, like a marriage contracted between partners with mutually conflicting expectations, was from the outset doomed to failure.

In 1909 Freud and Jung were invited to lecture at Clark University in Worcester, Massachusetts. They met in Bremen to embark on their transatlantic voyage, and it was during a luncheon discussion that the first sign of their future discord came to the fore. Freud was vexed by Jung's recital of a story of mummified corpses which had been discovered during a recent archeological dig. Then and there, Freud went into a dead faint. On coming to, he bluntly accused his companion of harboring secret death wishes against him.

Jung, still somewhat naive and impressionable, seems to have reacted with guilt feelings to the charge. He may again have wondered whether he was possessed of mysterious powers.

Some 3 years later, in 1912, his growing suspicion of his own "blessed or cursed" omnipotence of thought led to the ultimate showdown with Freud. During a visit in Freud's studio, Jung asked Freud for his views, concerning "occult" phenomena. "Because of his materialistic prejudice," Jung writes in his *Memoirs*, "he rejected this entire complex of questions as nonsensical and did so in terms of so shallow a positivism that I had difficulty in checking the sharp retort on the tip of my tongue..." And he continues: "While Freud was going on this way, I had a curious sensation. It was as if my diaphragm was made of iron and were becoming red-hot, a glowing vault. At that moment there was such a loud report in the bookcase which stood right next to us that we both started up in alarm, fearing that the thing was to topple over us. I said to Freud: 'There, that is an example of a so-called catalytic exteriorization phenomenon,' i.e., a case of what parapsychologists today describe as psychokinesis. 'Oh, come,' Freud exclaimed, 'oh, come, that is sheer bosh!' This was his only reaction." Provoked by Freud's intransigence, Jung proceeded to repeat his "poltergeist" performance with Freud's bookcase—and there was another "loud report" (p. 155).

COLLISION AND BREAK WITH FREUD

Yet Jung's poltergeist performance, real or imaginary, was more than merely an attempt at winning a point in a theoretical argument. His belief in the reality of his No. 2 personality, in his personal myth, in his mysterious powers, had become articles of faith for him. Doubts expressed on that score were a threat to his very sanity and emotional balance. Since starting his psychiatric residency in Bleuler's clinic in Burghölzli, he had secretly asked himself whether he was truly qualified to face his mental patients from the psychiatrist's side of the desk. He discovered a spiritual kinship with some of his paranoid schizophrenics and was worried about it. As a child, Jung had been the victim of sexual molestation by an older man. Since then he had been concerned about his masculine identity. His earlier correspondence with Freud held out the hope of sympathetic understanding from a man whose work he admired. He now turned to him not just for an exchange of ideas, but in search of guidance and approval that would have helped to dispel whatever doubts he had about his own mental health and the soundness of his philosophy.

Jung's vehement gut reaction, the "glowing vault" in his chest, dramatically expressed his inner turmoil at the moment of truth. Alas, Freud dashed his hopes for understanding and reassurance at the time of the bookcase incident. A letter from Freud written shortly thereafter only deepened Jung's hurt and despair. Granting that he had given the phenomenon serious thought, Freud wrote: "My credulity...vanished along with your personal presence. Once again for various inner reasons it seems to me wholly implausible that anything of the sort should occur. The furniture stands before me spiritless and dead, like nature, silent and godless before the poet after the passing of the gods of Greece." And he adds: "I therefore don once more my horn-rimmed paternal spectacles and warn my dear son to keep a cool head and rather not understand something that makes such a great sacrifice for the sake of understanding" (Jung, 1962, pp. 361-363).

In the end, Freud tries to soften his rebuke: "I . . . look forward to hearing more about your new investigations of the spook complex, my interest being the interest one has in a *lovely delusion* (my italics) which one does not share oneself." The tone of the letter is cordial as before, but from then on the ominous word *delusion* must have stood between the two men like an invisible wall.

Yet Freud's involvement with the younger man was by no means as detached, analytical, or even calculating as met the eye. He was greatly impressed with his exceptional gifts, with the sincerity of his motivations; he was attracted by his intense, brooding qualities, by his intuitive, imaginative approach to matters of common interest. Consciously or unconsciously, Freud recognized Jung as one of his inner "doubles," as a new incarnation of his soul mate Wilhelm Fliess, or rather as an alter ego with his prevailing left hemispheric orientation. He was both fascinated and dismayed by Jung's open display of his No. 2 personality. More than that: the facts behind more recently published reports of Jung's involvement with his ex-patient Sabine Spielrein, may have further contributed to their growing alienation.

I noted that Jung was equally taken by Freud's nimbus as the intrepid explorer of the world of the mind, by the depth, discipline and lucidity of his thinking. At the same time, Freud represented to him the challenge of a strict, demanding superego. But he may also have evoked memories of the black Jesuit priest, the bogey man—the Brown-Skinned Savage, if not the exotic Jew, the detested child molester of his childhood years—or the blasphemous dream of a depraved godfather defecating on his shiny cathedral: the world. Thus Freud's idea of anointing him as his "crown prince and heir apparent" was both a blandishment and a threat to Jung.

In any case, Freud's blunt refusal to endorse—or to even comprehend—Jung's message and his aspirations for a higher spiritual purpose, had dealt a fatal blow to their relationship from which both men were never to recover. To be sure, on the face of it, the scene in Freud's study was of an arcane though relatively trivial nature. Still, it brought the polarity of their temperaments, their respective ideologies and philosophical positions out into the open—with a bang.

We must also realize that in men of Freud's or Jung's intellectual caliber ideological factors had a far more powerful leverage than in ordinary mortals. It extended from the highest spiritual sphere—or the highest cortical structures of the central nervous system to the autonomous or gut level indicated in Table 1 in the introductory chapter of this book.

Still, both Freud's and Jung's post-confrontation reaction was slow in coming. In 1912 they both attended a psychoanalytic conference in the Park Hotel in Munich. In the wake of a seemingly minor difference of opinion, Freud again went into a dead faint, and fell on the floor. The strong-armed Jung carried him to the nearest couch. On coming to, Ernest Jones heard Freud mutter under his breath "How sweet it must be to die..."

The incident has given rise to a spate of conflicting speculations. Was it just a consequence of Freud's excessive cigar smoking? Did he sense again that his "beloved son" was out for the oedipal kill of the father figure? Was his fainting a masochistic surrender to the younger man's superior sexual prowess? Or else, did he respond to the lure of Jung's Dionysian raptures, to his cosmic flights of fancy, with a headlong rush into those "oceanic feelings" which he,

Freud, had hitherto kept under his right-left hemispheric control? Did his fainting aim at forestalling the danger of impending ego disintegration, and did its "sweetness" herald the taste of freedom from strict superego controls, sexual, intellectual, and emotional?

I am inclined to subscribe to the latter interpretation. If Jung responded to the incident in Freud's study with an explosive discharge of rage, including its physical and, perhaps, *para*physical concomitants, Freud's reaction was considerably delayed but no less explosive. It was a reaction to what Frazer and later Jung described as the *Perils of the Soul*: to what is here termed the return of the culturally repressed. Needless to say, a repressed homosexual undercurrent may have likewise entered the picture.

It is, however, of more than incidental interest in the present context that, according to Jones (1953), Freud had suffered two previous fainting spells in the presence of his erstwhile friend Wilhelm Fliess; the second reportedly occurred during an argument in the same room, in the Park Hotel in Munich, where Freud and Fliess had stayed during their periodic "congresses." Fliess had accused Freud of acting as a "thought reader" who had planted his own thinking in his patients' heads. Fliess's charge must have hit a vulnerable spot, since Freud himself had worried about such a possibility all along. Had the charge been substantiated, it could well have shaken Freud's system of thought to its very foundation.

Jung's delayed reaction to his confrontation with Freud was of an even more serious nature. In his *Memoirs* he repeatedly refers to his forebodings of the catastrophe which was to engulf Europe in World War I. He describes visions and fantasies and other omens as signs of "an unusual activation of the unconscious." For instance, he saw corpses placed in crematory ovens, then discovered that they were still alive (p. 172). Some of the dreams took him back into the 18th, and then to the 12th century, and seemed to confirm his Jungian (versus the Freudian) interpretation of the unconscious. He lived under steadily growing pressures, so much so that he thought that "there was some psychic disturbance" in himself. At the same time, he felt the need to return to his early childhood and his favorite games of playing with building blocks and assorted found objects. He felt he was rediscovering his own myth.

Towards the autumn of 1913 the atmosphere grew darker and darker. Jung was seized by a new rush of overpowering visions. He saw a monstrous flood, the floating rubble of civilization, and the drowned bodies of uncounted thousands: "the whole sea turned into blood" (p. 175).

PLUNGE INTO PSYCHOSIS OR SHIFT TO RIGHT BRAIN DOMINANCE?

Jung interpreted these apocalyptic visions as prophecies of things to come. But to a more objective observer they appear as typical phantasies of so-called cosmic catastrophes often seen in the opening phase of psychotic reaction: Jung was on the verge of falling victim to his No. 2 personality, gone mad. Yet he also notes that when he endured these "assaults of the unconscious," he had "an unswerving conviction" that he was obeying a higher will, and that feeling continued to uphold him until he had "mastered the task."

Significantly, he also notes that in the struggle with psychosis he had to describe his experiences of the archetypes "in the language of high rhetoric, even of bombast" (p. 178). It is a language he himself found embarrassing. Still, he had no choice "but to write everything down in the style selected by the unconscious itself." Evidently, it was the cognitive style of the right hemisphere seeking to find release through creative expression of his predicament.

In the further course, Jung was confronted with a succession of archetypal images he identified as projected parts of his own personality: *Siegfried*, the hero of Teutonic mythology; the *Brown-Skinned Savage*, representing the Shadow; they were followed by the *Wise Old Man Elijah*, and the blind girl *Salome—the anima*. They were joined by *Philemon*, the aged mate of *Baucis*, and others. Gradually the whole house was filled "as if there were a crowd present, crammed full of spirits...As for myself, I was all aquiver with the question 'For God's sake, what in the world is this?'" (p. 190–191).

The answer to Jung's question can at best be surmised. Among the ghostly visitors crowding in was the biblical prophet Elijah, one of the archetypes of the Wise Old Man—and by implication, of another "departed" prophet: Sigmund Freud. Did Jung leave an empty chair at his table, just in case Freud, the second Elijah, would care to reappear? He notes in his *Memoirs*: "When I parted from Freud, I knew I was plunging into the unknown. Beyond Freud, after all, I knew nothing; but I had taken the step into darkness..." It may well be that his psychotic break was an attempt to fill the vacuum left by Freud with the cast of several *dramatis personae* to substitute for the man who had rejected him, or from whom he himself had broken away: the many had to pitch in for the irreplaceable one who was missing.

In the years that followed, Jung withdrew from "the world of intellect," from his assignments at the university, from his private practice and all scientific activity, into complete loneliness and isolation. At about the same time he discovered the arcane significance of mandala drawings. Mandalas, for him, were coded symbols or "cryptograms" of the unconscious. They represented the wholeness, harmony, and centeredness of an integrated personality, steppingstones on the way to "Individuation." He proceeded to fill his *Red Book* and his *Black Book* with scores upon scores of mandala drawings. He did so for hours and days on end, and he felt that it helped him find his "center," to regain his emotional balance and peace of mind.

SELF-HEALING AND RECONCILIATION OF OPPOSITES

It is a moot question whether this discovery was Jung's special brand of sympathetic magic or a forerunner of present-day art therapy. The fact is that by the end of World War I he was able to resume his normal routine and to plunge into novel fields of psychological explorations: Gnosticism and medieval alchemy. Alchemy, in particular, became a rich source of new insights to Jung. He considered it as a science most congenial to his No. 2 personality, on an equal footing with the mainstream sciences of the modern world, holding the key for the resolution of the existential conflict between knowledge and wisdom, between Western and Eastern philosophy.

Another major project was his pioneering study of *Psychological Types* (1921). It is a monumental work of 725 pages, replete with scholarly quotes, references, and footnotes. It delineates in painstaking detail the dichotomy between the extroverted and introverted types, correlated with such basic functions as thought, intuition, sensation, and feeling. It is an example of a largely speculative armchair philosophy, aimed at bringing order into what he called the totality of the psyche—in particular his own—an attempt to counterbalance chaos with an elaborate, abstract, and rather pedantic system of psychology. Yet at the same time it is a graphic illustration of his power to compensate, and overcompensate with his left hemisphere for the occasional excesses and aberrations of the right.

Gradually Jung was able to resume his usual activities. But following a heart attack and a new series of visions, he felt the need to build for himself a new "castle of stone" on his estate on the Zurich lake. He called it Bollingen Tower, and it was to be a retreat for further maturation and individuation—symbolic of the womb. Yet even this retreat was not safe from the intrusion of hallucinatory voices and images from the collective unconscious. Neither the four walls or four phases in which his castle was built, or the arcane quaternity of his cherished mandala drawings—one better than the Freudian trinity of ego, superego and id—succeeded in bringing about the hoped-for annealing of the inner split between his No. 1 and No. 2 personality: the reconciliation of the opposites.

Freud's abiding achievement was the creation of an overarching internally consistent scientific system of thought. But he achieved it at the cost of excluding from it the *mysterium tremendum* of man's spiritual experience. Jung's grandiose project was to fill the gap left in Freud's left hemispheric universe of discourse. Yet despite his avowed scientific aspirations and record of spectacular scholarship, the ultimate synthesis of knowledge and intuition eluded him. Jung remained an essentially right hemispheric genius, an inspired prophet and dispenser of a beguiling personal myth in an increasingly demythologized technological age.

Summing up, it is this basic contrast of hemispheric preponderance which was at the root of the fateful conflict between their personalities, their hidden premises, beliefs, and systems of values.

Initially, all this seemed to augur well for the mutual attraction of opposites and for a viable complementary relationship between the two. But in the end both men found themselves caught in a web of popular misconceptions and misrepresentations that cast their growing incompatibility into the polarity of Jew versus Gentile, of Jahwe versus Christ, and set the stage for the replay of the age-old passion play of an anti-semitic confrontation.

Sadly, it has to be admitted that Jung did occasionally allow himself to be typecast into the uncongenial role of a Jew-hater, unaware that he was in effect merely misreading the promptings of his right cerebral hemisphere; and he himself protested vehemently against the reproach of anti-semitism. In turn, Freud remained equally unaware of the forbidding impact upon his "beloved son and crown prince" of his uncompromising left hemispheric orientation. This is how his—and Jung's—hopes for a joint enterprise to explore the scope and depth of the human mind came to grief. Their followers did little to bridge the gap between their respective philosophies, and exacerbated the differences between the two. It will be for posterity to shift the emphasis from discord and incompatibility to the common ground between Freudian and Jungian systems of thought and to throw into proper perspective the complementary aspects of their respective approaches and personalities.

7

MOZART,
FATHER AND SON
Talent Versus Genius

My lifelong fascination with Mozart prompted an earlier psychohistoric study of *Mozart: Father and Son* (1963). It was a time when split-brain research and the problem of hemispheric specialization were still waiting in the wings, and the exploration of genius was largely based on Freudian principles, with an added slant towards family dynamics.

It is humbling to confess that in the process I failed to pay attention to telltale signs in Wolfgang's life history pointing to circumstances which happened to be outside my original frame of reference. What are the salient facts emerging from the traditional psychoanalytic approach? And what are the new findings relevant to the issue pursued here?

CHILD PRODIGY WHO THROVE
ON CLOSENESS WITH FATHER

Mozart's genius, I suggested, has to be viewed in the light of his symbiotic closeness to, and subsequent rebellion against his father

102

Leopold Mozart. Leopold was a prolific but mediocre composer. He started his career as a valet with an influential, musically interested churchman, and soon made a name as a composer steeped in the Italian rococo and baroque tradition. He was later employed as an assistant conductor and court musician to the Archbishop of Salzburg and remained for 44 years in the same position. His more renowned contribution was a pedagogical work, *The School of Violin Playing*, widely used for the benefit of several generations of students. It was published in 1756, the year Wolfgang Amadeus, his second child, was born.

For Leopold, the discovery of the little boy's prodigious musical talent was a gift from the gods. It held the promise of vicarious fulfillment of his own dreams of glory, fame, and financial prosperity. The child was to become an extended part of the father's personality, a second chance life was offering him to accomplish what had been denied him in the past. The fact is, that short of having been Wolfgang Amadeus's father, Leopold Mozart would have remained one of the many forgotten composers of the 18th century (Biancolli, 1954).

Quoting from my earlier account (1963), the story goes that the child, aged five, listening to his father and two friends playing a trio for strings, suddenly piped up, asking permission to take the fiddle and play second violin in place of one of the men. Undismayed by their good-natured jibes, he insisted; Leopold's eyes filled with tears of rapture as he listened to Wolfgang's performance.

A few years later, during a stop in his travels with the child prodigy through the capitals of Europe, Leopold took *Wolfgangerl* to a country church to acquaint him with the intricacies of organ pedal technique. The boy pushed away the stool, placed himself in front of the instrument and played as though he had already had months of practice.

It took barely more than three or four years for Leopold, the professional instructor, to impart to his child all the technical skills he was able to muster. Apparently, Wolfgang started where the father had stopped in his own development. Musical notation, elementary theory and composition, were all part of the curriculum. Before Wolfgang was able to write the scores,

Leopold's trembling hand penned for the five-year-old child his first musical compositions—two minuets known today as Köchel listing 1 and 2. They were followed by more minuets scrawled in Wolfgang's own childish hand.

The father's symbiotic closeness to the son, his tendency not only to be his mentor and guardian, but also to live Wolfgang's life in his behalf, is illustrated by Leopold's undertaking to write his son's biography and collect all the documentary material which might conceivably have a bearing on Wolfgang's career. Some of the trips abroad were made by father and son alone. They must have further reinforced the intimacy existing between the two. At times, we are told, they were forced—or chose—to sleep in the same bed.

Wolfgang, in turn, responded to his father's guardianship and control in what can be described as a pattern of sharing. His reaction was one of ready compliance, if not unconditional submission and surrender. It was aided by the fact that Leopold's fanatic dedication to his task, his missionary zeal of instruction, was truly congenial to Wolfgang's genius. That which was transmitted from father to son through the strict discipline of his *Violinschule* and by the unrelenting routine of daily coaching and tutoring, had a potentiating effect upon what may have lain dormant in the boy's genetic endowment, waiting to burst forth in the fullness of time. We shall see that here, again, the right hemisphere was the repository of the child prodigy's native endowment. But we are also told by the musicologists that he too had to learn the hard way the laggard skills of the left side of the brain to reach the full flowering of his genius. Paradoxically, the child prodigy has in that respect been described as a late bloomer.

Yet Wolfgang was by no means unresponsive to influences reaching him from other quarters. Indeed, his ready susceptibility to flattery, to influences both good and bad, his gullibility and childlike trust in people were a major grievance to Leopold. He was a loving, but also possessive and jealous father, and he would not tolerate other father figures besides himself. He sensed Wolfgang's excessive dependency needs, his propensity to compliance, and sought to guard him against its consequences. At the same time there can be little doubt as to Leopold's own need to feed into Wolfgang's continued dependence on his father. The son was to remain his exclusive spiritual property once and for all, the consummation of Leopold's own frustrated artistic aspirations, the instrument on which he was to perform the triumphant cadenzas of his *magnum opus,* the crowning achievement of his faltering musical career.

Leopold's letters to his son reflect both his possessiveness and his genuine concern for his welfare. They show him as a man with a rigid, conservative turn of mind, a pedantic, nagging insistence on duty, diligence, and parsimony, coupled with the tendency to distrust the motivations of his fellow men. Some of his cautionary remarks to the young man trying to sow his wild oats sound like Polonius's sermons to Laertes refurbished in the spirit of the *ancien regime.* "A good-hearted fellow," he exhorts Wolfgang, "is inclined to express himself freely, and naturally, nevertheless, it is a mistake to do so. And it is just your good heart which prevents you from detecting any shortcomings in a person who showers praises on you, has a great opinion of you and flatters you to the skies and who makes you give him all your confidences and affection."

In another passage, he reminisces: "As a child and boy you were serious rather than childish and when you sat at the klavier or were otherwise intent on music, no one dared to make the slightest jest. Why, even your expression was so solemn that, observing the early efflorescence of your talent and your ever grave and thoughtful little face, many discerning people of different countries sadly doubted whether your life would be a long one."

It never occurred to the older man that the child's solemnity and seriousness was fortunately only a passing phase, reflecting his total merging with Leopold's personality, and that it was precisely the boy's gaiety and natural trustfulness—"the abiding charm and loveliness of his gaiety," as one of Wolfgang's admirers put it—that distinguished the son's genius from the father's talent. We shall see that theirs was in effect the contrast between an essentially left-hemispheric and an essentially right-hemispheric personality make-up.

WOLFGANG REBELLING

This basic cleavage between temperament and personal style had all the makings of ultimate conflict between the two. Still,

Wolfgang's open rebellion against father was late in coming. Unlike Beethoven or Pablo Picasso, he displaced his rebelliousness onto a more deservably hateable father figure: the tyrannical Archbishop of Salzburg, in whose service he, too, had been employed as long as he stayed in his home town. Only in Wolfgang's later years does W. Hildesheimer (1982), his latest biographer, discover evidence of a more critical attitude, even of duplicity, in Amadé's correspondence with the old man.

Wolfgang's mother, a loving and self-effacing German *Hausfrau,* died during their prolonged sojourn in Paris. On his return to Salzburg, he felt his father's gloomy outlook and the Archbishop's chicanery more difficult to take than ever before. Despite his sister's tears and Leopold's strenuous objections, he took off on his own to try his luck in Vienna.

Leopold himself was crushed by the breaking of the symbiotic tie with his son. In a letter written during his absence in Paris he had already complained of his poverty, of his material deprivations, and expressly clamored for the sympathy of his absent dear ones: "All my joy to hear you play and compose has gone and all around me is dead." His health began to fail and his letters became increasingly plaintive and accusatory: "You may believe and believe for sure, my dearest son, that I prefer to die without you and that if I had the pleasure of having you with me I'd lived longer by many years." He accused Wolfgang of killing him, the way the son's selfishness and lack of consideration had killed his mother. At the same time, he promised him greater independence in his musical activities and a chance for more liberal and uncensored correspondence with Aloysia Weber, the object of Wolfgang's infatuation during an earlier stay in Mannheim.

The final blow to his father was Wolfgang's sudden decision, following rejection by Aloysia, to marry Constance, Aloysia's younger sister. Yet the fact is that it was their mother, Frau Weber, who pulled the strings, who dictated the stiff marriage contract and took charge of the household of the newlyweds. Cecilia Weber was a scheming, controlling woman, described as the evil genius in Mozart's life, and she never lost her strangle hold over him. He in turn, had never learned to stand on his own feet. Once he made the break from Leopold's benevolent despotism, it was Cecilia who took over the reins. In that respect, one of his father's predictions did come true. Her principal function was in effect to usurp Leopold's place and to substitute for his symbiotic tie with Wolfgang one of predatory, parasitic exploitation.

As far as Wolfgang's relationship with his wife is concerned, it certainly lacked the wholesome, supportive, affectionate qualities that were characteristic of Leopold's attitude towards his son. She is described as a flighty, poorly educated, emotionally immature woman, completely lacking in understanding of Wolfgang's genius. Leopold did not attend their wedding in St. Stephen's Cathedral in Vienna. His health had turned from bad to worse, and his letters to his children made no secret of his condition.

News of his father's illness seemed to strike once more the chords of Wolfgang's close identification with Leopold. He wrote to the dying man: "As death is the true purpose of life, I have for many years made myself familiar with that best friend of man, and his face no longer holds terror for me, but is, if anything, calm and consoling to look upon. I thank God for his blessing...and never go to bed without thinking that perhaps on the morrow I may no longer be alive."

It is as though Wolfgang, who had taken it upon himself to live a substantial part of his own life on his father's behalf, was now trying to carry at least some of the burden of Leopold's death on his own frail shoulders. I can see no reason to doubt the genuineness of these sentiments.

Wolfgang's remaining years in Vienna are a chronicle of artistic triumphs in the face of adversity, of recurrent financial failures, of persistent mismanagement of his affairs and of shocking indifference and neglect by his beloved "little wife," Constance. His letters to his friends and patrons, begging for loans or outright handouts and charity, are pathetic documents of abject poverty and self-abasement. But it is also possible that his persistent failure to make ends meet was not merely due to bad luck, to the callousness of his contemporaries, to historic accidents, or to the scheming of his mother-in-law. It could be also attributed to the need to re-establish his relationship with a loving though controlling father, who had rewarded the son's continued dependence on him by the show and showering of affection, yet who reacted to every step in the direction of independence and self-reliance with nagging reproaches, anxiety, or outright castigation.

Despite Wolfgang's frustration with Leopold's unimaginative, philistine, if not compulsive, demands for prudence, order, frugality, and compromise with the powers that be, he seemed to miss his counsel, his stabilizing influence. "Pragmatic thinking was alien to him," as Hildesdeimer puts it. It is as though Mozart's right cerebral hemisphere, left to its own resources was missing the restraining, tempering trend of the left hemisphere which his father had provided by proxy, as it were, so long as he was alive. Needless to say, his rivalry with Salieri, the well-connected court composer could duplicate only the frustrating side of the father-son relationship.

THE BAESLE LETTERS: LETTING GO OF LEFT BRAIN CONTROLS

It is true that, as far as the elder Mozart is concerned, it is difficult to quote chapter and verse to substantiate such a statement. There is, however, more than speculative evidence of Wolfgang's fitful, if not preponderantly, right hemispheric orientation. Telltale signs to this effect can be found in the correspondence of the twenty-year-old with his girl cousin, Maria Anna Thecla, in Augsburg, but also with his sister, Nannerl, and even in some passages of letters to his father. The letters to his girl cousin, known as the *Baesle Briefe,* have, with their coarse ribald content, been a source of keen embarrassment for his Victorian (or Francisco Josefian) biographers. A letter of February 28, 1778, congenially translated by Emily Anderson (1938) is a typical example.

> ...Now I have the honor to inquire how you are and whether you perspire? Whether your stomach is still in good order? Whether indeed you have no disorder? Whether you can still like me at all? Whether with chalk you often crawl? Whether now and then you have me in mind? Whether to hang yourself you sometimes have in mind. Whether you have been wild? With this poor foolish child? Whether to make peace with me you'll be so kind? If not, I swear I

let off one behind (flatus). Ah, you are laughing! Victoria! Our arses shall be the symbol of our peacemaking. I knew that you wouldn't be able to resist me much longer. Why, of course, I'm sure of success, even if today I should make a mess, though to Paris I go in a fortnight or less. So if you want to send a reply to me from the town, of Augsburg yonder, you see, then write at once, the sooner the better, so that I may be sure to receive your letter, or else I'm gone I'll have the bad luck, instead of a letter to get some muck. Muck!—Muck! Ah, muck! Sweet word! Muck! Chuck! That too is fine, muck, chuck—muck!—suck—oh *charmant!*'' Muck, suck! That's what I like! Muck! chuck, suck! Chuck, muck, and suck, muck! (*Note.* From *Mozart's Letters*, E. Blom (Ed.) Farrar & Rhinehart).

Most offensive to Victorian sensibilities is, of course, the scatological content of such passages. They are closer to the sewer line than to stream of consciousness—a striking contrast to the perfection, the matchless beauty, and angelic purity of his musical output. Put in Freudian terms, it could be described as sublimation in reverse, a cathartic release of all pent-up and repressed, anal, coprophilic, destructive impulses issuing from the unconscious.

No less significant are, however, the formal characteristics of his free-associations gone on a rampage. They are illustrated by the following samples from a letter of November 5, 1777:

"Dear Coz Fuzz! I have received reprieved your dear letter telling selling me that my uncle carbuncle, my aunt, can't and you too are very well hell. Thank God, we too are in excellent health. Today the letter setter from my papa Ha! Ha! dropped safely into my claws paws. I hope that you too have got shot the note dote which I wrote to you from Mannheim. If so, so much the better, better than much so..." etc.

This exercise in verbal clowning and rhyming slang in Cockney style is followed by these rhetorical questions: "Why not—What?—Why not?—why should I not send it? Why should I not dispatch it? Why not? Strange! I don't know why I shouldn't—Well then, you will do me this favor. —Why not? Why should you not do it?—Why not? Strange! I shall do the same for you, when you want me to." There is much more in this vein.

He signs the letter *Wolfgang Amadé Rosy Posy*. By way of a

dateline he writes: "333 to the grave, if my life I save. *Miehnnam, Rebotco eht ht5 7771*"

This, of course, is a literal reversal of: *Mannheim, October the 5th, 1771.* It should also be noted that in the last sample Mozart elevates his ribald double-entendre from the scatological to the psychoanalytically more respectable erotic level. Still, it sounds very much like a caricature of a symphonic piece in which the melodic line of a *Tema con variazione* is punctuated by the flatulent *umph* of the basses and drums. It is as though the ordering principle of his musical idiom had given way to a well-nigh *Dadaist* principle of randomness and disorder, shedding all semblance of control and restraint, moralistic, esthetic, or otherwise, ordinarily exercised by the left cerebral hemisphere. This is further borne out by the playful reversal of both words and parts of sentences, in an otherwise exemplary letter to his father on October 3, 1777:

> "Well, I wish you a very restful night and I improve upon this good wish by hearing to hope soon that Papa is well quite. I forgiveness your crave for my disgraceful handwriting, but ink, haste, sleep, dreams and all the rest...I papa your, my hands kiss a thousand time dearest, and my embrace, the heart, sister I with all my brute of and remain, now and for ever, amen
>
> Wolfgang most obedient your
Amade Mozart son (sic!)

The letter shows that even the dutiful correspondence with Leopold could not dampen Wolfgang's high spirits. But it is unlikely that his right hemispheric (metaphorically speaking, left-handed) exercise in a contrapuntal grammar had amused his father; nor would it have won applause from *Monsignor* Martini, his erstwhile instructor in counterpoint.

Still, amidst all the havoc Wolfgang was wreaking on left hemispheric grammar and syntax, the part played by a musically informed right hemisphere is unmistakable. In his Dear Coz-letter the phrase, "If so, so much the better, better than much so" bears a striking structural similarity to the symmetrical structure of the celebrated finale in Act II of Figaro composed in 1786: E^b-B^b-G-C-F-B^b-E^b. Musicologists have specifically noted the mirror pattern of the E flat, B flat, B flat, E flat in the opening and closing phase of the piece (C. Rosen, 1979).

In effect, contrapuntal mirroring of musical phrases has been a recurrent theme of baroque music, and its original can be traced back to the Renaissance. It was a prominent feature of Bach's treatment of counterpoint in fugues and canons. A celebrated example is the Crab Canon in his *Musical Offering*: when played left to right it sounds exactly the same as played right to left. Such playful reversals have been described as *al rovescio* or *Cancrizans,* an allusion to the sidling forward and backward motions of the crab. Another example is the third movement of Haydn's symphony #47. It is specifically marked *al reverso* or *al rovescio,* that is, the first section is written in mirror form followed by its exact reversal. Significantly, Arnold Schoenberg's late compositions in the twelve-tone scale likewise include numerous *al rovescio* devices.

Such musical tongue twisters are more than whimsical products of the composer's ingenuity. They reflect his facility in shifting gears, vectors, or directional impulses, controlled as they are by the right or left hemisphere respectively. Such an ability has recently been described by Douglas Hofstadter (1979) as a characteristic of many creative artists and thinkers, from Bach to Goedel and Escher, and it is closely related to Rothenberg's Janusian thinking mentioned on a later page. Recent brain scan tests with radioactive glucose specifically confirm the role of the left hemisphere in professional musicians.

But delight in occasional forays into "dextraversion" versus "sinistraversion" seems to be their common denominator. Even former president Nixon who was certainly worlds apart from Mozart, showed a comparable need to seek explosive relief from his carefully guarded public image—and his "work-aholic," left hemispheric routine. He did so by abrupt shifts from presidential rhetoric to the colorful language ("expletives deleted") in the collection of his notorious White House tapes. In a way they are the grown-up equivalents of Wolfgang's adolescent *Baesle Briefe,* though they did not necessarily serve as backdrops to creative artistic expression.

Needless to say, genius is by no means constrained to such

limited, left versus right hemispheric alternatives. There is an infinite number of options between equally seminal projects or programs tucked away in the recesses of his cerebral organization. The choices range from viable innovations, to the comical, the bizarre, the frankly absurd, orchestrated by artistic intuitions and controlled by diverse neural networks or the incidental mix of neurotransmitters brought into play for the occasion.

Here is an example of Wolfgang's forays into the absurd. He closes his Baesle letter of February 18, 1778, with the following untranslatable word salad: "Ich bin, ich war, ich waere, ich bin gewesen, ich war gewesen, ich waere gewesen, o wenn ich waere, o dass ich waere, wollte gott ich waere, ich wuerde seyn, ich werde seyn, wenn ich seyn wuerde, o dass ich sein wuerde, ich wuerde gewesen, ich werde gewesen, seyn, o wenn ich gewesen ware, wollte gott ich waere gewesen, was?"

A veritable babel of mixed and fragmented languages is telescoped into the following letter to his sister Nannerl, dated Vienna, 12th August, 1773.

"Hodie nous avons begegnet per strada. Dominum Edelbach, welcher uns di voi compliments ausgerichtet hat, et qui sich tibi et ta mere emphehlen laesst Adio. W.M."

This shows once more the loosening of Wolfgang's free associations in moments of expansive mood, his freewheeling shifts from one linguistic frame of reference to another, coupled with attending comical effects. It certainly betrays his cavalier disregard of the rules and regulations of a strictly compartmentalized grammar and syntax, presided over by the left hemisphere.

BLENDING OF THREE I'S AND THREE R'S, TALENT EXALTED BY GENIUS

Viewed against the background of Mozart's works as a whole, such lighthearted capers seem to be trivial, insignificant lapses from grace. But they give us a behind-the-scenes glimpse into the workshop of genius. They suggest once more that the act of creation is the product of typical right-hemispheric inspiration and intuition, pressed into the mold of left-hemispheric order and discipline. If the first, right-hemispheric ingredient has sprung from the genes, like Pallas Athene from the head of Zeus, the second ingredient in Mozart's case was provided by his methodical training and instruction at the hands of Leopold. It was Wolfgang's patrimony of craftsmanship and professional skills without which his most inspired efforts would have fallen short of perfection. On the other hand, his verbal clowning; vulgarities and obscenities are indications of his need for disinhibition, for occasional explosive release from the tyranny of his left hemisphere, so that the right side or even the lower centers, could have a "ball." Unfortunately, the otherwise brilliant New York production of Schaffer's *Amadeus* failed to make allowance for this state of affairs.

Hildesheimer's iconoclastic Mozart biography calls attention to much the same puzzling inconsistencies in Wolfgang's personality. But I submit that, as with Beethoven's heroic versus antiheroic aspects, making due allowance for the right hemispheric, "sinister" origin of the purported mischief is apt to dispell at least part of the mystery. Yet while Beethoven's quest for sexual liberation seemed to be frozen in its tracks, Mozart's emancipation from left brain constraints was the photographic negative of the angelic beauty of his music. It went hand in hand (perhaps he would have referred to another bodily organ) with a rather earthy love affair with his Baesle, injecting into it an added human, if not all-too-human, 18th century dimension.

To repeat: the first ingredient of Mozart's genius originated from the native endowment of his right cerebral hemisphere. This is suggested first, by the anatomical findings reviewed in the first chapter, expressly linking musical ability with the right side of the brain (p. 8); secondly, by his impish propensity for punning, for versifying, from rhyming slang to parodies of poetic diction. This too seems to be a special prerogative of the right hemisphere, as opposed to the more sedate, measured, and disciplined style of the left side of the brain. Thirdly, there are sundry indications of fluidity and interchangeability of the right versus left hemispheric *directional impulses*. This is evidently one of the prime requirements for both composer and performer in the musical medium.

It should be noted, however, that all these considerations focus chiefly on cognitive, that is to say, more or less rational, aspects of the anatomy of genius. They ignore deeper, biological or instinctual levels of personality that supply fuel for the human enterprise in both its lowest and highest manifestations—including genius. Without the contributions of these phylogenetically lower—if you like, reptilian—centers of the brain, the creative impulse would never get off the ground, or would soon lose its momentum.

There are unmistakable signs of the part played by an uprush from these deeper, vegetative or limbic centers of the brain in acts of discovery, inspiration, or creation. Archimedes uttered his jubilant shout of *Heureka* stepping naked out of his bath. We are told that Leonardo da Vinci trembled when reaching for his brush to start a new painting. Einstein wrote about the "deep shudder of the soul in enchantments" associated with scientific discovery. Goethe alluded to his "burning innards" on trying to give poetic expression to his feelings. Carl Gustav Jung felt his diaphragm turning into a "glowing vault" when he sought to convince Freud of the reality of psychic phenomena. Indeed "gut feelings" have always been considered unfailing harbingers of emerging insights. They may call for the impulsive acting out, a victory dance or just a perfunctory jig, for instance, when Hitler thought that ultimate triumph over the Allies was just around the corner.

In the ideal case, the three levels of the central nervous system—and of human personality—operate in concert. This is evidently a *sine qua non* and crowning achievement of genius. Yet we have seen that even a genius of Mozart's stature had his occasional lapses from grace. His clowning and tomfoolery which were recurrent sources of annoyance to his father illustrate the point. They show his delight in letting "it all hang out," in playing the role of the *enfant terrible,* in reckless self-expression shorn of the checks and balances of the left hemisphere. They were unguarded moments when his right hemisphere seemed to be operating in high gear, parodying and caricaturing everything his father had stood for.

What Leopold Mozart stood for was the diametrical opposite of such conduct. Despite of the symbiotic closeness of father and son, he was the paradigm of a left-hemispheric, cognitive style, of dedication to law and order, to traditional values, to strict self-discipline and meticulous attention to detail. He was undoubtedly richly endowed with talent in his own right, but lacked the exuberance, the originality and spontaneity—in short, the genius—of Wolfgang. Indeed, we have seen that it was just the high-spirited, self-willed, nonconformist antics of his offspring that went most against Leopold's grain, and he bemoaned the passing of the time when a solemn-faced little Wolfgang was performing at the piano, "serious rather than childish," a miniature replica of his father's plodding but unflagging dedication to his calling.

We have his word for it that his son's departure to Vienna had drained his life of all its meaning. He died in Salzburg when Wolfgang was thirty-one years old. Wolfgang, in turn, was left struggling, destitute, and distraught in his modest quarters in Vienna, saddled with gambling debts and with a cold, ever-resentful Constance; with Cecilia, the shrewish mother-in-law, and two hapless children to take care of during Constance's prolonged absences in a nearby watering place.

Yet adversity did not seem to dampen Mozart's creative powers. He continued to pour out his dazzling array of symphonic pieces, concertos, and string quartets, interspersed with such operatic gems as *Don Giovanni* or *The Magic Flute*. In *The Magic Flute*, his last opera, he conjured up a carefree, enchanted world in which the loveless Constance was transformed into a loving soulmate, *Papagena,* confident that

> When the gods will bless our marriage
> With little babes to love and cherish
> Oh how happy will we be...*

He himself was cast into the role of *Papageno,* the chicken-brained (right-hemispheric) bird catcher, delighting audiences with his playful variations on the theme of *Pa-Pa-Pa-Papageno,* while for himself it was one more occasion to fall back on glorified baby talk, raised to the heights of an at least fitfully childlike genius. The alchemy of his music even succeeded in elevating the shrewish Frau Weber to the role of the *Queen of the Night,* and her nagging

---

* *The author's translation*

diatribes to coloratura arias that ever since have remained highpoints of the operatic literature.

Death caught up with Mozart at age thirty-five, before he could finish his *Requiem*. He was buried in an unmarked pauper's grave on a cold, drizzly December day. No mourners had ventured out to pay their last respects at his graveside. But there are unconfirmed reports that angels were singing his praise from above the leaden sky.

8

EINSTEIN

Genius Emerging,
Triumphant and Eclipsed

The idea occurred suddenly.... The breakthrough came suddenly one day sitting on a chair.... In two weeks, the correct equation appeared in front of me....

Einstein, 1922

Einstein wore his genius like an ill-fitting garment. There was a strange disparity between the exalted, heroic, more than life-size image perceived and embellished by his contemporaries, and the man in his crumpled sweater and baggy pants. At one of the banquets given in his honor, he was praised by the speaker in extravagant terms. Einstein whispered into a neighbor's ear: "But he does not know that I don't wear socks." We are told that Einstein was the greatest scientist of the 20th century, on a par with Newton, Kepler, or Galileo. But we also learn that he was childlike, naive, unsophisticated, even uneducated in conventional left-hemispheric terms of the German *Bildungsphilister*.

How do these two conflicting perceptions of Einstein jibe with the dual aspects of genius and the neurophysiological organization proposed here? There are four groups of data available for such an inquiry: (1) the slow, halting development of a seemingly backward child into the Nobel Laureate of 1921; (2) the formal qualities of Einstein's thinking, writing, and other productions; (3) the nature and

117

distinctive qualities of his work; and (4) the sampling of some earlier attempts at offering a psychological understanding of his personality.

On an earlier page, I ruefully noted that it would require genius to take the measure of genius. Needless to say, the present chapter has a more modest objective: it seeks to identify, however tentatively, the respective parts played in Einstein's cognitive style and written or verbal expressions of the left versus the right cerebral hemispheres.

GENIUS WHO WILL NEVER AMOUNT TO ANYTHING

Much has been said about Einstein's late blooming. He did not learn to talk until he was three years old. He was not fluent until age ten, and his verbal skills remained below the standard of his intellectual development. He was a mediocre student at grammar school. In his high school, the *Luitpold Gymnasium* in Munich, he excelled in mathematics and physics. But he rebelled against the rigid discipline and the authoritarian spirit of the school. His teacher of Greek told him: "Einstein, you will never amount to anything." Another teacher found that his presence in class was disturbing, and suggested that Einstein better leave the school. Einstein promptly complied. At fifteen, he dropped out without a diploma to join his parents who had meanwhile moved to Milan, Italy. He spent a year loafing and seeing the sights of the city and the surrounding countryside. He also taught himself the intricacies of integral and differential calculus.

But respite from the oppressive atmosphere of academic routine was only temporary. He failed the entrance examination in another institution in Switzerland and had to return to the classroom. He failed to obtain an assistantship at the Zurich Polytechnic Institute. Later he was rebuffed when he submitted one of his trailblazing papers on relativity to be appointed a *privatdozent* at the University of Bern. He obtained a modest job in the Bern Patent Office only through the intervention of a family friend. Up to his middle twenties he apparently had no marketable skills to offer to society.

What is to account for such an inauspicious start for one of the greatest minds of the 20th century? Here, again, the conjecture of a relative developmental lag of the left cerebral hemisphere is strongly suggestive. It would explain his delayed language development and the appearance of backwardness that caused anxiety to his parents. It could also be responsible for the prediction of his high school teacher in Munich of the dismal future in store for the young genius. It will be recalled that Nietzsche and Jung had to overcome the same hurdles in their development. Similarly, the novelists Herman Hesse and Konrad Ferdinand Meyer, or Thomas Alva Edison in this country—to say nothing of the emperor Claudius in ancient Rome—were considered backward children or social misfits in their youth.

However, Einstein also showed signs of precocious talent and originality. In his autobiography (1949) he recalls his fascination with a magnetic compass his father had given him at the age of four. At twelve, he got hold of a textbook of Euclidian geometry and found it an exquisite source of stimulation and abiding interest. At sixteen, he made his first faltering step towards the discovery of what he later called his "thought experiments." He projected himself in fantasy into a light beam and sought to resolve the paradox that the observer should see it "as a spatially oscillating electromagnetic field at rest," while methodical experiments and the Maxwell equations do not bear out such an expectation. It was from these beginnings that he developed a new approach to resolve the paradox. Indeed, he noted many years later that its resolution contained "the germ of the special theory of relativity" in 1905. And he adds: "For general reasons [I] was firmly convinced that there does not exist absolute motion and my problem was only how this could be reconciled with our knowledge of electrodynamics."

We are here evidently dealing with one of those leaps of scientific imagination that are usually attributed to intuition. Indeed, Einstein specifically went on record stating that it is courageous to use intuition "when there is simply no other guide available at all—[for instance when] one has tentatively to propose an axiom that by definition is unproven." He remarked to a friend, Janos Plesch: "When I examine myself and my method of thought I come to the conclusion that the gift of phantasy has meant more to me than my talent for absorbing information" (qu. from M. Stern, 1980). On another occasion, he conceded that it is instinct or a sense of "smell" which may put the scientist on the right track. He repeatedly noted that a breakthrough, an idea would "suddenly come" to him, that an equation would "appear in front of him," out of the blue; he was keenly aware of his ability "to *visualize* the effects, consequences and possibilities" of his conclusions.

Critics have noted that occasionally Einstein's computations were incorrect yet that, surprisingly, he nevertheless usually proved to be right. David Hilbert, the noted mathematician of Göttingen, remarked, tongue in cheek, that every schoolboy in the streets of Goettingen understood more about 4-dimensional geometry than Einstein. Still, in spite of that, Einstein did the work, and not the mathematicians (French, 1979, p. 111). Hilbert's accolade referred to Einstein's general theory of relativity, developed in the years 1913-1917. It was a monumental sequel to his theory of special relativity and was described as an achievement of supreme originality and grandeur.

Yet Einstein remained by no means an exclusively right hemispheric *wunderkind*. If mathematical ability is a measure of left hemispheric competence, it had certainly contributed a fair share to the global range of his genius, Hilbert's criticism notwithstanding.

Whether he was also aware of the pitfalls of exclusive reliance on intuition, is an open question. While he was still engaged in his work on general relativity and trying to develop an overarching unified field theory, a new generation of physicists led by Niels Bohr, Heisenberg, Schroedinger, and others were developing a new revolutionary approach to the quantum theory. Although Einstein's early work dealing with the photoelectric effect and the photon had laid the groundwork for this approach, he was unable or unwilling to accept probability in lieu of causality as a new law of nature, and vehemently opposed Heisenberg's principle of indeterminacy. Yet the fact is that his objections were largely based on intuitions. "An inner voice tells me," he wrote to Max Born, another pioneer of the quantum theory, that "it is not the true Jacob," that is, not the final solution of the quantum puzzle. He criticized Born's method of matrix algebra as a "witches' calculus," and raised one objection after another against the arguments put forward by Bohr and his associates. Authorities in the field sadly note that the aging master's objections were usually refuted by his adversaries.

Still undaunted, Einstein continued to place reliance on his "inner voices" and intuitions. They had served him well from the beginning to the heights of his creative period. He declared that "glimpses into the secrets of nature" were an act of grace divinely ordained. After the spectacular experimental confirmation of the deflection of light during the eclipse of the sun in 1919, he was asked what he would have to say had the astronomers failed to do so. His answer was, "I would have had to assume that the Lord made a mistake." Other confirmations, based on the celebrated formula $E=mc^2$, followed suit. The equation expresses the convertibility of matter into energy, and vice versa. It was the curtain raiser of the atomic age, with its vast consequences for good and for evil. It must have further reinforced Einstein's trust in his intuitions, though the mushroom cloud billowing over Hiroshima and Nagasaki would cast a cloud of guilt over the rest of his life.

Right Hemisphere and Genius Triumphant

Einstein's faith in the validity of his intuitions was indeed closely akin to religious belief. His was a belief in order, beauty, and goodness in the universe. "God is subtle," he stated, "but he is not malicious." (A. Pais, 1982). He never tried to define the nature of his hunches·and intuitions, but he noted that they were largely based on unconscious reasoning. He also observed that his thinking usually involved visual and spatial imagery, including muscular clues and a ceaseless play of combinations and recombinations. If this is true, it would point once more to the part played by the right hemisphere in the processing of both incoming information and of information retrieved from the individual's earlier experiences. Gerald Halton (1978), in his classical study of the Scientific Imagination describes Einstein as the foremost example to illustrate this point. In Einstein's case it can even be surmised that the "three I's" were aided by the "wisdom of instinct" derived from deeper, phylogenetic levels in the DNA in every fiber of the body, not just the gray matter of the brain. It may well be that it is the positive survival value of such archaic or archetypal dispositions which bestowed on him the apodictic certainty that his intuition told him the truth.

Yet he was in the fortunate position of having at his disposal the assistance of a no less solidly endowed left hemisphere. His developmental history suggests that the left hemisphere, after initially lagging behind, soon caught up with its supposedly junior partner. In the end it was their harmonious, synergistic operation which was responsible for his superb feats of scientific discovery culminating in the *annus mirabilis* of 1905.

There are, however, a few more clues to the original preponderance of his right hemispheric orientation. He possessed marked musical abilities. Despite the anecdote of a fellow member in a string quartet asking him "Herr Einstein, can't you count?" he was better than an amateur violinist. We are told that music was, next to physics, one of the most important things in his life. "Whenever he felt he had come to the end of a road...he would take refuge in music."

Sailing was another escape from his professional self. But he was dead set against speed, competition, or the setting of records. "He had a childlike delight when there was a calm and the boat came to a standstill or when the boat ran aground" writes one of his boating companions. Or else, he would, on a sudden impulse, play a perilous prank with the vessel which would bring it to near-collision with another boat. Of course, he invariably avoided it. Also, he never looked at a compass, and never studied navigation. (Clark, 1971, p. 633-35). Here, again, we are told that "an intuitive knowledge," perhaps based on practical experience, had taught him how to handle a boat. Clearly, sailing meant to him to take a complete vacation from his left cerebral hemisphere.

Another refuge was his knack for versifying. His humorous quatrains, *Knuettelreime,* are in the tradition of the German humorist Wilhelm Busch or reminiscent of Lewis Carroll, the Oxford mathematician's secondary personality, made immortal by his existential shifts into *Alice in Wonderland,* with its profusion of typical right hemispheric punning and nonsense verse. Banesh Hoffmann (1972). Einstein's congenial biographer, reproduces one of his quatrains celebrating the 300th anniversary of Newtons's birth:

Behold the stars in the heavenly sphere
They teach us Newton to revere
They follow the course the master charted
Before in silence they departed.

(author's translation).

His mordant wit is reflected in another quatrain

> When I contemplate the Jews
> I'm afraid I get the blues
> When the others come to mind
> I am glad I'm not their kind.

(author's translation).

Nothing can throw the contrast between Einstein's and Isaac Newton's personalities into sharper relief than such snippets of the 20th century's Jewish sage's heartwarming sense of humor, and the 17th century's puritanical genius's irascible attitude and legendary jaundiced view of his contemporaries. The contrast may well be due to more than a mere change of venue and of the *Zeitgeist* in which the two were immersed.

In the years following the Holocaust he was closely associated with Zionism. But when in 1948 he was offered the presidency of the Jewish state, he politely declined. By then he had been satisfied with playing the role of the "Jewish saint"—or else with masquerading as what, in a fit of self-mockery, he called an "artist's model:" at the height of his fame and the beginning of his eclipse, he was hounded by painters and photographers who wanted to take his picture.

Einstein's scientific interests were by no means confined to physics and mathematics. They extended to keen curiosity in the working of his own mind and in the nature of creativity. His writings (1934) and conversations with such authorities as J. Hadamard (1945), G. Holton (1978), Max Wertheimer and others have elicited illuminating comments by them, by Arthur Koestler (1964) and more recently by the psychiatrist Albert Rothenberg (1979). Some suggested that Einstein's thinking more closely resembled primitive, preverbal modes than adult patterns. Psychoanalysts stressed the "tendency to regress in the service of the ego." Others emphasized his habitual resort to visual and geometric i.e., "lateral" or "divergent" thinking. Rothenberg went beyond such more or less generalized formulations. He presented persuasive evidence of Einstein's striking ability to "actively conceive" two or more opposite ideas or images simultaneously and/or existing side by side "as equally operative or equally true." This is what Rothenberg describes as *Janusian* thinking.

He chose Einstein's imaginative quantum leap from special to general relativity as his illustrative example (1979, p. 39).

It is based on Einstein's account, dated approximately 1919, entitled *Fundamental Ideas and Methods of Relativity Theory, Presented in their Development* (1979); and found after his death among his personal effects. Einstein starts off with Faraday's observation that when a magnet is in relative motion with respect to a conducting circuit, an electric current is induced in the latter—regardless which of the two happens to be in motion. Closing in on his principle of relativity, he argues that the generation of an electric field was a "relative one."

Years later when he tried to modify Newton's theory of gravitation to fit it in with his own theory, "the happiest thought" of his life occurred to him: An observer in free fall would likewise be unable to decide without further clues whether a gravitational field would be in existence during his free fall, e.g., from the roof of a house. Viewed from the angle of Einstein's theory, the hapless observer would in effect be justified in considering "his state as one of rest."

Einstein's account and Rothenberg's analysis of it should be read in the original. It shows, among other things, Einstein's detached, depersonalized attitude toward human affairs, though it is possible that it is percisely such an attitude which he himself would have adopted even under such extreme conditions. More relevant in the present context is that even the present condensed summary illustrates two important points made by Dr. Rothenberg: (1) in the quoted passage Einstein made a creative leap of thought from electromagnetic induction to gravity; (2) in both instances, he was able to "conceive actively" two or more opposite or antithetical ideas or images simultaneously." In short, he presented a classical example of *Janusian* thinking, or Koestler's "bisociation"..

Rothenberg rightly notes, furthermore, that on the face of it, there was no evidence of an altered state of consciousness, of "regression in the service of the ego," nor of a switch into archaic or primary process reasoning. What happened was that Einstein was able actively to espouse two antithetical or oppositional ideas, both pertaining to a perfectly legitimate order of logical conjunction. At the same time, they were, as Rothenberg and Holton pointed out, *"intrinsically symmetrical"* (my italics).

If this is true, the suggestion is at hand that Einstein's example of Janusian thinking is closely correlated with his underlying right versus left hemispheric dichotomy, coupled with the successful resolution of the dichotomy. It points to the two respective hemispheres rising to the occasion, operating in tandem, and making their respective contributions on equal terms. They reveal symmetry, organization, and structure where otherwise chaos and confusion would have reigned. It was their teamwork that brought the two strands together, weaving them into the magnificent tapestry of his overarching special and general theories of relativity. That he failed to conjoin them in an all-encompassing tryptich of Unified Field Theory was perhaps the greatest frustration of an otherwise richly rewarding scientific career.

Rejects Quantum Theory: "God Does Not Play Dice"

Einstein's life work testifies to his consummate skill in resolving and reconciling the two opposing aspects of his Janusian thinking and of his right versus left hemispheric orientation. This, coupled with his abiding faith in the meaningful nature of the universe, made him one of the true heroic figures of our time, bridging the gap between science and humanistic endeavors—between C. P. Snow's two cultures. Though his special and general theories of relativity cannot legitimately be described as works of art, Einstein, at the peak of his creativity, was on a par with—if not one above—Leonardo da Vinci in resolving the dichotomy between the two. He created masterpieces of logical coherence and consistency as well as of beauty and elegance—works which are likely to stand the test of time and not be destroyed by the heat and humidity of the Cloisters of the Santa Maria delle Grazie, that chipped the pigment off the Last Supper, nor by the blunderbusses of the rowdy mercenaries who had used Leonardo's Great Horse for target practice.

That a new generation of theoretical physicists found growing evidence of decline in Einstein's creative powers is another matter. J. Robert Oppenheimer (1979), the brilliant theoretical physicist and one-time director of the Princeton Institute for Advanced

Studies, paid tribute to the master in his centenary volume. He lists the achievements of the twenty-six-year-old clerk in the Bern Patent Office that culminated in his two theories, followed by the rich harvest of general relativity from 1913 to 1917, leading up to the dramatic confirmation by astronomers of the deflection of light in the sun's gravitational field in 1919.

But Oppenheimer sadly notes that in his last 25 years Einstein's "tradition in a certain sense failed him...And this, though a source of sorrow, should not be concealed." (p. 46). The papers published during Einstein's remaining years in the Princeton Institute have not measured up to the standards of his earlier work. He remained critical of the new findings of Bohr and his associates, trying to prove the inconsistencies and incompleteness of the quantum theory. When that did not work, we are told by Oppenheimer that Einstein simply said "he did not like the theory." He did not like the elements of Heisenberg's indeterminacy. He did not like the abandonment of causality in Bohr's probabilistic approach. And Oppenheimer goes on to say "These were things that he had grown up with, saved by him...and to see them lost was very hard on him, even though he had put the dagger in the hand of the assassin by his own work." Indeed, using a less bloodthirsty metaphor, it could be stated that it was Einstein's conception of the photon that started the ball rolling that ended up in the quantum physicist's ball park.

Abraham Pais (1982), Einstein's latest biographer, writes about the last decade: "On rare occasions, he would give a seminar about his work at the Institute...the seminars themselves were lucid, inconclusive, and otherworldly. Those were the days of striking advances in quantum electrodynamics and important discoveries of new particles, days when the gap between Einstein's physics and the younger generation was widening" (p. 474).

Needless to say, I am in no position to comment, and even less to take a stand, on an historic debate comparable in magnitude—though not in acrimony—to the dispute between Newton and Robert Hook in the 17th century. But Einstein's dislike of the quantum physicist's position is clearly relevant to our issue. Oppenheimer did not try to go into the apparent reasons for Einstein's openly admitted pique. But his much quoted insistence that God does not play dice; that he is subtle but not malicious, provides a clue to the problem.

Evidently, in the years of his adolescent rebellion, and throughout the peak periods of his creativity in his twenties and thirties, his genius had been under the spell of his triumphant right hemisphere. But in his remaining years in Princeton a more conservative and more disciplined left hemisphere had taken the upper hand. Like most physicists (and nonphysicists) of his generation, he found a probabilistic universe, capped with Heisenberg's principle of uncertainty, an intolerable thought. He was unwilling to surrender his serene, law-abiding, well-ordered universe to a capricious Demiurge who threw causality to the winds, who permitted dissonance and randomness to drown out the music of the spheres—and hemispheres.

We know today that such an attitude extended from physics to his philosophy, religion, and politics. It even colored his views on telepathy and related phenomena of the ESP type. In two letters Einstein wrote to me in 1946 (1978a), he expressed doubts on several grounds about the validity of J. B. Rhine's card-calling tests. One was that "the subject's spatial distance proved wholly irrelevant to the success of the procedure." This aroused his suspicion that a "hitherto undetected systematic source of error may have been at play." The other reason was that "in the large scale statistical experiments...the discovery of a minute systematic error may upset everything" (1978a, p. 138).

However, in the same letter he notes that telepathic productions of patients in the analytic situation "seem to be important to me." He was intrigued by reports of telepathy between Ilga K, a retarded girl of nine, and her mother. He also noted that "the (Upton Sinclair) experiments with drawings seem to be of greater weight than the large scale statistical experiments (of the ESP type)."

What, then, is to account for Einstein's doubts about ESP of the card calling type as opposed to his greater readiness to accept the occurrence of so-called spontaneous, macropsychological phenomena, versus micropsychological, laboratory incidents? The fact is that in both instances results are independent of distances involved, and though it is true that in statistical tests minor errors of calculation "may upset everything," mistakes in observation may do the same thing in spontaneous phenomena. (This is precisely one of the reasons why experimental parapsychologists place their greatest emphasis on the quantitive approach, on the statistical evaluation of results). Yet I submit that this, also, was the reason for Einstein's preference for cases of the Ilga K. or Upton Sinclair type. Telepathy between mother and child or husband and wife made more sense to Einstein. Moreover, the Sinclairs were his friends, and he was ready to trust their observations.

By contrast, Rhine's ESP tests were capricious, random, psychologically meaningless events. It is a case of quantification substituting for understanding. Indeed, elsewhere (1978) I described them as flaw-determined, due to incidental minor imperfections in the screening functions of the ego, or of what has been described as the Bergsonian filter on several levels of the central nervous system, designed to ward off the intrusion of biologically irrelevant information into our mental organization.

If this is true, Einstein's misgivings about ESP were largely due to his emotional bias against a capricious universe condoning disorder and lawlessness, upsetting both his equanimity and tidy field equations. Such a world struck him as just as objectionable as the world of the quantum physicists. If Einstein went on record against God playing dice, he must have disapproved even more strenuously of Dr. Rhine playing games with Zener cards in his laboratory.

GENIUS ECLIPSED: THE LEFT HEMISPHERE
IN ASCENDANCE. HE DIED FROM A RUPTURED AORTA
WHILE GOD WAS APPARENTLY PLAYING DICE

Thus, in this respect, the foe of the quantum theory found himself in the same camp as some critics of parapsychology. Yet in other respects he sided against them: "One must not go with blinders through the world," he wrote in his letter of July 1946. On the other hand, such modern authorities of quantum theory as Wolfgang Pauli, Pascual Jordan, Henry Margenau or E.P. Wigner have gone out of their way to confirm the possibility or even the reality of psi phenomena. By the same token, a new generation of parapsychologists find that there is nothing wrong with micropsychological psi phenomena of the ESP type, and have objected to my describing them as flaw-determined.

Einstein's increasing commitment to the discipline of the left hemisphere is also reflected in the intriguing observation that while the brilliance of his early work was occasionally marred by trivial errors in calculation, the record of his later years is free of such blemishes. But it also lacked the hallmarks of his originality and genius. This may in part be due to the handiwork of his younger assistants who were assigned to him. But viewed in the broader perspective of his personal development, it suggests once again that Einstein's early output was indeed under the sway of a spectacularly endowed right hemisphere, with the left hemisphere having a hard time to keep pace with the exploits of the right. It will be recalled that in typically left-hemispheric linguistic skills Einstein had always lagged behind. He lacked the verbal dexterity and sophistication of some who intellectually were far below him. Yet by the time he had reached his peak, the left hemisphere had apparently caught up with the right side. It must have imparted a stricter intellectual discipline and a greater measure of authority and deliberation to his work. But it may have also slowed down the soaring flight of his genius. It marked the decline of his creative period—the beginning of the end.

Einstein himself was painfully aware of this new turn of events. Work on his unified field theory bogged down after countless promising but false starts. In the past, he recalled, he had rebelled against authority. Now, in his fifties and sixties, he had become an authority himself—one who started to find faults in the ideas of other up-and-coming geniuses. It is true that the aging Einstein's new role as an elder statesman of science, of a "Jewish saint"—if not a much photographed artists' model—had only added to the aura of his personal nobility and grandeur. But he knew full well he was past the peak of his career, all was vanity, nothing but vanity. It was overshadowed by the memory of his broken first marriage, to Mileva Maric, by his sorrow over a schizophrenic son—and of a mushroom cloud over Japan.

He died in Princeton at the age of seventy-six from a ruptured abdominal aorta. It was one of those capricious, random events for which he was reluctant to make provisions in his philosophy. He bequeathed his brain to the neuroanatomists for study, and I am sure he would have been greatly interested in their findings. My guess is that, had they been able to lay hands on it when he was in his twenties or thirties, they would have found a somewhat enlarged right hemisphere, as compared with the left, especially in what Norman Geschwind described as the temporal plate. Either way, it would tell us little about his genius. Even his brain may have worn his genius "like an ill-fitting garment," bearing no discernible relationship to its wearer.

9

WHO WAS PABLO PICASSO?
—A Case of Multiple Identities

In Chapter 2 I noted that Beethoven was the first creative artist who put me on the track of the part played by the right hemisphere in the making of genius. But years before that, my fascination with Picasso's work had brought me close to such a conjecture. In a book dealing with neurosis (and genius) in the family (1963), and in an earlier paper (1967), I pointed to the emergence of several "secondary" personalities in Picasso's career. They were responsible, I suggested, for his seemingly erratic shifts of style and modes of artistic expression over the years. It appeared as though in his Rose or Blue or Cubist or "African" or neoclassical periods, a succession of different artists had taken control of his brush, pen, or chisel, with nothing but his superb craftsmanship as the common denominator.

Critics and art historians have sought to account for these perplexing changes by reference to such environmental influences as his encounter with the art of Catalan primitives at home, with the

Fauves and Impressionists or ancient Minoan or Greek artifacts in Paris and elsewhere—or merely with the change of the leading lady in his love life. But viewed in the present context, Picasso's chameleon susceptibility to external factors suggests another explanation. It implies recurrent existential shifts due to the absence of sustained stabilizing left hemispheric controls and the prevalence of right hemispheric flights of fancy, spontaneity, and loosening of inhibitions.

It is sea-changes of this order which led Picasso to recapture the roots of his archetypal Mediterranean heritage. The mythical images swept up in the process are veritable diagrams of the unconscious in both the Freudian and Jungian sense, the fingerprints of Picasso's soul. They are the pictorial counterparts of Mrs. Eileen Garrett's Four Voices, or of the perplexing productions of Patience Worth, the 17th century "ghost writer" of Mrs. John Curran, an early 19th century American housewife and automatist. (see chapter 11).

How, then, in the light of newly emerging insights into the workshop of genius, can we account for the beauty, the brilliance, the originality—and the abominations, the ugliness, and abrasiveness of subject matter in Picasso's oeuvre? The following pages taken from an earlier publication, attempt to throw the origin of the first of Picasso's secondary personalities into sharper perspective. Though barely acknowledged by art historians, it was none other than Pablo Picasso's father, Jose Ruiz.

PICASSO: FATHER AND SON

Don Jose Ruiz, a painter, curator, and teacher at the Barcelona Academy of Fine Arts, is described as a moody, retiring individual who suffered from recurrent depressions and anxiety states. He was an accomplished craftsman, painting in the strictly representational, academic manner of the late 19th century. He was "a painter of dining room pictures" as Pablo Picasso put it, "with partridges, pigeons, pheasants, and rabbits." Even in his formative years he did not conceal his disapproval, if not contempt, for this "mockery of art."

Yet one of his earliest childhood memories, as told to his friend, secretary, and biographer, Jaime Sabartés (1948), is of one of Don José's paintings of this genre. "An enormous picture, swarming with pigeons. Imagine a cage with a hundred pigeons, with thousands and millions of pigeons..." According to Sabartés, Picasso liked to tell this story "a thousand—no, a million times." He did so "after a period of 50 years and from a distance of 1000 kilometers over and over again."

It is not likely that Sabartes has been familiar with Freud's celebrated study of Leonardo da Vinci's childhood recollection. Nevertheless, he was moved to do some research on his own. He found out that Don José's canvas was a fair-sized (though by no means "enormous") painting, showing no more than nine pigeons and a dovecote, executed in his characteristic smooth academic manner.

I myself was unable to trace the Ruiz original in the museums of Barcelona. But I found a black and white reproduction of the painting which suggests that, unless there exists another version of the canvas, Sabartés's census of pigeons also was erroneous. There are no more than three birds and a dovecote in the picture. The rest was clearly a product of Picasso's imagination.

What is behind this striking falsification of Pablo's childhood recollection? Is it merely the telling and retelling of a "tall story," exaggerating the accomplishments of a once admired idol? Is it a screen memory alluding to Don Jose's superior prowess—sexual artistic, and otherwise, as it was imprinted on the little boy's mind at an early age? In either case it is an unintended tribute to the older man who had served as a teacher and mentor in his formative years and who had been the model after whom both Pablo's art and personality had been fashioned. We are told by Sabartés that long before Pablo could talk, he asked for a pencil and started to draw. It may have been a first hint at a relative maturational lag of his left cerebral hemisphere. He may in effect have been a latent left hander or ambidextrous.

We also learn that Don Jose liked to call on the six-to-seven year-old to help in his work. Dissecting dead pigeons for the painting of still lifes was part of the procedure. He would pin their severed feet on the drawing board and instruct Pablo to copy them in the required position. Under his father's expert guidance Pablo's drawings soon attained a perfection "almost unbelievable in one so young." He became a child prodigy—as had little Wolfgang Amadeus Mozart under the tutelage of his musician father. In any case, Pablo's drawings and paintings that have come down to us from his years of apprenticeship with Don José show him a faithful follower in his father's footsteps.

Yet there is another side to the picture. Sabartés gives a few revealing glimpses of Pablo's well-nigh symbiotic relationship with his father in his childhood years. As a little boy, he literally clung to Don José's coattails. He refused to go to school unless accompanied by him. He had to be dragged to the schoolhouse, and the moment of parting invariably led to the same "battle scene" between them. Pablo insisted on keeping his father's paintbrush and walking stick, or even one of his pet pigeons as pawns in order to make sure that Don José would come and fetch him from school at one o'clock. Sabartés describes the child's poor progress in the three R's; his inability to concentrate, to his fear father would fail to come and pick him up.

All this became a veritable obsession to the boy. He was sick and vomiting in the morning; or else he feigned illness to avoid the dreaded separation from Don José and from the security of his parental home. In short, Pablo developed unmistakable symptoms of a school phobia—the early childhood counterpart of his father's neurosis.

PABLO REBELLIOUS

When Pablo moved into adolescence a radical change in the father-son relationship took place. He became increasingly rebellious toward Don José. He rebelled against what by now had become the "stifling atmosphere" of the parental home; he was critical of Don José's set ways; of his philistine outlook; of his old-fashioned artistic standards and the classical academic tradition in general. In one of his diary letters to his parents, written at age fifteen, Pablo sketches a gang of young hoodlums engaged in a fight, with knives drawn. A middle-aged gentleman watches the fight in horror. The sketch bears the caption *Todo Revuelto—All in Revolt*.

Three years later, at the age of eighteen, the youth was ready to make the break from his ailing father, from his doting mother, a nondescript older sister, and meddling uncle who had tried to interfere with his artistic education. He moved to the Bohemian quarters of Barcelona, joined a group of artistic and literary friends, the forerunners of "angry young men," the later hippies, or leftist radicals. Shortly thereafter, in defiance of his father's wishes—though perhaps with his mother's tacit approval—he exchanged his "digs" in Barcelona for the glamour of Paris and for the squalor of an unheated and poorly lighted studio in Montmartre. It was the end of his first, academic, strictly representational "Ruiz" period.

In keeping with a Spanish custom, his early canvasses still show the signature *Pablo Ruiz Picasso,* featuring both his father's and mother's surname. But soon he was to drop the name *Ruiz* altogether and sign his paintings by his mother's name only. Art historians tracing his artistic development date to his final break with the academic tradition from the canvas *Les Demoiselles d'Avignon*, painted in Paris in 1907. It may be no coincidence that its title contains a veiled reference to the *Rue d'Avignon* in Barcelona's red light district. At the same time it ushers in his Negro or Cubist period and stands at the threshold of one of the most revolutionary chapters in the annals of modern art.

With the meteoric rise of Pablo's genius, Don José's artistic work as well as his health went into a gradual decline. He became increasingly morose, withdrawn, and depressed, staying away for weeks from his job at the Academy of Fine Arts. (It will be recalled that Leopold Mozart reacted much the same way to the departure of his son from Salzburg). He died in 1913, a bitter and disappointed man. Pablo did not return to Barcelona to attend his father's funeral.

Viewed against this background, Pablo Picasso's rebellion against his father, against both the neurotic heritage and the academic tradition he had stood for, may well have been a crucial factor in his personal as well as artistic development. He was bound to make the break from a compulsive-controlling parent, lest he remain saddled for the rest of his life, not only with the neurotic contagion, but also with the sterile artistic influence emanating from him.

Nevertheless, there is considerable evidence of neurosis in

Picasso's own personal history. We learn from Sabartés, Penrose (1958), and especially from the memoirs of Francoise Gilot (1964), that he was plagued by recurrent scruples and anxieties. In one of his nightmares he dreamed that his legs and arms "grew to an enormous size and then shrunk back just as much in the other direction. All around me," he told Miss Gilot, "I saw other people going through the same transformations, getting huge or very tiny." She rightly remarks that some of the grotesquely distorted figures with small heads and big limbs of gigantic infants, etc., may have been influenced by these experiences. To the psychiatrist they are strongly suggestive of a precariously integrated body image whose disturbances tend to be projected into the outside world.

Other symptoms seem to be more directly related to his father's pathology, handed down to him by way of neurotic contagion. Francoise Gilot, who lived with Picasso over a period of ten years—and may have known him nearly as well as an analyst knows his patient—describes in some detail his morning depressions, his tendencies to obsessive rumination, his compulsive rituals, his inordinate dependent needs, combined with his inability for sustained object relationships, and occasional undisguised spells of sadistic acting out. Both Sabartés and Penrose tell about his pleasure in cruel pranks; his uncontrollable tempers and his tendency to cut corners in his business affairs. He liked to keep pets in the house but seemed to take the same delight in dogs, goats, or pigeons as in the female models whom he made to sit for him. Nor did he seem to show much compunction in treating his women in a way reminiscent of the plight of the pigeons whose severed limbs his father had nailed to the drawing board to suit his artistic purposes.

Still, these tendencies were usually kept at bay by Picasso's seemingly incongruous squeamishness and show of concern for the welfare of others. One day he was told of the unexpected death of his friend, Maurice Reynal. Picasso was deeply perturbed by the news. He confessed that he had been in the habit of going over the names of his most intimate friends every morning. On that particular day he had left Reynal off his list. "But you did not kill him by just omitting his name," said his companion. Picasso remained disconsolate. "Still, I forgot him this morning." Gilot's account of his anxieties lest his son, Claude, sleeping in the room next door, might suddenly stop breathing is another variation on the same theme.

Pablo Violent

On the other hand, some of Picasso's work amounts to a virtually undisguised show of violence, perhaps more so than the art of any of his predecessors, including Goya or Delacroix. Inevitably, it is aimed in one of two directions: either at the viewer of his work, or at the object which served as the original stimulus for his anger—and its artistic expression. There is the dying horse with its protruding entrails in his *Guernica*. There are the mutilated bodies of human victims, the tortured forms of houses, furniture, trees and flowers. There is the awful shape of a ferocious cat carrying a lacerated, fluttering bird (Don José's pigeon?) in his mouth. And there are the distorted shapes of a wide variety of monsters—part human, part animal—whose occasional resemblance to one of Picasso's friends or mistresses is only apt to enhance their shock value.

Violence directed against the observer is illustrated by one of his collages from 1926. It represents a guitar and a coarse dishcloth perforated by nails "whose points stick out mercilessly from the picture." According to Penrose, Picasso had originally thought of embedding razor blades at the edge of the canvas so that whoever tried to lift it would cut his hands with it. It is a matter of esthetic judgment whether this sort of artistic expression is in the nature of mere neurotic acting out—of violence directed simply "to *Whom It May Concern*—or whether it can still be taken as a feat of more or less successful sublimation of the Freudian love and death instincts blended in the improbable witches' brew of Picasso's personal alchemy.

Perhaps the most savage show of violence is featured in Picasso's celebrated *Guernica*. It may be no coincidence that here, for once, he could hide behind the avowed message of the canvas: "It is you, Generalissimo Franco, not I, who are the perpetrator of all these unspeakable horrors!" One is reminded of another dictator exclaiming at the sight of Rotterdam, destroyed by the divebombers of the *Luftwaffe*: "How cruel must have been those who forced me to take this action!" Yet the difference is that in one case unbridled violence was the real thing, with death, destruction, outrage, and worldwide condemnation in its wake. In the other, it was confined to two-dimensional icons of artistic imagination, serving as cathartic release for its author, followed by worldwide admiration and acclaim.

At the same time, it is perhaps the *Guernica* which shows the emergence of the ultimate Pablo Picasso personality at its best. It is the triumphant expression of a new, reconstituted physical reality in the wake of the destruction of both Guernica, the ravaged city, and of Picasso's paternal heritage—classical art. Rudolf Arnheim (1962), the art historian, described the *Guernica* as "a marvel of organized complexities," and Howard Gardner (1980) compares the preliminary sketches for the real work with "the creative efflorescence" of Dostoevsky's notebooks or Beethoven's sketchbooks.

I submit that it is in effect the consummation of a perfect fusion of the creativity of his right, and the craftsmanship and discipline of his left cerebral hemisphere. It is the quintessential synthesis of Picasso's multiple personalities that had made their appearance over the years.

Certainly, the blend of violence, death, and destruction is only one of the ingredients of Picasso's artistic output. Indeed viewed from the present vantage point, there are four major factors that went into its making. One resides deep in the wellsprings of his biological makeup: in his predominantly right hemispheric orientation and the attending fluidity of his body image. The effect of El Greco's alleged astigmatism upon the painting of his elongated figures is debatable. But Picasso's recurrent nightmares of swollen or shrunken human forms may well have been responsible for some of the purely anatomical extravaganzas of his paintings and drawings.

Another factor was Picasso's rather transparent oedipal conflict: his lifelong love-hate affair with his father; his lingering admiration combined with his overt rebellion against the painter of "dining room pictures," against the "mockery of art," and the whole academic tradition he had stood for. The son's rebellion against the father's well-ordered universe of conventional shapes, colors, and contours, handed down to him on a silver platter, as it were, was perhaps the major source of Picasso's iconoclastic fervor. He literally hacked to pieces Don José's representations of human and animal forms, of animate and inanimate objects. He made mincemeat of them all—including his own sensory impressions. He wrought havoc with the laws of perspective, with space, time, and causality itself.

Yet this apparently was one of the prerequisites for the emergence of some of his most prominent secondary personalities: analytic and synthetic Cubism, followed in due course by Abstract Expressionism, collages and assemblage painting in the years to come. They were necessary steps, preceding the rearrangement and restructuring of the world according to Picasso's own idiosyncratic vision, in a dazzling array of shapes, curves, crystalline forms, and color combinations, springing to life like new mutations in the experimental geneticist's laboratory. We know today that the process of wholesale disorganization—both spontaneous and artificial—of the perceptual world tends to have a twofold impact upon personality. It leads to the fragmentation of the ego, to the impairment and downgrading of its hierarchy of defenses. But at the same time it may also be conducive to the influx of primary process material from the unconscious—or the reptilian brain—to the emergence of a variety of archaic forms and mythological themes.

I have noted that precisely this can be seen in Picasso's art—in his case, obviously without the aid of mescaline or LSD. In fact it may well be argued that it is his unmistakable tendency to "regression in the service of the ego," with its attending liberation of primitive, quasi-mythological material, which shows Picasso at his creative best, in contrast to the dreary host of his imitators who rarely, if ever, go beyond the stage of studied distortion and disorganization of artistic expression.

There is a fourth major factor which can be discerned in Picasso's work. It is a factor without which his total output would perhaps lack an important dimension. By his own account, Picasso spent a major part of his life engaged in the struggle against the stagnation or "death" of art, equating it, as he did, with the legacy of his father's academic painting. Yet I have hinted that Pablo, despite his protestations, had never been able to emancipate himself completely from the influence of the "red-bearded giant" of his childhood years; from the omnipotent creator of the "enormous" canvas swarming with hundreds, thousands if not millions of doves, conjured up as by magic from Don José's palette. Emulating his example, catching up with him, and ultimately surpassing the accomplishments of his idol may well have remained Pablo's secret goal. This may account for the fact that drawing, carving, painting, and sculpting doves and pigeons in many and varied forms and media had been one of his lifelong passions. It is as though the seed—or the avian image—planted in the child's mind, was to grow and multiply with the passage of years, pressing for endless expressions. If we are justified in viewing Pablo's childhood memory as symbolic of his desire to put himself in his father's place, it must have been endowed with something like a prophetic, precognitive quality of his right hemisphere.

Picasso has literally attained his goal as far as the imagery of thousands, if not millions, of pigeons is concerned. In 1949, some 50 years after the time of the story told to Sabartes, he was asked to design a poster for a peace conference organized by the Communist Party in Paris. It was for that occasion that he prepared a wholly representational lithograph of a white dove. It was subsequently printed in thousands of copies, posted on the walls and billboards of numerous cities of Europe and even won a medal sponsored by the Philadelphia Museum of Art. Since then Picasso's doves of peace have flown all over the world. They were reproduced in pottery and ceramics, engraved on postage stamps in China and other Communist countries.

MULTIPLE PERSONALITIES

These, then, are the four major vectors which can be discerned in the parallelogram of forces that has gone into Picasso's work. It has often been stated that the seemingly capricious changes of his style and technique defy all attempts at placing them in any chronological scheme, at linking them with any particular personal idiom or period of his life (John Berger, 1965). Yet the difficulty can readily be resolved if we realize that his whole artistic career had indeed been determined by the succession of his multiple personalities and by the opposing forces described above. This is why he appears to have worked under the alternating spell of two—if not more—secondary personalities. We have seen that the first was Don Jose. He was followed by recurrent changes of Pablo's own problematic identity—neurotic or otherwise—as a rebel, iconoclast, and seeker after new expressions and self-expressions. This also is the reason why art historians have been at a loss to describe his development in one unbroken line of progression—or regression. We have seen that Picasso's portrait as a young man is that of a follower and imitator, first of his father and then of others, greater and bolder than Don Jose. If his earlier academic efforts were made under the remote control of José Ruiz, Picasso's subsequent style—his Rose and Blue Periods—brought him under the sway of the French Impressionists, from Toulouse Lautrec to Monet, Gauguin, Cézanne, and Van Gogh. Thus, despite the striking success of his early attempts at emancipation from father, they still fell short of Picasso's own idiom.

On the other hand, even his subsequent wholly original artistic output has been interspersed with a recurrence of traditional, classical, or neoclassical forms, harking back to the years of apprenticehship—and symbiotic closeness—with his father. Like a mediumist control, Don José's personality seemed capable of taking over and reasserting itself, time and again, even though it was hidden behind the camouflage of an Ingres, a Ribera, a Velasquez, or even of the unknown painter of an ancient Grecian urn. Thus the seemingly erratic meanderings of Picasso's art were in effect due to his alternating submission to a motley group of multiple personalities, demanding obeisance to their respective styles, guiding his brush, inspiring his pen, or wielding his chisel.

Robert Schumann, the celebrated 19th century romantic composer and author of several volumes of music criticism, is another case in point. In both his writings and compositions he attributed parts of his output to such fictitious personalities as Florestan, Eusepius, Raro and others, using them as ventriloquist dummies to express his own ideas, shifting gears—or musical keys—from one to the other, or even letting them engage in dialogue when the spirit moved him. Schumann also spoke eloquently of the dichotomy of the composer's creativity: his output may express the same basic experiences, ideas or mental states in either non-verbal, musical, terms (in terms of the "soul"), or else in literary, verbal terms, expressing his intellectual concerns and preoccupations (E. Lippman, 1964). In effect, Schumann seemed to anticipate intuitively some of the recent findings of split-brain research.

He suffered two or three mental breakdowns; at 23, in his mid-30s, and the last one in his early 40s. He died at 44, leaving the question of his true or core identity unresolved. Undoubtedly, Picasso was made of sturdier stuff, but his underlying obsessive-compulsive trend may have merely masked an ego likewise prone to splitting or fragmentation.

Who Was Pablo Picasso?

With so many conflicting influences crowding in, the question of Picasso's ultimate personal identity becomes even more perplexing. D.D. Duncan, author of the volume *Picasso's Picassos* (1962) devotes seven pages of his book to the rhetorical question "Who is Pablo Picasso?" Obviously, it is his very chameleonlike susceptibility to changing lights, shades, meanings, and messages impinging upon him from without (and alternating with his ceaseless quest for self-realization) which comes closest to providing a key to the puzzle. Picasso is many personalities, styles, and modes of existence—not just one. He is the purveyor of a striking succession of what I have described as existential shifts.

The problematic nature of his very personal identity is also illustrated by the fact that the mature artist seems to have studiously avoided submitting to the searching scrutiny of the self-portrait which reveals so much of the character of a Rembrandt or Van Gogh. Barr's, and Boeck and Sabartés' richly illustrated volumes contain three or four sketches showing Pablo as a youth of eighteen in a Paris street; as a young man in his twenties caught in profile, standing in a great coat, or reclining on a bench. A brooding introspective canvas, executed in the spirit of the French Impressionists, shows the artist, aged twenty, sad-faced, wearing a beard. A later portrait representing Picasso at twenty-five, foreshadows the style of *Les Demoiselles d'Avignon*, but betrays, as yet, little tendency to distortion.

Apart from his last self-portrait (which I haven't seen), I know of only one sketchy drawing of the artist as mature man. It is dated 1943, and portrays him from a bird's-eye view while he sits sketching in his studio. This time Picasso avoids playing his customary tricks with perspective. His back is turned on the viewer with only the balding head showing. It is as though giving the onlooker a glimpse of his innermost vision of himself would have been an invitation to encroach on his privacy. Yet it is also possible that Picasso would have winced at the thought of subjecting his own anatomy to the awesome forces of artistic distortion meted out to others. His apparent castration anxiety, his hypochondriacal trend, and the very brittleness of his body image may have forced him to develop a measure of immunity against such influences. Indeed, "doing unto others" what he did not want to happen to himself may well have served as a defense against a recurrence of the nightmares of bodily disintegration described to Françoise Gilot. By contrast, his younger contemporaries, Salvador Dali and Joan Miró, have been much less squeamish in this respect. Dali has gone on record with a veritable Surrealist nightmare of a self-portrait; nor did Miró, in a similar effort, hesitate to play havoc with his self-image.

Nevertheless, the fragmentation of Picasso's ego into secondary personalities, the chameleonic changes of his style and modes of artistic expression have remained the dominant theme throughout his career. He seemed to be operating under the influence, not just of one, but of at least half a dozen signs of the Zodiac. This, more than anything else, made Pablo Picasso one of the representative figures of the 20th century, a contemporary of James Joyce, Franz Kafka, Arnold Schoenberg, of the Dadaists, Futurists, of a perpetual avant-garde, a harbinger of Pop and Op art, offbeat psychotherapies, and of a rapid succession of psychedelic, cultist and other fads on the lunatic fringe of our culture.

Such social critics as Marshall McLuhan, Alvin Toffler, Theodor Roszak, and many others have described this breathless scramble for change, for novelty for novelty's sake, as one of the foremost characteristics of our time. They suggested that it is largely due to the spectacular proliferation of the electronic media; to the acceleration of our means of communication on a planetary scale; to the massive use of psychotropic drugs, and to the universal crisis of authority, in the family, in the educational establishments, and in our culture at large.

We have seen that precisely this is brought into sharp focus in Picasso's personal history and artistic career. At the same time, the diversity of his styles and modes of expression, the fitful emergence and alternation of a motley group of secondary personalities seems to bring a brand new element into the history of western culture. No great artist, writer, composer, painter, or sculptor, either in ancient Greece, Rome, the Renaissance, or in modern times, has a record of diversity, coupled with abrupt existential shifts, and crowded with conflicting artistic styles and identities, comparable to those of Pablo Picasso. The art and craftsmanship of Michelangelo, Titian, Leonardo, or Dürer grew steadily and in linear fashion over the years. It attained increasing depth and maturity with their advancing age, but their work carried the imprint of the same personality throughout life, with no abrupt changes or deviations from the main thrust of their genius.

DISOWNS PRODUCTS OF OWN RIGHT HEMISPHERE

Picasso's staccato career did not measure up—or did not care to emulate—the classical beauty of the Old Masters. Indeed, we have seen that he looked down on it. Nevertheless, in a conversation with Gertrude Stein (1938), the early sponsor and admirer of his art, he confided that he was frankly repelled by the work of other painters who tried to emulate his style. "With one's own pictures," he remarked, "one knows the reason why they are bad. And so they are not hopelessly bad" (p. 9). Apparently, he faulted his imitators for the very aberrations which he had condoned in his own works.

It is an attitude reminiscent of certain olfactory afficionados who take pleasure in sniffing their own bodily excretions but find those of other people thoroughly objectionable. At the same time, Picasso projected the "badness" of his own output onto his rivals and imitators.

There is another story that brings an added accent to his ambivalence about his own productions. In 1951 he confessed in an interview with a prominent Italian critic, Giovanni Papini (1951), that ever since his Cubist period he was ready to cater to the needs of those "who sought the strange, the scandalous, the oddity" in art. This is how he became rich and famous. "I became an *amuseur public*, a public entertainer, who understood the imbecility, the vanity and the cupidity of my contemporaries and let them be taken in by me." And he added: "Mine is a confession more painful than it may appear but it has the merit of being sincere" (p. 268).

These astonishing off-the-cuff remarks seemed to have caught Picasso himself off guard. They have apparently passed unnoticed in the Picasso literature and have not, as far as I know, been publicly refuted. But they echo the most acerbic comments of some of his critics. No less significant in the present context is that they reflect the master's own surprising failure to understand the wellsprings of his genius. They are utterances in which his left hemisphere disowns and repudiates the productions of the right. He sees them as odd, strange, scandalous, and relegates them to the realm of falsehood and fakery, if not of the excremental. And here again he shifts the responsibility for their failings to his contemporaries. It is their stench, not his.

The aging Giorgio de Chirico's attitude towards his early output reflected an even more radical change of heart when he rejected the trailblazing surrealistic paintings of his early years together with those of the contemporary avantgarde.

It will be recalled that Freud, in a moment of self-doubt, had likewise dissociated himself from his (right hemispheric) intuitions and labelled them as "aberrations." We shall see that, in a similar vein, Franz Kafka, shortly before his death, had implored his friend and biographer Max Brod, to destroy his unpublished manuscripts. He too had dissociated himself from the dark, nightmarish productions of his right cerebral hemisphere. He wanted to erase them from his legacy to posterity.

Another example is a poignant passage in the closing chapter of a book on *Paranormal Foreknowledge* by Jule Eisenbud (1981), the noted psychoanalyst and parapsychologist. After presenting an ingenious though highly unorthodox theory of precognition, telepathy and psychokinesis or "mind over matter"—the culmination of his life's work—he writes: "I . . . have no liking for the results of such a search . . . a vital part of me rejects the whole thing as pure nonsense . . . When I leave the solitude of thought and return to the everyday world . . . the sum of everything that has been chiseled out and elaborated appears to be strange and remote from truth . . . An illusion-fed ego . . . can hardly be expected to react favorably to something that challenges its ingrained, culture-bound premises" (p. 331, 332).

Read "left hemispheric" for "culture-bound," and Eisenbud has spelled out the thesis which is presented here. And he goes on to say "Surely there is something inhuman about this position. Such thoughts are by definition the stuff of paranoia" (p. 238). His reference at this point is to the idea of psychokinesis and its potential nefarious effects in social relationships. Yet the revolt of the "culture-bound" left hemisphere against the "sinister"impact of the right side of the brain could not have been put in starker or more eloquent terms.

Be that as it may, Picasso's ambivalence toward his work should not obscure his lifelong, unremitting quest for perfection as he saw it. Throughout his career he was engaged in an inner struggle between the forces of destruction, disorganization, and entropy on the one hand, and beauty, balance, and innocence on the other. As with Beethoven or Jung, it was a struggle to safeguard the integrity of his ego, his art, his sanity, and peace of mind. Paradoxically, the very failure to attain his goal of self-healing and self-fulfillment acted as a thorn in his flesh driving him on and on to his old age. He continued the struggle even in the face of the decline of his innate right hemispheric endowments. Incidentally, this may account for the sterility, the repetitive quality, and the endless perseveration of the works produced in his declining years, particularly stressed by John Berger.

Both Child and Grandaddy of Our Time

Yet apart from his compulsive trend, Picasso was a typical representative of his time. Both his virtues and vices throw the plight of modern and postmodern man into sharper perspective. He was not alone in his quest. Scores of contemporary writers, composers, painters, and choreographers have gone 'through intrapsychic and interhemispheric conflicts and existential shifts of the same order. Arnold Schoenberg oscillated between the romantic 19th century musical idiom and his forbidding, austere, atonal 12-tone scale. Max Ernst did the same thing in his lifelong meanderings between representational and Abstract or Surrealist painting, sculpture, and collage. So did Kandinsky, Paul Klee and some of the major figures of the Dadaist movement. Jackson Pollock's progress from representational to his brand of Abstract and Surrealist painting is a matter of historic record. His forays into archetypal and mythical expression have rightly been compared with Picasso's. But Pollock's archetypal language, despite its brilliance, has obviously been reinforced by doctrinal compliance from his Jungian analysts.

We cannot tell whether his frantic acting out and explosive release of passion, rage, and creative frenzy resulted from a loosening of left hemispheric structure, discipline, and controls and the attending decline of the Freudian superego, in the first place, or whether it was a climactic crisis of the *Zeitgeist*, of the prevailing Kuhnian paradigm of science and philosophy, that had thrown the inter-hemispheric balance of Picasso—and of postmodern man he stands for—out of kilter. Yet whichever came first in the chain of causal events, it points once more to the commanding position of the left hemisphere in human affairs.

It should be noted, however, that there are two hidden, seemingly contradictory assumptions in such a suggestion. One is that Picasso's predicament (and the predicament of postmodern man) is essentially due to the fragmentation and erosion of established ethical, religious, and esthetic standards and, in the last analysis, of individually held or socially ordained superego demands. Alternatively, it implies the proposition that the crisis originates from an altogether different level of discourse: from the decline of one of the major achievements of western civilization—the dominance of the left hemisphere in Western man.

But the two rival interpretations are by no means mutually exclusive. We shall see in Part III of this book that the left side of the brain is in effect the home and habitat of the Freudian superego—"Under New Management," as it were.

Picasso died at ninety-one, well past the proverbial biblical age. One should think that would have left him ample time to put his house, his real estate holdings, and assorted art treasures in order. He did not. Nor did he file a Last Will: leaving a motley group of heirs, both legitimate and not quite legitimate, in a battle royal for their appropriate shares in his estate. The ensuing scenario was his last dismal masterpiece: it set the stage for years of family feuds, more bitter and more bizarre than any one of the cartoons or canvasses painted by Daumier or Hogarth, but lacking the comic relief of Puccini's *Gianni Schicchi* who thumbed his nose at his would-be inheritors. There can be little doubt that here, again, one of Picasso's Puckish, if not demonic, secondary personalities was at work adding the seeds of strife, despair, and in two cases, suicide, to his bequest. This apparently was to be the punishment for their temerity in surviving after the demise of their master.

Yet apart from the monumental record and priceless artistic value of his legacy, it set two records unique in the annals of history: his legacy yielded the richest monetary rewards ever amassed by an artist in his lifetime and the greatest wealth ever accumulated by a card-carrying Communist.

10

KAFKA'S CONFLICTS
Theme and Variations

Some 40 years after Freud's exile from his beloved and hated Vienna, the City Fathers decided to honor his memory with a plaque on his house at Berggasse 19. At about the same time the representative literary circles in Prague decided that Franz Kafka, who had written all his works, including the dreary reports of his workman's compensation cases, in the German language, was a Czech writer after all.

Such belated recognition is a doubtful honor. It usually comes at a time when a great man's reputation is already past its peak and his position shifted from the revolutionary to the commonplace. The brightness of Kafka's star was, however, subject to considerable fluctuations due to changing atmospheric conditions, to the vantage point of the observer, and dependent on his ethnic or personal equation.

Born in Prague in 1883, the son of Herman Kafka, a self-made man, well-to-do Jewish shopkeeper and manufacturer, Franz Kafka remained virtually unknown outside his circle of friends.

Throughout my undergraduate years in Prague, I walked through the same winding cobblestone streets of the Old City, riffled through the same library shelves, and frequented the same coffee houses as Kafka had some twenty years earlier, but I never heard his name. Only years after his death in 1924 did I come across the first psychoanalytic study of his work, and fell under his spell.

This is admittedly the wrong approach to a great literary figure. Decay and putrefaction can never account for the beauty of a flower—of a Flower of Evil—that has grown out of it. His sickness may have been an inescapable corollary of his work, but it does not help to understand or define it. Indeed, a purely clinical approach would merely "factor out" Kafka's genius from the total picture, leaving nothing but a case history of a guilt-ridden, alienated, obsesssive-compulsive personality whose death from TB at the age of forty-one had saved him from suicide or a schizophrenic break.

More congenial to Kafka's personality and personal predicament is the Existential approach. It helps to place him alongside such writers as Kierkegaard, Nietzsche or Dostoevsky and to give him his due as the originator of a new, dreamlike, or nightmarish form of artistic expression. It will be supplemented by added reference to bihemispheric perspectives.

Psychoanalytic Perspectives

Psychoanalysis has contributed at least a tentative key for the decoding of some of the more puzzling features of Kafka's communications in both his books, letters, and diaries. Perhaps his most poignant complaint was his pervasive sense of loneliness and abandonment. He was longing for closeness and intimacy with mother, father, with male friends, or women, but, at the same time, he recoiled from every opportunity that had come his way. In the 5-year record of twice-broken engagements to Felice Bauer, Kafka laments that he is unable to live either with her or without her. He describes marriage as an incarceration, and compares a wedding with capital punishment. As a twenty-seven-year-old, he runs out in panic from a visit to a Paris bordello. Throughout his relationships with women he was haunted by the fear of impotence.

Max Brod (1970), his loyal friend and biographer, describes his irresistibly winning smile, but also his oversensitivity to noise, his insomnia, headaches, vegetarianism, and intolerance of alcohol. On visiting an aquarium, he reportedly told the fishes: 'I haven't come to eat you, just to look at you." As a little boy, he would get into fights on his way home from school. A casual reprimand from a servant girl with the courtesy title of governess, sufficed to stop his aggression in its tracks. His impressionable mind registered any message reaching him as if it was imprinted on wax. But, in fact, it became engraved on harder stuff, never to be forgotten. The do's and don't's of his father and mother left an indelible mark on his behavior. But this impressionability also laid the foundations for his neurosis.

Viewed from the Freudian angle, many of Kafka's personality traits were derived from what must have been a harsh toilet training, leaving him guilt-laden over the minutest failure to observe "the Law." It led to the development of what has been described as "sphincter morality:" "I am just a shitty little boy and nobody can possibly accept me the way I am." This anal guilt may have been exacerbated by his sense of rejection when he was replaced by several siblings in his mother's affection in the ensuing years. But his worst feeling of rejection stemmed from his mother's total subservience to his bullying, overbearing, insensitive father. The older man's explosive tempers, his yelling and screaming, and his contempt of the shy, puny little boy were an endless source of terror and frustration to the child.

Such analysts as Helmuth Kaiser (1931), Harry Slochower (1940), and a growing number of subsequent analytic contributors to the American *Imago* and elsewhere, placed the main emphasis on what they described as Franz's oedipal conflict. In a 100-page letter addressed to his father, he summarized an endless list of grievances against him: "In front of you I lost my self-confidence and exchanged it for an infinite sense of guilt. In the recollection of this infinity I wrote about someone quite truly, 'He is afraid, the shame will even live on after him...'" In another passage he noted, "My opinion of myself depended more on you than on anything else, such as, for example, any outward success."

He recalls, "We often undressed together in the same bathing hut—I, skinny, frail, slight, you strong, big, broad. Already, inside the hut I thought myself pathetic—not only to you but to the whole world, since for me you were the measure of all things. But then, when we stepped out of the cabin in front of the people, I holding your hand, a small skeleton, uncertain, barefoot on the planks, afraid of the water, unable to copy your swimming movements which you, well-meaningly but profoundly humiliatingly, kept on demonstrating, I was desperate, and at moments like this all my bad experiences of all kinds came egregiously together" (*Dearest Father*, 1954).[1]

The little boy's intuitive perception of the older man's brutally competitive attitude toward his offspring was perhaps quite accurate. We are told that writers like Heinrich von Kleist or Marcel Proust had similar problems with their fathers, though none may have been affected more deeply than Franz's experience with his progenitor. He certainly was not a "chip off the old block." Every fiber, every cell of his organism seemed at loggerheads with Herman Kafka's genes. There was a well-nigh genetic incompatibility between the two and, not surprisingly, Franz was the loser in the unequal struggle.

He showed little open rebellion against his father's despotic regime. He vacillated between bizarre sadomasochistic fantasies and abject surrender to the superior male. At times these reactions assumed a distinctly passive-feminine coloring, reminiscent of Freud's celebrated Schreber case, an equally pathetic victim of an obsessive-compulsive, brutal father. But while Freud's case culminated in the patient's full-fledged schizophrenic breakdown, Kafka found solace, if not cure, in the artistic expression of his plight. In *In the Penal Colony*, the torturer first inflicts untold suffering on his victim, but subsequently he himself succumbs to the ministrations of his diabolical torturing device. Some of Kafka's masochistic fantasies are, if possible, even more bizarre. He is bound, gagged, burned, and raped in his dreams. "I was rolled back and forth several times and they pulled on my legs so that I writhed with pain." He confesses his enjoyment of the fantasy of a knife penetrating his heart—and being turned in the wound. Elsewhere in his diary he spells out his credo that the freedom of the weak person is to seek salvation in defeat. "Victory is prohibited; all calculations originate and end in impotence."

The Metamorphosis, written in 1912 by the twenty-nine-year- old while he was still living in his parental home, is a culmination of his masochistic degradation and self-debasement. Turning into a cockroach is symbolic of regression beyond the stage of infantile dependence into a pre-human, insectlike existence. He chooses to eat garbage, is covered with dirt and detritus, a stinking outcast whose sight and smell even his closest family members cannot stand. In the end, he is fatally hurt by a missile thrown at him by his father and he starves to death in a dark corner of the room.

Franz seemed to have always been a finicky eater, given to food fads and vegetarianism. His excessive thinness had evidently been a matter of great concern to him, but the underlying psychodynamics are more reminiscent of anorexia nervosa seen in adolescent girls than of a genuine desire for "the leopard to change his spots." The paradox is even more intriguing when we recall that in his story *A Hunger Artist* the typically Kafkaesque anti-hero starves himself to death while faced with the growing indifference of his public. As it happened, some 12 years later, Kafka himself met his untimely death through starvation resulting from terminal tuberculosis of the larynx.

The Freudian symbolism of self-starvation, or anorexia nervosa, is obscure and it will be noted that, in Kafka's writings, it figures merely on the metaphorical level. Still, post-Freudian analysts tried to go beyond the classical sexual interpretation of dream imagery or neurotic symptoms in general, and to look for the existential messages hidden somewhere under the psychoanalyst's couch. Erich Fromm's analysis of Kafka's *The Castle* is a case in point (1941). The hero of the novel wants to get in touch with the mysterious inhabitants of the place. They should tell him what to do, show him his place in the universe. But, despite his frantic search, he never succeeds. He is a castaway "thrown" into the world, hopeless, perplexed by the absurdity and futility of existence. It will be noted that this is a sensitive existential reading of *The Castle*. Fromm's interpretation of *The Trial* (1951) hews more closely to the psychoanalytic line. He describes Kafka as an orally regressed or "arrested" individual in both senses of the word, suffering from what Fromm has termed an "authoritarian conscience." Thus, Fromm tried to reconcile the existential and psychoanalytic approach.

EXISTENTIAL PERSPECTIVES

Not surprisingly, existentialists dismiss the psychoanalytic reading of Kafka's work as irrelevant for the appreciation of its message and artistic significance. So, incidentally, do many psychoanalysts; so did Kafka himself. "All these so-called illnesses, sad as they may seem, are matters of faith," he stated. "They are an attempt by man who finds himself in distress to find moorings in some material soil." He also questioned the value of psychoanalysis as a therapeutic procedure. Hermann Hesse, one of Kafka's early admirers, noted that "interpreting" is an intellectual game, but it never finds access to the inner substance of a work "because they (the interpreters) stand at the door trying to open it with a hundred keys and do not see that the door is already open" (quoted from Franz Baumer, 1971, p. 11). Baumer cautions against taking Kafka's *The Judgment* simply as the embodiment of an infantile father complex and to view the notion of God it nurtures in psychoanalytical terms alone. For Kafka, God is more than a delusion born of a compulsion neurosis. Kafka's achievement, he suggests, is "taking the phenomena of the numinous and demonic out of the isolated sphere of the esthetic and realistically portraying them as actual forces in our own lives."

But the fact is that, by and large, it was the demon who had the upper hand in Kafka's life. In contrast to fairy tales in which the frog is turned into the prince, in Kafka's nightmares the hero, Gregor Samsa, is transformed into a subhuman creature. Albert Camus, another early admirer of Kafka's, saw in him the embodiment of modern man's predicament—a predicament that drove him "from hope to grief, from wisdom to despair, to intentional (self-imposed?) blindness" (Camus, 1964). Camus was touched by the "emotionally moving face of a man fleeing humanity," while at the same time he lamented the fate of being excluded from humanity.

For Edwin Muir (1969), Kafka's congenial translator, Kafka illustrates "the complete incompatibility of the ways of Providence and of the ways of man." The result is an attitude of estrangement, existential anxiety, closely akin to Soren Kierkegaard's *Fear and Trembling*, Sartre's *Nausea*, or Camus' *Myth of Sysiphus*. But

Kafka's skewed perceptions of reality also show a close affinity with the distortions of Picasso's canvases or with the disparity between meticulous craftsmanship, realistic presentation, and surrealistic content in Dali's or Magritte's paintings.

Kafka never went on record with a systematic statement of his philosophy. By default rather than by design, he left it for others to do so. His very obscurities, his metaphorical, right hemispheric style, was an invitation for literary critics, theologians, and psychoanalysts to try their hands at his exegesis. The present bihemispheric approach may not be the last attempt along these lines.

Bi-Hemispheric Perspectives

Kabbalistic lore describes the Bad Self, *Jezer Ha-ra*, as opposed to the Good Self *Jezer Tov*, standing on the left and the right side of a person respectively. They are aspects of the demonic versus the divine elements in man. At the same time, they are unmistakable projections of the individual's right- versus left-hemispheric *doubles* or *alter egos*, as described in an earlier chapter.

Kafka's world was certainly overflowing with irreconcilable opposites. He was a battlefield of the numinous and the demonic, with possession by the demonic tending to have the upper hand. He used to say that writing for him was a form of prayer. But he also wrote that it was "payment in the service of the devil, a descent to the dark powers, the unleashing of spirits by nature chained, of dubious embraces, and everything else that may be happening below about which someone above no longer knows anything when he writes stories in sunlight..." And he adds, "Perhaps there are also other kinds of writing, but I know only of this one; at night when terror prevents me from sleeping. I know only this one..."

It must have been this ambivalence towards the demonic aspect of his work that prompted him to implore Max Brod to assist him in an act of ultimate self-destruction. "My Dear Max," he wrote to him a few months before his death, "burn everything (except works already published in periodicals, papers, manuscripts or letters...) everything without exception is to be burnt, preferably unread (I won't stop you from looking at it, but in any case, nobody must see it)—I ask you to burn it all as soon as possible." It was a deliberate gesture of rejection and repudiation by the left hemisphere of his creative, right-hemispheric brain children, but also a last tribute paid by the son to a despotic father who had considered his writings nothing but worthless scraps of paper.

Fortunately, Brod refused to comply with his friend's death sentence on his literary output. He knew all about Kafka's ambivalence and was well aware of the blissful moments and hours which had brought him under the spell of his creativity. They were moments, hours, or days of labor in which he gave birth to a progeny "covered with slime and filth," but which had given him surcease from the anal or filial or existential guilt he had carried throughout his life. They were times when Kafka knew abandon without fear of reprisal, reproach, or the need for self-torture and masochistic self-debasement; when obliteration of the ego meant paradise, nirvana, not hell and damnation.

But back in the numbing routine of his work as a law clerk or supervisor at the Workmen's Compensation Office, he had to face what he felt was the distressing reality of a skinny, malfunctioning body, a wretched appearance, an ill-defined, forever vascillating, doubt-ridden self. This is how his self-image was ultimately transformed into the awesome nightmare of Gregor Samsa's *Metamorphosis*.

There is no consensus about the origin of such distortions of a person's body image. My own experience points once again to anomalies in right-hemispheric functioning. There are my own cases of organic lesions of the right hemisphere as well as those of Elliott Ross and others. There is my adolescent half-Gentile patient who developed conversion hysteria during the Nazi era, complaining that the left, hemianesthetic side of his body had turned into his Jewish side. There are a few drawings recorded in Kafka's diaries which show striking evidence of fragmentation of the body image. Yet, in Kafka's case, the entire body image had become evil, castrated, sick, subhuman. This is why, in the nightmare of the Hunger Artist, it had to be punished, liquidated, starved to death. This is why, by some mysterious fluke of fate, Kafka's terminal illness ultimately led to death from self-starvation.

There is, however, ample evidence of the saving grace of the right hemisphere occasionally taking over from the harsh rule of the left; the image of the benevolent *Jezer Tov* stepping in for the ill-starred *Jezer Ha-ra* of the Kabbalists. We have Kafka's word for it that he, like Nietzsche, like Blake, Mozart, or Walt Whitman, produced his best creative work in a state of ecstasy or trance. Indeed, I have noted that the stylistic analysis of his writings shows all the hallmarks of right-hemispheric dominance. They can be contrasted with the following sample of a typical left-hemispheric communication from an office memorandum. It was included in Brod's Kafka biography:

> "Our illustrations show the difference between square spindles and cylindrical spindles as it affects the technique for the prevention of accidents. The cutters of the square spindles are connected by means of screws direct to the spindles and rotate with exposed cutting edges at speeds of 380 to 400...etc., etc." (p. 83).

Another example that comes to mind is the contrast between Mrs. Eileen Garrett's flowery trance utterances and her comments in the waking state. It is painful to contemplate that Kafka's parables and the office memo were written by the same person.

It is true that his literary prose is plain, lucid, factual, propositional. But the austere form cloaks a rich panoply of myth, metaphor, and allegory, the emblems of the right side of the brain. There is never a hint of artifice, of conceit, never a jarring note to detract from the authenticity of his message. Yet the message reveals a dreamlike world in which subject and object seem to merge, in which the laws of left-hemispheric logic, the categories of time, space, and causality are suspended. This is what psychoanalysts describe as the primary process, characteristic of the dream, of the mentality of the child and the neurotic. It is also a world inhabited by such psychic or psi phenomena as telepathy, clairvoyance, and precognition studied by the parapsychologists.

DEATH FROM STARVATION FORESEEN BY THE HUNGER ARTIST AND THE SAVING GRACE OF CREATIVITY

Kafka himself had expressed at least passing interest in such incidents. He consulted Rudolf Steiner, the theosopher, during

Steiner's visit to Prague. Steiner suggested that Kafka's writings were done in a clairvoyant mood—whatever that was supposed to be. Though Kafka was unimpressed, there are many indications of intuitive flashes, premonitions, and inspired "hunches" in his work. Some sanguine critics tend to read veritable prophetic qualities into his description of the *Penal Colony,* equipped as it is with all the paraphernalia of the cold, mechanical cruelty of a Nazi concentration camp, run as it is for no purpose other than destruction and self-destruction. Ultimately it engulfed the commander himself in an avalanche of filth, blood, and corruption.

While we are told that *The Trial* reflects Kafka's painful experience during a "tribunal" held by the Bauer family that led to the break of his second engagement with Felice, some critics see in it yet another premonition of man's ultimate debasement and destruction by a soulless court of law in which guilt is always taken for granted and the defendant is always kept ignorant of his crime. Here, too, allusions to the descent into the holocaust have been detected. They are not unlike Jung's claims of having prefigured in his dreams the advent of a "sea of blood and destruction" during World War I. Still, in both cases, the purported prognostications are too ambiguous, dreamlike, and nebulous to justify bestowing the badge of a soothsayer on the dreamer. The question of true precognition must remain undecided.

But there is an ominous theme in Kafka's writing that does seem to anticipate tragic things to come in his own life. On an earlier page, I hinted at the food fads and the distressingly skinny physique of Franz Kafka as a young man. Coupled with his recurrent fantasies of self-imposed starvation, e.g., by Gregor Samsa in *The Metamorphosis,* and later by *A Hunger Artist,* they seem to anticipate a hidden predisposition for anorexia nervosa, a malady occurring more frequently in adolescent girls than in boys. Gregor Samsa turned into a cockroach and eventually refused to feed on the garbage offered to him. At the same time, he could no longer stomach food that was fit for human consumption. He shriveled to an empty husk and was ultimately disposed of by the charlady. The *Hunger Artist* chose starving to death as his higher calling, while meeting with nothing but indifference and disbelief by his public.

The final clincher is, however, the concatenation of a set of improbable circumstances that culminated in the complication of his terminal illness by a severe tubercular laryngitis. It literally choked off all possibilities of food intake and led to the selfsame form of death he had inflicted on two characters of his fiction.

Had Kafka's intuitions been at work informing him of what the future—his own demon, or *Jezer Ha-ra*—had in store for him? Was he, himself, weaving the web that was instrumental in his undoing? Directly aware as he was of his own unconscious, he had suspected all along that his tuberculosis was one of the stratagems enabling him to escape from the dreaded prison of marriage. His first pulmonary hemorrhage occurred in the wake of one of his last major clashes with Felice in 1917. It made him ask in his diary whether his "lungs and his brain had been in secret collusion" behind his back. By the same token, we may well ask whether or not the macabre denouement of his tubercular infection likewise sought to meet a secret timetable of the Hunger Artist's plan for self-destruction.

There is a striking parallel of Kafka's predicament with what Nietzsche has called his own fateful "inoculation" with insanity, with a syphilitic infection—the venom of the Tarantula—that may have had a hand in lifting his spirit to the heights of Dionysian raptures but which ultimately caused his descent into madness. If so, were both Nietzsche and Kafka in effect prophets, if not agents, of their own downfall or *Untergang*? Ronald Hayman, (1982), the author of one of the latest major Kafka biographies, describes the agonies of his terminal illness in graphic terms. Hayman also has a highly praised biography of Nietzsche to his credit. I wonder whether he would agree that there was indeed a prophetic—or self-fulfilling—quality to both Kafka's and Nietzsche's premonitions.

If so, it could be argued that the right hemisphere carries the seed of the future in its womb, while the left hemisphere is busy planning it. Unfortunately, there are no conclusive, non-falsifiable data to bear out such a suggestion. The ambiguity of myth, metaphor or parable is wholly consistent with the cognitive style of the right side of the brain. But if there is such an animal as an average reader, he or she may well be left wondering about the fascination, bewilderment or even the touch of terror aroused by Kafka's writings. It may all stem from the reader's own intuitive response to the material, making logical, analytic, left-hemispheric understanding unnecessary. Such a response may be reinforced by Kafka's restrained, factual prose and by the explosive meaning of his hidden message. We may be repelled by the face staring at us as we look into the distorting mirror, but we may suspect that the distorted image is our own.

Has there been nothing to dispel the pervasive gloom of the author of *The Trial, The Castle, The Metamorphosis,* and countless other writings? Yes, there has been. It was *writing* itself that dispelled his gloom; the moments, the hours, the days when he was in the grip of his creative powers. Call them trances, ecstasies, altered states of consciousness—when self-loathing and self-doubt (the nagging voice of his father) were replaced by the authentic experience and self-expression of Kafka himself.

Such moments must have occurred at the confluence of his inner, right- and left-hemispheric promptings, marking the reconciliation of opposites, the resolution of conflict, the blending of his austere, factual, propositional language with the dark incandescence of his imagery, of his parables, myths, and metaphors. They must have been the stellar hours of his genius.

11

EILEEN GARRETT
Four Voices of a Medium

It is one of the paradoxes of recent studies in lateralization of brain functions that in women they are more heavily weighted in favor of the right hemisphere—the cradle of genius—than in men. Yet at the same time genius, as it is commonly understood, still seems to be the preserve of the male establishment.

It makes me feel a little like an American government official who is called upon to fill a job with a minority applicant but has difficulties in finding one qualified to take his or her place alongside Beethoven, Einstein, Leonardo da Vinci and company. Despite their indisputably superior right hemisphere endowment, few women have claimed their place on a par with the great creative minds of their time or the shakers and movers of their societies.

In any case, our dominant left hemisphere society has refused to surround a George Sand, Madame Curie, Simone de Beauvoir or Golda Meir with the aura required for admission to a redesigned unisex Hall of Fame. Joan of Arc and St. Teresa of Avila were respectively burned at the stake and canonized by the church, but certainly not nominated as candidates for the mantle of genius. Mrs. Garrett was at least neither beatified, burned at the stake nor declared immortal by the French Academy.

PSYCHIC, AUTHOR, BUSINESSWOMAN

Thus shifting the spotlight from some of the great personages in the *Who's Who* of Western civilization to the Irish-born American author, publisher, and noted "sensitive," is apt to raise eyebrows as well as questions of perspective and propriety. Even Mrs. Garrett, though used to hobnobbing with celebrities both in this country and in the United Kingdom, would perhaps be startled to find herself in such illustrious company. Yet the reason for her inclusion in the present volume is not to pay a posthumous compliment to her accomplishments, but to call attention to two (if not more than two) separate and sharply defined aspects of her personality: on the one hand successful business executive, woman of the world, foundation president, lady bountiful; and mystic, trance medium, gifted "psychic" on the other.

Whether or not there is a corresponding right versus left hemisphere polarity in her neurological makeup, is a question that will be pursued in the pages that follow.

The available evidence is drawn from two sources of information. First, there is the record of a rich life, spent in the raising of a family, the pursuit of psychical research, the writing of several books and autobiographies, and many articles of both professional and general interest. To this has to be added the feat of enlisting the munificence of wealthy sponsors, enabling Mrs. Garrett to become the president of a multimillion-dollar research foundation. And there is, further, the record of her numerous mediumist seances whose tape-recorded transcripts have been published in journal articles and in a major monograph by Ira Progoff (1964), a Jungian psychologist.

This is perhaps the best introduction to Eileen Garrett's four favorite trance personalities: *Ouvani, Abdul Latif, Tahoteh,* and *Ramah.* Stripped of their esoteric, spiritualist embroidery and

Victorian curlicues, they are highly imaginative, dramatized products of mental dissociation. They emerge either in hypnosis, autohypnosis, or as a result of what I have described as doctrinal compliance by a suggestible subject with the hypnotists' subliminal suggestions or "demand characteristics." Mental dissociation, culminating in hysterical trance states, has from time immemorial formed a veritable breeding ground for secondary personalities. Such trance states have served as a mouthpiece for the medium's own unconscious wishes, hopes, and expectations, but also for diverse ecstatic, visionary, or prophetic utterances, or, for Julian Jaynes' hallucinatory voices of the gods earlier mentioned. In rare cases they may be possessed of a veridical quality and contain elements suggestive of extrasensory perception.

THE FOUR VOICES

Mrs. Garrett's first trance personality called himself *Ouvani,* a 13th century Arab soldier. He spoke in an Arab or Spanish accent, but offered little more than romaticized Victorian folklore to enlighten us about his purported background. By the time he made his first appearance in Dr. Progoff's *"Conversations"* with Mrs. Garrett, Ouvani had already assumed distinct personal characteristics. Here is a typical fragment from the transcript: speaking through the voice of the medium he introduces himself: "It is Ouvani, greetings, friend..." Warming up to the occasion, he goes on to expatiate about "change:" "I think it is fairly obvious to you that before there is any great change in the outlook of those who inhabit this little earth, you would call it, before great changes, has it not always been that there are those who come in the voice of prophetic assurance? Rather in a sense are we not in our appearance those who enter with the change of the change, before the change, and during the change? Are we not in a sense the dramatic experiment through which and by whom changes are made in the methods of man's thoughtfulness?" (p. 14).

The fragment is typical of the rambling, disconnected, chaotic quality of trance communications. At the same time, it shows a characteristic rhythmic cadence which, in other passages, assumes the quality of poetic diction. *Tahoteh,* another of Mrs. Garrett's trance personalities, introduced into the session by Ouvani, speaks in a wholly different voice, in a portentously archaic style: "I am he who wishes to be called Tahoteh...My nature is universal...It is the breath of the elements. It is the breath of life. It is the breath of the stars."

Another quote from Ouvani has a quaintly poetic quality, interlaced with metaphors and rich symbolic imagery: "In each one of us is the knowledge that sometimes shows itself in sleep that we are not only the doers but the creators also, and that if there is already within the little seed the perfume and the color of tomorrow's flower as yet unseen, so there is in all men the way, or the many ways, if you like the many routes, that he may take for the eventual road that he will lay out for himself in the dreaming state" (p. 18).

The passage is less confused than the previous quotation. But it is interesting to note a confusion about his sexual identity as he continues. The speaker, Ouvani, suddenly refers to himself as a woman (i.e. as Eileen Garrett), for instance, when she talks about "*her* petulance which...causes *her*self difficulty...*she* seeks knowledge," etc. (p. 18). Indeed, on one page of the transcript I counted six male and seven female references reflecting the uncertain gender of the purported speaker. As we shall later see such an alternation between male and female identification throws the psychodynamics of Mrs. Garrett's secondary personalities into sharp relief.

Responding to a question asked by Dr. Progoff, Eileen-Ouvani remarks:

> "When I am called upon and because even when the instrument is sleeping or waking or dreaming, do not forget this polished bowl is very vulnerable. A pathway has been cut to the door, a pathway has been made into what we will call the mental presence..."

Here, again, the speaker tries to convey her meaning through a string of metaphors, mixed and unmixed, as the case may be. And here, again, the symbolism of the polished bowl is distinctly feminine.

It is interesting to compare these rambling, flowery, metaphorical communications with Mrs. Garrett's ordinary discourse in the waking state. It is illustrated by the transcript of one of her conversations with Dr. Progoff *before* entering the trance state: "...When people come into the room to sit with me, like yesterday, I have no idea who she (the next sitter) is. She calls. I give her an appointment because she is the cousin of a man I had six years ago..." and so on and so forth. It will be noted that her speech is coherent, factual, propositional. It is a typical left hemispheric communication. This is how I remember my own conversations with her, and this is how she performed as a public speaker.

However, entering the trance state requires a brief period of "warm-up." It usually starts with heavy breathing, groaning, moaning, interspersed with a few more inarticulate grunts. It is a performance which readily conveys to her listener the impression of a person in the throes of a powerful emotion, of pain, suffering. On the other hand, a skeptical, clinical observer may merely view it as the opening phase of a fit of conversion hysteria. Still, far more revealing is its interpretation in terms of what elsewhere I described as an *existential shift,* closely associated with a shift from left hemispheric to right hemispheric functioning.

More recent neurological studies in this country by Elliott Ross and M.M. Mesulam (1979) and others have shown that "a painful, groaning, plaintive voice" is a characteristic feature of right hemispheric utterances (p. 148), trying to make up for the loss of left hemispheric speech functions. By contrast, lesions of the right hemisphere tend to erase the emotional coloring, the affective component, of the patient's speech.

Abdul Latif, who introduces himself in Mrs. Garrett's trance state as a 17th century Persian physician, is the second of her trance personalities. His style and manner of speaking is a variation on the Ouvani theme, with the difference that he tends to engage in the discussion of medical matters. On one occasion, he sounds like a consultant giving a second opinion about one of Dr. Progoff's patients. Though expressing himself in the vaguest right-hemispheric terms, some of his statements apparently impressed Progoff with their veridical quality.

Tahoteh and *Ramah,* the next two secondary personalities in Mrs. Garrett's repertoire, are less sharply defined. Tahoteh is described as the *Giver of Words,* Ramah as the *Giver of Life.* According to Progoff, they represent deeper levels of the medium's personality as well as of her trance state. Progoff compares Ramah's utterances "with an initiation into the secret doctrine of mystery religion." Showing an admirable objectivity and tolerance for the rambling quality of such pronouncements, he notes that Ramah is "the ultimate cosmic principle as carried symbolically through the psyche as he expresses a primal level of depth of the psyche itself" (sic!) (p. 326). Indeed, I think Ramah himself could not have put it in more right-hemispheric terms.

Progoff adds, however, that such utterances are "not measurable in terms of truth or falsity." He suggests that on occasion Mrs. Garrett spoke with the tones of a god (p. 151) indicating an inflation of her personality, that is, a tendency to ideas of grandeur, if not paranoid mentation. Tahoteh, in particular, tended to speak with a "transpersonal quality as though a *god was speaking*," (my italics). The reader familiar with Julian Jaynes' thesis of the *Bicameral Mind,* mentioned in earlier chapters, will note that such a formulation is in full accord with Jaynes' ideas, and indeed anticipates by more than a decade his conclusions about the hallucinatory origin of the gods.

THE "REAL" EILEEN GARRETT

Is there a unifying bond between Eileen Garrett's assorted secondary personalities and the "real" Mrs. Garrett functioning on the plane of her ordinary daily experience? To answer this question, we have to take an at least cursory look at her personality development. Mrs. Garrett's autobiographical writings amplified by my personal contact with her, make such an approach somewhat easier than with most other personages that have come within the purview of this book.

Elsewhere (1948), I have presented her case history as a "*Portrait of a Psychic*" in more detail. A brief summary will suffice in the present context. Eileen started life under tragic circumstances. Her mother, the youngest of a family of 13, came from strait-laced Irish Protestant stock, but had married a Spanish Catholic of doubtful character. For this she was disowned by her family, and committed suicide soon after giving birth to the child. Six weeks after her mother's death, Eileen's father took his life by shooting himself. The orphan was brought up by an aunt in a farmhouse near Dublin, and it appears from her account in *My Life in Search of Mediumship* (1939) that her foster mother lacked all understanding of the sensitive and imaginative child. Her uncle, more sympathetic, and perhaps more readily acceptable as a father substitute, seems to have done little to make her life easier.

Eileen grew up as a withdrawn and lonely child, seeking refuge in daydreams and fantasies in the company of what she called the "unseen children:" a boy and a girl, who came to visit her any time she summoned them. They obviously were the forerunners of the trance personalities whom she conjured up in later life. So firm was her conviction of the reality of her imaginary playmates that she was deeply hurt when her aunt questioned their existence and called her a liar. In the absence of friends to play with, and of real people on whom to lavish her affection, she became more and more entangled in her world of fantasies and grew increasingly resentful of her aunt. She became a "behavior problem," and continued as such when placed in a boarding school. At the age of thirteen, she and other girls were involved in a nightly escapade, meeting boys from a nearby college. She was expelled from school.

At sixteen, she married a man much older than herself, in order to escape from an intolerable continued dependence on her aunt. Owing to sexual difficulties, but also to her continued pattern of escaping into daydreams and fantasies, her marriage soon turned out to be a failure. By that time, her imaginary playmates were replaced by a rush of "sensing and visioning," no less vivid and colorful. She was "seeing" not merely the physical bodies of people, but noticed that each person was set "within a nebulous egg-shaped covering of its own. . . The state of the covering altered according to the variations of people's moods." At times, she felt that she was surrounded by "singing sounds; globules of light dancing like midget stars in space." Sometimes she would feel that she herself was drawn into their movements, or that she would split up "as though divided into little pieces, and each piece was located in a different place."

On other occasions she had typical experiences of depersonalization, with loss of feeling of reality of her body image. At times, this was associated with what textbooks of psychiatry term autoscopic hallucinations: "I was sitting one day in a chair in a quite relaxed and passive state, wondering whether I should get up, when looking ahead of me I saw a shadowy replica of myself." Later on, she suddenly realized that she could see more easily and clearly "with my fingertips," or through the nape of her neck than through her eyes: or else "hearing came" to her through her feet and her knees.

Experiences of this order came precariously close to delusional ideas. She felt that she possessed an "all-discerning eye" which penetrated beyond men's ordinary vision. Many pages of her autobiography are devoted to pursuing this theme. At the same time she felt that she was "surely heading for madness." Her condition was further aggravated by three consecutive pregnancies and the death of two infants soon after birth. She seemed to be heading for a mental breakdown.

Yet all along she claims that her hallucinatory and delusional experiences were interspersed with veridical, telepathic or clairvoyant incidents. Incidents of this order occurred as early as the age of seven or eight. A typical example involving her second husband happened during the first World War, shortly after he had left for the front. "I seemed for a moment to have lost my own identity and was caught in the midst of a terrible explosion. I saw this gentle, golden-haired man blown to pieces—I watched the pieces fall: I swam out of a sea of sound—I knew that my husband was killed . . . Two days later my husband was reported missing. A week later . . . he was listed as dead."

Whether or not it was recurrent "psychic" experiences of a more auspicious nature which helped Mrs. Garrett to head off a mental breakdown must remain a matter of speculation. The fact is that the subsequent systematic development of her mediumistic faculties seemed to channel her propensity for mental dissociation—if not psychotic disorganization—into a means of creative self-expression. If so, they may have served a truly restitutive function. It is true that at times even these "heteropsychic"—that is, telepathic or clairvoyant—experiences became too much for her, and she complained of the "unbearable strain" of being the unwilling recipient of impressions of this kind. But in the end her methodical training as a trance medium in the British Center of Psychic Science in London seemed to relieve the pressure. It was also the time when her trance personalities *Ouvani* and *Abdul Latif* made their first appearance.

At the same time, she developed a growing interest in the scientific exploration of her unusual abilities. Her first trip to the United States in 1934 took her to Dr. J.B. Rhine and his laboratory at Duke University, Durham, North Carolina. Although she thoroughly disliked laboratory tests of the card-calling type, she did well under telepathic conditions and was in a class with Dr. Rhine's "very best" subjects. "Altogether the work with Mrs. Garrett was among the most interesting we have done," reports Dr. Rhine (1938), "her averages, omitting a final week during which she was manifestly ill, were about 10.1 for telepathy in the waking state, and 9.1 in trance. In more than 8,000 trials with clairvoyance, she averaged only 5.7 correct hits in 25 trials in the waking state and 5.6 in trance. But even so, results with such a large number of trials are significant. During the high point in her curve, for a 3-day period, she rose to an average of 6.3 in clairvoyance in 3500 runs, and to 13.4 in telepathy." Dr. Rhine adds that, on the whole, her work passed the mathematical criterion of extra-chance results.

Although we are still inclined to invoke statistical evidence, critical ratios or the chi-square test as the ultimate arbiters of truth, I have pointed out in my book, *The ESP Experience, A Psychiatric Validation* that the acid test of laboratory findings is more likely to dissolve the living tissue of psychological truth than to prove it. Nevertheless, the combined record of Mrs. Garrett's life as a trance medium and experimental ESP subject has gone far to suggest the reality of her paranormal abilities.

Yet if this is true, it points once more to the part played by the right hemisphere in the processing of so-called psi phenomena discussed in earlier chapters. At the same time, it is in keeping with the newly emerging views about the hallucinatory voices of the gods, of the prophetic utterances in the Old Testament, and, last but not least, of the creative self-expressions of genius reviewed here.

"Psychic" Exploits and Personality Needs

What is the significance of Mrs. Garrett's trance productions? What is their contribution to the economy of her emotional life and to the maintenance of her sanity and mental balance? The part played by the forerunners of her trance personalities, the imaginary playmates of her childhood years, speaks for itself. She had conjured them up to meet the desperate needs for companionship of an isolated and unloved child. Their appearance was so sweet and soothing that it called for the repetition of her conjuring trick over and over again.

In the ensuing years her cast of characters was undergoing changes appropriate to the changing needs of her psychosexual development. Ouvani's exotic background and Spanish (or Arabian?) accent is strongly suggestive of what to her was the mysterious Spanish origin of her father. Abdul Latif, the noble Persian physician, marked the next step in her idealization of the father figure. At the same time, her own preoccupation and recurrent experimentation with "psychic" healing points to her unconscious identification with him.

The fact is that her favorite trance personalities were all men. They were evidently projections of Eileen's own unrealized masculine potentialities and aspirations. Put in Jungian terms, they were representations of her *animus* (Progoff, 1964). Yet I have also mentioned the wavering of her trance productions between male and female identities. They were in effect graphic illustrations of her underlying ambiguity about sexual roles. This is also borne out by incidents of sadomasochistic game playing in early childhood and by a few tomboyish escapades in her adolescent years mentioned in her first autobiography. It may well be that a latent masculine undercurrent had been at the roots of the sexual difficulties that caused her later marital maladjustment. But it may also have helped her to embark on her career as a business executive, publisher, and foundation president. Nor did it prevent her from establishing wholesome emotional ties and working relationships with a few remarkable women who came her way. They may well have played the role of surrogates for the good mother she never had.

Yet I have also noted that the emergence of her trance personalities served another purpose. It prevented the disorganization and fragmentation of her personality, by channeling disruptive inner forces into the *dramatis personae* of her trance productions. It is these dramatic impersonations of conflicting trends in her personality makeup, and their projection into the outside world, that served as a major safety valve. In so doing, it had a restitutive, self-healing value, and saved her from the danger of a possible psychotic break.

Still, such a conventional psychiatric reading fails to do justice to equally important creative aspects of her personality. The quartet of her four voices, despite their confusion, incoherence, and pseudoprofundity, had all the hallmarks of a flawed effort at artistic self-expression in poetry, prose, or a mystery play. It showed a close similarity to the more polished literary outpourings of such automatic writers as Patricia Murphy, the voice of Mrs. Pearl Curran, the St. Louis housewife who insisted that her writings originated from a secondary personality operating through the Ouija board. On a more exalted plane, such productions can be compared with the poetry and surrealistic drawings of William Blake; with Nietzsche's incandescent prose, with the allegorical messages of Kafka's novels and short stories, or with the emergence of sundry secondary personalities in Picasso's art.

By the same token, some of the cryptic utterances of Tehoteh or Ramah seem to tap the deepest levels of the medium's personality. They hark back to the sacred texts of ancient Indian, Celtic, or Hebrew tradition; they echo the cadences of Vedic chants, of Homeric hymns, of the songs of the Psalmist; they recapture the ambiguities of Delphic oracles, of Hebrew prophetic tradition; of Sufi mystics; of the raptures of medieval Christian saints. In short, they carry all the hallmarks of the three I's; Intuition, Inspiration, and Imagination, which we have learned to associate with the repertoire of the right cerebral hemisphere.

"PSYCHICS," "HOLOPHRENICS" AND THE RIGHT HEMISPHERE

Evidently, Mrs. Garrett's quartet of voices fell short of the measure of the men of genius reviewed here. If so, it appears that in her case the right hemisphere, enveloped in the Delphic vapors of the trance state, tried to do its own thing without the saving grace, the austere discipline, and the organizing skills of the left hemisphere presiding over the three R's.

At the same time it may be as well to realize that Mrs. Garrett's trance productions were merely the garden variety of an historic tradition that reached from the great Hebraic prophets to Jesus or Mohammed, or to Mary Baker Eddy in more modern times. The difference is that Mrs. Garrett merely claimed to be the recipient of messages from "spirit controls," while Mohammed was fully convinced that he was the mouthpiece of Allah himself. But here again, the voice may or may not have been that of the divinity, but the cognitive style, the syntax, the grammar of the message was that of the right hemisphere.

Thomas Carlyle, whose credentials include his enthusiastic advocacy of hero-worship, complained that on perusing the "best English translation" of the Koran, he found that it was the worst reading he ever encountered. "Much of it" he noted, "is rhythmic, a kind of wild, chanting song...(and) it is difficult to see how any mortal ever could consider this Koran as a book written in Heaven...or indeed as a book at all, and not a bewildered rhapsody...written as badly as almost any book ever was" (1840, p. 199). In short, it was a typical right hemispheric utterance, with a few of the saving graces of the left side of the brain.

Carlyle notes that, according to Muslim tradition, Mohammed was illiterate. Whether or not he really was is irrelevant in the present context. But Carlyle's exasperation with the text is typical of the intolerant, knee-jerk reaction of a pedantic, less than sympathetic left hemispheric critic to the ecstatic utterances of an essentially right hemispheric religious genius.

What, then, are the conclusions from our re-examination of Mrs. Garrett as a "psychic," "trance medium" or just the subject of psychiatric case history? Evidently, the standard clinical approach scratches the surface only. It is true that her mental dissociation, her "spirit controls"—and their underlying psychodynamics—would suggest the presence of a conversion hysteria. Her colorful reports of hallucinations, interspersed with delusional material, may have brought her to the verge of a psychotic break. But invariably, she bounced back from such episodes, with the core of her personality unimpaired. Similarly, she attained a remarkable control over her trance states and would snap back into her "ordinary" identity at the drop of the conjurer's hat, as it were. Her apparent split into dual or multiple personalities would again be replaced by a seamless whole. If a clinical label was needed, she could be described as a *holophrenic* like Joan of Arc, Saint Teresa of Avila, or C.G. Jung: the only aberration left would be her striking capacity for existential shifts along these lines.

In one of our last conversations she turned to me and remarked, half in jest, half in earnest "I know, Jan, you think I'm crazy, but I love you anyway." Eileen was wrong with the first part of her remark. But I am sure she sensed my boundless admiration for what she stood for. She was an explorer of uncharted territories, where others had merely studied the maps. She walked a tightrope between the extremes of madness and genius—and she did it with grace and an Irish smile.

12

CORTES AND MONTEZUMA
A Tale of Two Hemispheres

The historic meeting of Cortes and Montezuma is a morality play enacted on many levels of meaning. In the present context it illustrates an improbable encounter of two disparate personalities and civilizations, one literate, controlled by rigid left hemispheric programming and ideologies, the other by what Julian Jaynes (1976) called the bicameral mind presided over by the right hemisphere, the sounding board of the hallucinatory voices of dead kings and immortal gods.

The disparity embraces nearly 2,000 years of time lag between the two societies. One had absorbed all the appurtenances of classical Greco-Roman heritage, compounded with such novel technological advances as the gun and gunpowder, and at least lip-service to the Ten Commandments and the Golden Rule. The other, with its clock—or Calendar Stone—set back to a technology without the wheel, to an architecture without the arch, to martial prowess without fire power, to communication without the written

174

word, but committed to a religion drenched in the blood of human sacrifice and ritualistic cannibalism.

An attempt to reconstruct such a scenario, the confrontation of two hemispheres in both the anatomical and geographical sense of the word, must make due allowance for these intertwining historical, cultural, and psychological complexities as they were highlighted in Jaynes's *Bicameral Mind*. They led to the "collision between two god-programmed peoples, marching to a different drummer," as Hampden-Turner (1981) put it.

In the Spring of 1519 Hernan Cortes, leading an army of 600 Spaniards with 16 horses and some artillery, landed near Vera Cruz on the shores of the Gulf of Mexico. Six months later he had brought about the downfall of the Aztec king Montezuma, forced the surrender of an army of hundreds of thousands of fierce Indian warriors, and had established himself as the representative of King Charles V on the American continent.

How did this spectacular feat of conquest, unprecedented and unsurpassed in the annals of history, come about? W.H. Prescott (1856), the celebrated historian of these events, stresses the inherent weaknesses of the vastly extended Aztec empire, comparing it to an ill-proportioned edifice "ready to fall before the first blast of the tempest." He contrasts the "imperfect tactics and rude weapons of the barbarians" with the "advanced science and engineering of the most civilized nation of the globe." A hundred years later, G.C. Vaillant (1956) points to the "inexorable European world of steel" which hopelessly outmatched the military resources of the Aztec empire—based as they were on Stone Age tools and used for practicing ceremonial forms of warfare in which the taking of live prisoners was more important than strategic victory and the destruction of the fighting powers of the enemy. Other historians point to the lose organization of Montezuma's alliances; to the threat emanating from his vassals and rival tribes; to the preoccupation of his people with bringing in the harvest; and to their belated realization of the deadly peril attendant upon the invasion of their land by this handful of foreigners.

According to A.J. Toynbee (1947) it was the very developmental stage of the Aztec state at the time of the conquest which carried the seeds of disintegration within itself. Others, again, stress the part played by smallpox and other diseases that decimated the native Indian population.

All historians agree, however, on one point. This is the role of the legend of Quetzalcoatl's return in the subsequent downfall of Montezuma's empire. Quetzalcoatl was the Aztec culture-hero, the teacher of arts, the god of such spiritual things as civilization and learning. As a result of some internal struggle in the Aztec pantheon he was exiled from the country, but on leaving, promised his followers that he would return on his boat made of serpent skins, and bring back to them the Golden Age of Bounty. Quetzalcoatl was pictured as tall in stature, white-skinned, with dark hair and flowing beard. "The Mexicans looked confidently to the return of this benevolent deity," writes Prescott, "and this remarkable tradition deeply cherished in their hearts prepared the way...for the Spaniards."

Montezuma, preliterate like all Aztecs, but a man of priestly learning, is said to have been thoroughly familiar with the legend and deeply disturbed when receiving news of the landing of bearded white men on the shores of his country. This, to him, was an indication that Quetzalcoatl had indeed kept his word: he had returned to resume the rule over the land of his ancestors. The 16th century Codex Florentino contains a picture showing Montezuma as he plays a ritual ballgame with the chief of Texcoco, the outcome of which was to prove that the dire predictions of his downfall were correct. The story of Quetzalcoatl's expected return is told with such consistency by all primary sources of the conquest, from Ixtilxochitl, Bernal Diaz (1956), Diego Duran, and De Sohagun to W. H. Prescott, and, thereafter by G. C. Vaillant (1956), S. Madariaga (1955), C. H. Haring, or Jacques Soustelle, that there can be little doubt as to the historic reality of the legend itself, even though it may, for obvious reasons, have been promoted and further disseminated at the time of the conquest by the Spaniards.

What, then, was the psychologic significance of the legend, and how are we to account for its apparent impact upon the minds of Montezuma and Cortes, the two principal protagonists of the historic events which it seemed to anticipate—or at least to rationalize—by way of a prophecy after the event?

Hernan Cortes

Viewed from the vantage point of the 20th century, Hernan Cortes appears as the prototype of the daring knight-errant, of the intrepid hidalgo, growing in stature to become the far-sighted statesman and colonizer of the New World. Seen in historic perspective, he is the son of a nation steeled in seven centuries of life-and-death struggle with the Arab invaders, of a nation which finally succeeded in driving them into the Mediterranean, 'and in establishing what at that time was the most powerful empire of the western world. He was the child of a century in which medieval dogmatism was supplanted by the spirit of bold scientific inquiry; in which the young and adventurous began to shift their attention from the "true stories" of chivalry to the breathtaking accounts of seafarers and explorers venturing across faraway oceans to exotic lands. He is the military version of the Renaissance Man, equally versatile with the sword and the pen. His biographers compare his military genius—as well as his cunning—with that of Hannibal, while at the same time ranging the elegance of his reports to his sovereign alongside the historic comments of Julius Caesar or the memoirs of Napoleon Bonaparte.

But his most outstanding character trait was undoubtedly his boundless self-confidence, the belief in his capacity to achieve the impossible. This, in turn, may account for his reckless daring, to the extent of literally courting disaster, and suggestive of a gambler's unconscious trend to self-destruction. In fact, we learn from his biographers that Cortes had been given to gambling with cards and dice long before he was in a position to play for such high stakes as ships, armies, and the lives of his associates as well as for his own life.

There is another trait of his character closely connected with his propensity to reckless gambling. Cortes, like many men of action, was, to put it in modern terms, accident prone. In one of the many amorous adventures of his youth he trespassed over the roof of a neighbor in order to see his lady love. On losing his foothold he fell or jumped from the roof, sustaining injuries which immobilized him for months to come. During his Mexican campaign, while pacing his room during a sleepless night, he fell into a hall below and nearly broke his neck. In one of his battles he fell from his horse and fractured his arm. These and many more injuries have to be added to those which he suffered from the hands of his enemies in countless bouts of hand-to-hand fighting, often against over-whelming numerical odds. Time and again, he was only saved by the self-sacrifice of his soldiers or lieutenants, some of whom lost their lives in the venture. A classical example of reckless daring bor-dering on self-destructiveness is his order to burn the ships that would have taken him and his soldiers back to the safety of his home port so as to make sure that those faint of heart were prevented from forcing him to return. At least twice in the course of the conquest he threw all precautions and military judgment to the winds to embark on impulsive punitive expeditions which brought him—and the fruits of his labors—to the brink of disaster.

It is certainly not to detract from the stature of Cortes the man, if analytic scrutiny is concerned with the unconscious forces which may have been responsible for such a spectacular show of mascu-line prowess and personal courage. The interpretation of such character traits in terms of defenses against a secret propensity to passivity, to a latent feminine trend, is readily at hand. He was a sickly child, brought up in an environment which set the highest store by proofs of the fighting spirit, virility, and personal bravado. In these circumstances the achievement of these attributes may well have been the result of a successful denial of fears and compen-sation of weaknesses which would have debilitated a man without Cortes' ego resources. We know that the flaunting of masculine prowess often merely masks the latent homosexual tendencies of a Don Juan or Casanova. It may lead to sexual promiscuity and athleticism, or else to deeds of spectacular daring on the battle field—or in the bullfighting ring.

There is no evidence in Cortes' personal history, however, which points to overt neurotic difficulties that would stem from such conflicting drives. The little we know about his psychosexual devel-opment presents a man who was equally versed in the arts of love, courtship, and chivalry, as in the tactics of diplomacy or warfare. We know that he married his first wife, Catalina, under the pressure of a highly-placed relative who threatened to jail him otherwise. His expedition to Mexico entailed 3 years of separation from Catalina. When she rejoined him in Mexico, their marriage ended in tragedy. After a violent scene with her husband, she committed suicide by hanging herself. Rumor had it that it was Cortes himself who had strangled her with a necklace. His second marriage, to Doña Juana, a woman of wealth and high aristocratic standing, is said to have been one of convenience to suit his ambitious plans.

Doña Marina, a Mexican-born slave girl given to Cortes by an Aztec chief, was another important woman in his life. Her knowledge of both Aztec and Mayan dialects, and later of the Spanish language, was an invaluable aid to Cortes' dealings with the natives. She served as interpreter in most of his contacts with Montezuma and was his steady companion and concubine in the early years of the conquest. Here, as in Cortes' dealings with his male friends, it is apparent that he sought to combine pleasure with business. That ultimately he gave away Doña Marina as a gift to his friend Puertocarrero throws this tendency into still sharper relief.

The fact is that he had an unfailing flair for winning the unswerving loyalty and devotion of his associates, his captains and lieutenants, as well as of a motley crowd of soldiers of fortune, and of common mercenaries and adventurers. They followed him through thick and thin in the quest of adventure, for gold and for good times. But they submitted to his leadership even when times were hard and the gold was slipping from their hands. In effect, his capacity to gain friends even among his enemies, and to influence people, surpasses the boldest success story of a Dale Carnegie. Salvadore Madariaga's (1955) sensitive biography of Cortes abounds with examples of his mesmeric effect upon people. The charm of his personality seems to have been as irresistible to those under his command as to his adversaries, sent by a scheming superior or a suspicious king to restrain or depose him.

Throwing his arms around a friend or impulsively seizing the hands of a defeated enemy was one of his characteristic gestures, as described by eye-witnesses. It is as though Cortes, the man, had met with singular success in the job of integrating a latent feminine—or right hemispheric—undercurrent with the rest of his personality. Instead of driving this tendency underground, he found a way of reconciling it with his prevailing aggressive, left hemispheric trend and to turn it into an ally in his unrelenting struggle for power. He appeared to derive genuine pleasure from the company of men and from the exchange of such tokens of intimacy as a piece of jewelry, a war trophy or a captured slave girl shared with one of his captains. The gratification of his passive-feminine needs, far from constituting a threat to his personality, seems in effect to have added to his ebullience and zest for living.

Occasional spells of tearful moods, fits of temper, or acts of outright cruelty, reluctantly recorded by his biographers, are not altogether out of keeping with such a personality. Rather, they round out and complete the picture of Cortes, who won an empire through his personal valor and who conquered people—both friends and enemies—by browbeating, charming, or seducing them into submission.

MONTEZUMA

The figure of Montezuma appears to us through the mist of the intervening centuries and through the distorting medium of chroniclers separated from him by well-nigh impenetrable linguistic, cultural, and religious barriers. The Aztec scribes who might have told his side of the story have gone down with him in the holocaust of the conquest and most of their records were destroyed by the iconoclastic zeal of inquistitors and book-burners who followed in the wake of the conquest.

There is an added difficulty. Our picture of Cortes conjures up the image of a man embedded in the Spanish Renaissance, that is, in an epoch, a civilization, a language familiar to us. We have no such things to go by with Montezuma. Nor can we take his uniqueness, as an individual in our sense, for granted. Montezuma is the product of a dazzling, creative, but essentially pre-literate right hemispheric, bicameral civilization. He and his people left no articulate, written record for posterity. As a result, his figure strikes the contemporary observer like an archeological find: broken, discolored, weatherbeaten shards, laboriously pieced together by their discoverers. The restored artifact leaves us puzzled and discomfited. Montezuma's inner contradictions—the cleavage between ferocity and meekness in the same person—are alien to our western sensibilities. We are shocked by the reported ritual cannibalism of the Aztecs, but we perceive Montezuma as the innocent victim of predatory western man and we project unto him our own image of a heroically embellished lost civilization.

A more recent relativistic or structural approach to "primitive," preliterate societies provides us with a more balanced perspective, but still leaves us with the feeling of a gulf between the world and values of the Aztecs and our own. Viewed in the present context, one of the crucial differences derives from their lack of writing skills. Whatever scripts they left behind are mysterious glyphs or pictographs, only a few of which have as yet been deciphered. They do not have the unidirectional quality of western writing, nor do they alternate between the left and right orientation of a given line characteristic of the ancient Greek "buostrophedon." We now suspect that the lack of written records is closely associated with a relative cultural or developmental lag in the left hemisphere of preliterate peoples. That the Aztecs nevertheless possessed considerable mathematical skills and astronomical and architectural competence admittedly complicates the picture. It suggests a relative deficiency in only one of the three R's and that the Aztecs were in effect straddling the fence between illiteracy in one area and proficiency in another.

Nevertheless, all the available evidence indicates that, measured by modern standards, their mentality did not surpass the level of pre-Socratic or Homeric civilizations. Indeed Julian Jaynes (1976) has made a persuasive case for an apparent arrest of most pre-colonial Central American societies at the stage of what he called the *Bicameral Mind,* that is, when the dominance of the left hemisphere had not yet been established and the individual was still under the control of the "hallucinated" voices of the gods issuing from the language centers on the right side of the brain. We don't have to subscribe to all the arguments with which Jaynes tried to substantiate his thesis. But the historic record shows that his description of men in Homer's *Iliad,* with their rudimentary sense of identity and lack of introspection, applies with equal strength to the protagonists of ancient Aztec, Olmec, Mayan, or Inca societies. "The characters of the *Iliad,*" writes Jaynes, "do not sit down and think out what to do. They have no conscious minds such as we say we have, and certainly no introspections." For example, "It is one god who makes Achilles promise not to go into battle, another who urges him to go, and another who then clothes him in a golden fire reaching up to heaven and screams through his (Achilles') throat across the bloodied trench at the Trojans" (p. 72–73). In another passage, Agamemnon, the King of Kings, complains: "So what can I do? Gods always have their way." Similarly, Montezuma "seemed to take leave of mankind and enter mythology," as Maurice Collis put it (1954).

What would happen if Achilles met Socrates, the rationalist, spokesman of a more sophisticated, literate civilization, face to face on his walk to the agora? The scenario would be a challenge to any science fiction writer. The encounter of Cortes and Montezuma on a sun-baked street in his capital city is nearly as improbable. But it is an historic event with surpassing consequences for those involved and for generations to come.

It also was a meeting of two different modes of existence, of two cultures—and two hemispheres, in both geographic and neuro-anatomical connotations of the term.

As it happened, the available reports present us with two conflicting versions of Montezuma's character. One is the picture of the fierce warrior, of the tyrant who reigned in haughty isolation over a people cringing before him in superstitious awe; the other is the picture of an effeminate coward who meekly surrenders to the superior prowess of his enemy. Prescott compares Montezuma's household to that of an Asiatic despot, or to the splendor of the court of Louis XIV, *le Roi Soleil*. We learn that Montezuma had gone through the rigorous training mandatory for the priestly caste and was later admitted to the highest military order of the Aztecs, an honor only bestowed on those possessed of uncommon martial prowess. Reports concerning his wanton cruelty with hapless subjects who ran afoul of his orders, or with slaves and prisoners of war—thousands of whom he had committed to death on the sacrificial stone—have to be taken with a grain of salt. Such treatment was an integral part of the Aztec religion, based as it is on an unmistakable sadomasochistic concept of life in a world in which sadistic and masochistic behavior may, in effect, have come close to representing the social norm.

From all we know about this religion, its values are impossible to calibrate against Western concepts of good and evil, or to compare with Christian notions of sin and salvation, of cruelty or compassion. The Aztec gods were unbending and inscrutable in their ways of determining, for better or for worse, the destinies of their people and of the world at large. The people themselves lived on borrowed time, with the inevitable end of the world bound to come in ever-recurring cycles of 52 years. Only feeding the gods with the most vital (and therefore the most nourishing) parts of the body—with living hearts plucked from the chests of human victims—was thought to avert catastrophe. Killing prisoners for ritual purposes was thus in the interest of the very survival of the nation, if not of the world. As Bernard Shaw's Warwick assures Joan of Arc in her execution: it was not meant to be a personal insult but a political necessity.

In effect, Aztec ritual demanded essentially similar acts of mortification and self-torture from its priests and devotees, from men, women, and children alike. Montezuma had undoubtedly submitted to them in his youth and early manhood. Prescott remarks that human sacrifice, however cruel, was not degrading to its victims. It was sometimes voluntarily embraced by them "as the most glorious death and one that opened a sure passage into paradise."

While few students of modern comparative religion would go along with this interpretation, there can be little doubt that these religious practices had a profound influence upon the formation of Aztec character—or to put it the other way around: they were outgrowths of an essentially sadomasochistic structure of the Aztec character itself. Indeed, unlike the distinctive trend to self-denial and self-moritification characteristic of Vedantic Indian tradition, a recurrent cycle of sacrifice inflicted on others alternating with self-sacrifice, seems to have been the prevailing mode of Aztec existence.

Another feature, deeply rooted in his cultural conditioning, was Montezuma's tendency to be swayed by omens and portents in all his decision making. This included both his private life and affairs of state. On one occasion, a vision prompted him to break up a military campaign and to return to his home base in order to put to death some of his courtiers for a minor infraction. He was terrified by the black magic of the rival sorcerer king Nezahualpilli, and of his forecasts of disaster: "You will see that wherever you wage war, you will be defeated...before many days you will see the signs in the sky."

He relied on visions produced by hallucinogenic mushrooms or on the prognostication of his astrologers, though he did not hesitate to have them killed when they ran afoul of his expectations. Yet the evil portents did not come from them alone. Comets, flocks of birds that obscured the sun, a talking boulder, conveyed to him the same message of doom. Above all, they predicted the return of Quetzalcoatl, the exiled Aztec god and culture hero, to his land.

There is another aspect of Montezuma's personality which seems to be wholly inconsistent with his savage, essentially sadistic-destructive personality-makeup which has emerged from these legendary accounts. It is his ready masochistic submission to the Spanish conqueror, his apparent cowardice in the face of a handful of armed horsemen and at the sound of a few cannons and blunderbusses sending black smoke into the translucent sky of a Mexican summer day. His meek compliance with Cortes' demands to relinquish his palace and to surrender as a virtual prisoner to the uninvited guests to his capital city is indeed unintelligible unless it is recognized as part of a self-imposed sacrifice *ad majorem gloriam* to Huitzilopochtli, the Aztec god of war. So is his yielding to the ultimate degradation of letting himself be locked up in irons, and of surrendering some of his loyal captains for execution by Cortes' henchmen, while still protesting his undying loyalty and love for his captor and torturer, the reincarnation of Quetzalcoatl, the rival Aztec deity.

Most historians of the conquest seek to explain this paradoxic behavior by reference to an apparent change in Montezuma's personality. They see in it a sign of the gradual corrosion of his stamina, of his waning powers resulting from a sybaritic life amidst the splendors of his court at Tenochtitlan and of his summer retreat in the shady park of Chapultepec. Or else they charge him with outright cowardice and effeminacy. Prescott quotes the outcry of Montezuma's own disillusioned subjects cursing him in his hour of dying: "Base Aztec...coward, the white men have made you a woman, fit only to weave and to spin.'' According to another version, his attempts to placate the irate crowd was greeted with the revealing words: "What is this Spaniard's wife talking about. He is a vile man and should be punished.''

These, then, are the two conflicting and apparently incompatible aspects of Montezuma's personality as they can be gleaned from reports of those who saw him at the height of his power and who subsequently witnessed his pathetic decline and downfall brought about by his beloved friend and betrayer Hernan Cortes.

Yet I have hinted that the two conflicting pictures of Montezuma's personality, colored though they were by the bias of his admirers or detractors, are thoroughly understandable. To Montezuma, Cortes was not a stranger nor an alien intruder. He had come, as one presaged by the oracle, to consummate a fate no power on earth could avert. Cortes was in effect Quetzalcoatl, the Great White Father, the benevolent god who had returned to take his rightful place as the chief of the Aztec people. In fact, it may not be a far-fetched conjecture to suspect that, besides being the reincarnation of the Plumed Serpent, the feared and revered deity, Cortes also stood for Montezuma's father, Axayacatl, and for his uncle, the powerful and vicious Ahoicotl, whom Montezuma had succeeded as the ruler of Anahuac.

Yet Montezuma's puzzling dual personality is readily understood when we realize the complete "other-directedness" imprinted on him by his Aztec tradition. His hallucinatory or ancestral voices made him act like a will-less automaton when he was confronted with specific social situations demanding the suspension of his personal needs and motivations in compliance with their command; He was brainwashed, mesmerized by his captor.

Such an interpretation is in keeping not only with his seemingly incomprehensible attitude towards Cortes, the reincarnation of Quetzalcoatl. It applied with equal strength to the peculiar dichotomy of abject masochistic submission and wanton cruelty directed toward the outside world—or toward the self. It is a dichotomy which runs through the whole Aztec national character, culminating in the bloody ritual of human sacrifices on the altars of Huitzilopochtli.

MEETING OF TWO MYTHS

How, then, did this strange interplay of the two protagonists of our drama come about? What is it that prompted one to put his head voluntarily into the hangman's noose; what is it that gave the other the confidence that his victim was going to perform exactly according to his plans? What is it that gives the contemporary spectator the impression that it all happened as though by mutual consent of the participants? Stripped of its accessories and reduced to its essentials it involved the ubiquitous pattern of dominance versus submission, surpassing the boundaries of a given culture, race, or animal species. The spoken word must have played a secondary role as their means of communication. More important than the verbal exchange was their general demeanor, the symbolic right hemispheric messages conveyed by their body language by prosody, facial expression, or intonation of voice. And it may well be that this exchange had been aided by a psi factor involved in their relationship.

In particular, Montezuma's notion of the Return of Quetzalcoatl may have been one of those emotionally charged complexes—or personal myths—which, I have elsewhere tried to show, are apt under otherwise favorable psychologic conditions to pass from one person to another without the aid of sensory channels. They are all the more likely to do so if they happen to meet half-way, as it were, the personal myth, the unconscious wishes and expectations held by the recipient of such communications. This was exactly the case with Montezuma and Cortes.

To Montezuma, Cortes was more than the ambassador of his Catholic Majesty, King Charles V. He was Quetzalcoatl the God Incarnate, whose return he had dreaded and wished for from the depth of his heart—from the depth of a heart ready to be torn out and burned on the sacrificial stone of the temple. Again, somewhere at the back of his mind, the victorious Spaniard seems to have been aware of Montezuma's wish. And somewhere at the back of his mind he knew that he himself was destined to meet Montezuma's wishes: to act out on the symbolic level the role of the god, both terrifying and benign; to accept Montezuma's sacrifice and to deliver, despite his own protestations of love and friendship, the heart of his victim to a Christian god certainly less terrifying than Huitzilopochtli, but not altogether averse to receiving sacrifices, real or symbolic, from the faithful. In effect, they were sacrifices in the nature of empires conquered by his crusaders, of souls saved from perdition by baptism or by the ultimate remedy of the Inquisitors, burning at the stake.

Put in more specific terms: Montezuma's *idée fixe* concerning the coming of the Aztec messiah had its exact counterpart in Cortes' personal myth which prompted him to play, in actual fact, the part of the Great White Father, of the messiah, in the western tradition, and to assume the reign over a prostrate Montezuma and his subjects in the fullness of time. It is reasonable to assume that it was this symbolic meeting of Montezuma's and Cortes' myths which, more than anything else, accounts for the spectacular course of events which culminated in the Spanish conquest.

But there was a fatal flaw in the "fit," in the dovetailing and interlacing of their respective myths and personality makeups. We have learned from the ethologists that the posture of abject masochistic surrender by the defeated partner tends to arrest aggression by the attacker. It is a characteristic feature of intraspecies behavior, and may even be at the roots of the Christian commandment to turn the other cheek to your assailant.

Clash of Two Hemispheres

Unfortunately, the scenario of the Cortes-Montezuma encounter did not conform to this pattern, nor to the propositions of the ethologists. The signals exchanged between the two men and their interpreters got badly garbled in transit. It was as though the left side of Cortes' brain tried to communicate with the right side of Montezuma's, while the latter was listening to hallucinatory ancestral voices and paid no attention to the voice of the Great White Father in the flesh. Nor did Montezuma realize that Cortes' crusade was in effect a camouflage for another mission: to deliver all the riches of the Aztec empire to Mammon, the occidental pagan deity, in order to quench his insatiable thirst for gold—much in the same way that the Aztecs were duty bound to quench Huitzilopochtli's thirst for the blood of their sacrificial victims.

This is how Montezuma and the men who shared his beliefs in omens and portents fell victim to their faulty reality testing. In the end it was the Spanish conqueror and his dominant left hemisphere—both anatomically and geograhpically speaking—that prevailed over those who were taken in by hallucinatory promptings from their right hemisphere.

The pattern is not unique. Conquest and subjugation of "primitive," preliterate peoples by civilized, technologically advanced nations is a recurrent theme in the annals of history. It has led to undying bitterness among the conquered—the peoples of the third world, if you will—and to what the philosopher Georg Steiner described as the guilt of civilization among the conquerors. It could also be described as contrition over the rape of the right hemisphere by the dominant left side of the brain.

The broader implications of the case of Cortes versus Montezuma are largely conjectural. Is the presumably primitive, preliterate mentality tied to a lower level of left hemispheric control than the mentality of literate people? Is the "primitive" mind indeed under the prevailing control of the right hemisphere? If it is, is the difference between them due to cultural conditioning or to a difference in native endowment? Further, are some of the characteristics of primitive mentality associated with a generally lower level of individuation and ego control? If they are, do they result from a developmental lag of the left cortical centers as proposed by Popper and Eccles in their theory of the left hemisphere presiding over the executive functions of the ego? By the same token, are these functions stuck on an immature, childish level of primitive man's personality development, or do we have to assume that the Nazi phenomenon, Jim Jones' Temple cult with its *folie a deux, a trois,* and so forth, as well as other features of mob mentality, are regressions, throwbacks, to a primitive, preliterate level of personality organization and to control by what MacLean described as the reptilian brain?

Clearly, this long list of questions goes far beyond the scope of the present inquiry. Still, some are intimately connected with points raised in the preceding argument. They will be discussed on a later page.

13

LEADERS, MIS-LEADERS AND THE REPTILIAN BRAIN
A Digression into Pathology

Cortes and Montezuma were in part legendary figures and their interpretation must of necessity remain conjectural. I submit that more can be learned by focusing on leaders and mis-leaders closer to home. Great leaders are usually described as persons with superior qualifications for their calling, but who resist the temptation of using these gifts primarily for goals of self-aggrandizement. Those whose leadership had a major impact upon the course of history may then qualify for the mantle of genius. Unfortunately, the subjective nature of such a value judgment is an obstacle to reaching consensus on that score. For this reason, and even more for reasons intrinsic to the present inquiry, the neural organization of the leaders and mis-leaders of men must likewise be a matter of conjecture.

LEADERS: CAESAR, NAPOLEON, CHURCHILL, ET AL.

Julius Caesar had the burning ambition to emulate Alexander the Great's conquest of the world. He was at least partly successful in

189

reaching that goal and had at least a modicum of concern for the common weal. He was influenced by such right-hemispheric promptings as dreams and apparitions in his decision making, but he also possessed marked qualities of leadership, spectacular military talents, personal valor, and the ability to win friends and influence people. He also was a splendid orator and author of renowned historic tracts. He reformed the Roman calendar, codified existing laws, beautified Rome, and drained the Pontine marshes around it. Undoubtedly, such a record is predicated upon the optimal cooperation and integration of both the right and the left hemisphere. A considerable element of cruelty included in this repertoire completes the picture of his martial prowess.

Napoleon Bonaparte seemed to embody much the same mixture of personality traits. Though his achievements point to the overriding dominance of his left cerebral hemisphere, there are tell-tale signs of right hemispheric influences adding up to the picture of a bi-hemispheric genius. In addition to his marked (though by no means unfailing) intuitions as a military leader and to his superb administrative abilities, he was also actively involved in cultural, artistic, and scientific matters. His legendary gift for face recognition, the persuasive power of his oratory, likewise point to his rich, right-hemispheric endowments. Yet here, again, his callous detachment from the hecatombs of human sacrifices that bedeviled his march toward world conquest are indicative of the insidious influences of subcortical, reptilian centers on an otherwise well disciplined, sophisticated mind. It must have been this combination of ingredients which was responsible for one of the most spectacular careers in history.

Sir Winston Churchill's personality suggests much the same superb right- as well as left-hemispheric endowments. They range from those of a hard-nosed political and military strategist through the gifts of rousing oratory, to his accomplished style as a writer and as a painter of better than dilettante canvases.

Does Mahatma Gandhi belong to this exclusive club of great leaders? Measured by his impact on history, he does. But in view of his chiefly intuitive, right-hemispheric orientation, with less evidence of left-hemispheric contributions, he falls short of the criteria of genius as they are proposed here. So does, for a variety of reasons, Hernan Cortes, mentioned in the preceding chapter.

MIS-LEADERS: HITLER, STALIN, AND THE REVEREND JIM JONES

> When the psychiatrist bids the patient to lie on the couch, he is asking him to stretch out alongside a horse and a crocodile.
>
> MacLean, 1962

Yet instead of further belaboring a point which may by now have become sufficiently obvious, we may as well turn our attention to the opposite end of the leadership scale, to its miscarriage by mis-leaders of men. Unfortunately, there is no dearth of illustrative case material of this order: Hitler, Stalin, Mussolini, Ayatolla Khomeini, the Reverend Jim Jones, to mention only a few.

Adolf Hitler, leader or mis-leader of the German nation, is perhaps the best researched case study among them. He was variously described as a neurotic psychopath (Langer, 1972), given to sado-masochistic, coprophagic perversions; as a paranoid schizophrenic (Bychowski, 1965); as a narcissistic individual given to destructive and self-destructive acting out, a clinical necrophiliac with an ominously defective sense of reality-testing (Fromm, 1973); a man suffering from malignant incestuousness centering on his doting, indulgent mother (Binion, 1973). This, incidentally, should account for his paranoid hatred of the Jews. According to Binion, it stemmed from his resentment of a Jewish doctor who had failed to cure his mother's terminal cancer, and thereby poisoned and ravaged both her and the German "motherland."

But all this ingenious analysis and psychiatric name-calling does not account for the ominous miscarriage of Hitler's leadership and his stranglehold over his people. What then is its correlation to his neurophysiological organization?

Hitler was a man of the spoken word, of the barked command, more than of written communications. He was given to impulsive, precipitous action and hyperaction, more than to logical analysis and mature contemplation. By contrast to his passionate, frenetic oratory, his written work is uninspiring. His turgid, rambling, pretentious prose lacks clarity and organization. It would barely meet the criteria of informed polemic or even effective political pamphleteering. Like his early water colors or later forays into architectural design, his style is conventional, if not dilettantish. Apparently, his left hemisphere had a hard time keeping up with the creative potential of the right. He reportedly had a phenomenal memory, a quick grasp of problems and personalities. A voracious reader, he claimed it was sufficient for him to peruse the last chapter of a book in order to know its content. Still, he was a poor student, and flunked in mathematics and French in his *Realschule*. Letters preserved from his adolescent years show him as a poor speller. He wrote *dan* instead of *dann; soffort* instead of *sofort; den* and *denoch* instead of *denn* and *dennoch*. His use of capital letters was wholly arbitrary. E. Davidson (1977) describes his handwriting as childish: "He was not a Wunderkind...but a boy whose allegedly wide reading had slid off his skull." (p. 20)

Evidently, Hitler's forte was not the manipulation of concepts, of grammar and syntax, but the control of individuals and masses in meetinghalls and military barracks, in personal encounters and war councils. It was the capricious nature, the fitful operation of his higher, left-hemispheric centers that had become his undoing. Indeed, it may well be that the deceptively logical quality of his paranoid system had been one of the major contributions of the left side of his brain, while at the same time the unshakable conviction of the reality of his delusional ideas was contributed by the right side.

HITLER: "PSYCHIC," SHAMAN, OR PARANOIAC?

Yet it was perhaps Hitler's very right-hemispheric temperament which was responsible for his mesmeric influence upon his fellow beings. Some of his more critical observers were wondering whether the people around him had the "sixth sense." A hard-nosed German industrialist noted, after an encounter with Hitler, "The Fuehrer has an antenna to tune him in directly to the

Almighty." H. Rauschning (1940), an early follower, remarked that Hitler's henchmen "gave more and more play to his quality as the 'supreme magician.'" Hitler himself was firmly convinced of his supernatural gifts. We have his word for it that many of his minor and major decisions were guided by his intuitions, hunches, and prophetic visions. There is a much quoted passage in his *Mein Kampf* in which he reports that while in the trenches during the first World War, he suddenly heard a voice commanding him to leave the site of a grenade explosion that was to kill his comrades a few seconds later. He did not care to tell his comrades about it, but he had certainly saved his own skin. But for him the incident was an indication that he had been chosen by Providence to become the savior of the German people after the war.

A second incident of the same order, less noticed in the literature, occurred on November 8, 1939, at a meeting of the Old Guard in the Buerger Brau Keller in Munich. A bomb planted by assassins went off next to the podium where Hitler had given a speech. Yet he was once more saved when he departed from the Keller a few minutes ahead of the official schedule. I heard the speech on the radio and it is an intriguing detail that it was heavily laden with premonitions of impending death for some of those present. "None of us knows whether it is going to hit him next," was one of his concluding remarks. In the ensuing explosion, eight of those present were killed and scores injured.

Both Hitler's and Goebbels' propaganda machine made the most of this "miraculous" escape. It is evidently impossible to tell whether it was true telepathy, precognition, or yet another example of the Fuehrer's intuitive flashes that played its part. But for Hitler it was one more proof that providential intervention had saved his life. A fortnight later he spoke like a man of destiny, "In all modesty...I must name my own person; irreplaceable...I am convinced of my powers of intellect and decision...No one has ever achieved what I have." And he added by way of an afterthought, "In the last years I have experienced many examples of intuition. Even the present development I see as a prophecy...If we come through this struggle victoriously—and we shall—our time will enter into the history of our people. I shall stand or fall on this struggle. I shall never survive the defeat of my people." (Bullock,

1962, pp. 567–568). By contrast to Hitler's prophecy of the Thousand Year Reich, this part of his prediction was indeed to come true by his own desperate act of self-vindication through self-destruction.

A third incident involved Hitler's disenchanted "fellow architect" and erstwhile Minister of Ammunitions, Albert Speer. Realizing the hopelessness of the German situation, Speer made a last attempt on Hitler's life in February 1945. The Fuehrer and his closest entourage had virtually entombed themselves in their bunker in Berlin. Under cover of darkness, Speer attempted to filter poison gas into the bunker to bring the agonies of the war to a sudden end. Yet he discovered to his dismay that, at the last moment, Hitler had ordered the erection of a 12-foot-high chimney that led to the air vent, thus thwarting his scheme (Speer 1970, p. 509,ff).

The factual evidence of incidents of this order is debatable. Nor do they bear out Hitler's claim of supernatural calling. But they once more call attention to the part played by his underlying mystical, right-hemispheric bent.

Indeed, while some of his feats of intuition had all the hallmarks of rational inferences, their accuracy was often incongruous with his spotty education and poorly disciplined mind. Even in his last message to posterity, in his testament written prior to his suicide, Hitler struck a surprisingly accurate prophetic chord: "With the defeat of the Reich, and pending the emergence of the Asiatic, the African, and perhaps the South American nationalisms, there will remain in the world only two great powers capable of confronting each other—the United States and Russia."

Yet, as is frequently the case with right-hemispheric intuitions, they have at best a 50-50 chance of being correct. When it came to the crunch, Hitler did not allow sober reality testing—the domain of the left hemisphere—to take charge of his decision-making processes. He relied on the gambler's throw of the right cerebral hemisphere, reinforced by the promptings of the reptilian brain.

Paradoxically, Hitler seemed to have his own misgivings about his prevailing right-hemispheric orientation. Yet, as is often the case with paranoid personalities, he disposed of the problem by projecting it onto others. Like some of the patients discussed in the introductory chapter, he denied the reality of his own shortcomings, flaws, or passive feminine tendencies and displaced them into the outside world. In the process they were transmogrified into pernicious, homosexual or Jewish traits. They became a catchall and code word for everything that was evil, and contemptible in the universe—and in himself. This had to be excorcised, eradicated, like the cancer from his mother's body (Helm Sterlin, 1976). Much has been made by the new functionalist school of history of Hitler's failure to go on record with a written order for the notorious "final solution" of the Jewish question. But this is in good keeping with his dislike of bureaucratic routine, and knack for oral—or rather, barked or shouted—commands to his aides.

There has been speculation about an actual Jewish strain in Hitler's ancestry. It has never been confirmed. Yet more important is his overreaction to imaginary, social, or sexual impurities around him. It gave rise to both the Roehm purges of homosexuals in the Nazi party and to his obsessive preoccupation with his mission to find a "final solution" for the Jewish question. The destruction of the Jews (and the homosexuals) would then take care of his own repudiated, sinister, right-hemispheric tendencies. His excessive emphasis on masculine prowess, on the virtues of Nietzsche's "blond beast," was a natural corollary of the need to compensate and overcompensate for his own deficiencies. The phallic symbolism of the raised and rigidly outthrust arm in the Hitler salute is a dramatic expression of these factors.

What do these fragmentary glimpses of Hitler's life and psychological *modus operandi* add up to? They show a man ready to lay his and his nation's life on the line in blind reliance on the intuitions of his right hemisphere and deeper brain structures. At times, he seemed to do so to the exclusion of the critical voice of the left side of the brain presiding over analytic reason and sober reality testing. Put in analytic terms, Hitler on such occasions operated on the level of primary processes characteristic of the dream, the neurotic, or the child, instead of on that of secondary processes geared to the exigencies of waking life and the reality principle.

In the long run, this led to the gradual erosion of both right- and left-hemispheric checks and balances that would have controlled the influx of raw instinctual drives into his mental organization. At critical junctures, Hitler seemed to be completely under the sway of subcortical centers, of the limbic lobe, of the reptilian brain.

Historians may wonder about factual, documentary evidence of such a proposition. But watching and listening to audiovisual records of his speeches and harangues to his followers conveys a graphic picture of Hitler, the twentieth-century statesman and war leader, being transformed into a primitive shaman or medicine man. This is how the anthropologist, Bronislaw Malinowski (1954), described the original prototype in action:

> If the spectator were suddenly transported to some part of Melanesia and could observe the sorcerer at work...he might think that he had either to do with a lunatic or else he would guess that here was a man acting under the sway of uncontrolled anger...

Malinowski adds, by way of an explanation:

> For the sorcerer has an essential part of the ritual performance not only to point the bone dart at his victim, but with an intense expression of fury and hatred he has to thrust it in the air...Thus not only is the act of violence of stabbing reproduced but the passion of violence has to be enacted. (p. 173–174)

In Hitler's case the fury and the passion are the same and serve the same purpose. But the bone dart is replaced by his Panzers and Messerschmidts; by the awesome power of his war machine; by the stagecraft of the Nuernberg rallies and by his harangues to the host of enthusiastic followers. Yet magic ritual, uncontrolled acting out, and right hemispheric emotional gesturing were only part of Hitler's repertoire. Another feature was what neuropsychologists describe as *prosody*—the emotional ingredient of speech itself. His major addresses, film and radio performances, were accompanied, and at times drowned out, by a cataract of growls, grunts, snorts, snarls, hissing, and spitting noises—the native vocabulary of the limbic lobe and the reptilian brain. They went beyond the vocabulary of the right hemisphere, they were the call of the wild, assorted animal sounds rather than communications controlled by the language centers of the brain. They expressed turmoil, rage, elemental fury geared to whipping up similar passions in members of the same species, skin color, stripe, or political persuasion, to strike terror into the hearts of lurking predators. Evidently, no laboratory experiments are needed to confirm the origin of all this sound and fury from lower, subcortical centers, or their emblematic stand-in—the reptilian brain.

At the height of his performance, Hitler seemed to lose all coherence, as though passing through a phase of bilateral psychic lobotomy, leaving him to mouth his paranoid message like a broken phonograph record. Even on coming to, he would still remain under the spell of the muted drumbeat of the lower centers of the brain, of the background music of Richard Wagner's *Ring of the Nibelungen*, if you like. It is this split in the vertical which distinguishes Hitler's near psychotic break from the horizontal split in neurotics, or from the dialectics of interhemispheric tension and its creative resolution in genius.

Thus, Hitler and his followers, with all their military prowess and technological sophistication, were out of step with their time. In the end, the twentieth century caught up with them in their luxuriously refurbished and streamlined Stone Age cave—the underground bunker in Berlin. It was to become the tomb and funeral pyre of the Fuehrer, of Eva Braun, of the Goebbels' and their children and their assorted pets—to say nothing of the dream of the Thousand Year Reich.

Their downfall shows once more that an approach to human affairs—and particularly to affairs of state—geared to hunches, inspirations, or intuitions (to the three I's) contains the seeds of self-destruction itself. It lacks the critical scrutiny and the tempering influence upon lower centers by the neocortex, and specifically by the left hemisphere, as the ultimate arbiter of human conduct.

I noted in preceding chapters that such a pattern is the privilege of the creative artist, of the prophet, the "psychic," or sensitive. But in leaders of humankind it is closely akin to madness. In Hitler's case, the rumblings of the reptilian brain, the "call of the wild," had drowned out the gentler voices of Broca and Wernicke, and the strains of Wagnerian music had deafened his ear to the screams of his victims in the gas chambers of Auschwitz or Treblinka. Nor could the thin veneer of his architectural drawings or water colors mask the sight of corpses piled up in the mass graves of Babi Yar, or vie with the ruins of Coventry or Rotterdam. In the end, the horrors of Buchenwald had the upper hand over the legacy of Goethe's Weimar, next door, but worlds apart.

MIS-LEADERS AND THE REPTILIAN BRAIN
ON THE RAMPAGE

I noted that Hitler is perhaps the most dramatic illustration of a right-hemispheric individual who ran afoul of his mission as a leader—of the reptilian brain on the rampage. Yet this does not indicate that predominantly left-hemispheric leaders are less prone to excesses due to the breakdown of cortical controls and to the uprush of reptilian forces from the deep that would make a dinosaur blush and a crocodile weep. Joseph Stalin was such a left-hemispheric leader. He therefore rates at least passing mention in the present context.

The son of a brutal, tyrannical Georgian shoemaker, he grew up with a burning hatred of his father. "He soon learned to hate," says Gustav Bychowski (1965) in his study of *Dictators,* but "he also learned to wait for the proper time to give vent to his hatred." Stalin felt that he had to save his doting mother from her tormentor and he transferred this sense of mission from his family to the country at large. An expelled Russian Orthodox seminarian, he displayed early signs of a sadomasochistic predisposition, became a full-time revolutionary, and showed much the same cruelty with himself as with others.

In contrast to Hitler, he had no artistic interests or aspirations. He was a mediocre speaker and his writings are typically plodding, pedestrian, left-hemispheric products of a limited, pedantic intelligence. His main instruments in the arduous climb to dictatorial power were cunning and cruelty, making sure that all potential rivals were liquidated or otherwise cleared out of the way. If Hitler's victims were millions killed on the battlefield, in air raids or concentration camps, those who perished in Stalin's Gulag Archipelago are said to be multiples of Hitler's score.

We are told that Stalin, too, showed symptoms of an insidious paranoid and megalomaniac trend. But here again, diagnostic labels are unrevealing. All we know is that as a result of his unlimited and unchallenged dictatorial powers, the leverage effect of his personal pathology had ultimately assumed catastrophic dimensions. In other respects, the family resemblance between Stalinist and Hitlerian terror is unmistakable. The color of the shirts or uniforms of their henchmen may have been different, the principles proclaimed by their theorists of power may have been at variance, but their practice of violence was the same. As in sadomasochistic perversions, there is only a limited repertoire of pain and humiliation to inflict, and an even smaller number of body openings to invade, of torture instruments to wield. Even the subtle difference between the diverse Nazi or Bolshevik or anarcho-syndicalistic ideologies of violence are only skin deep. They all aim at the ultimate spiritual annihilation and physical destruction of the individual.

Shifting the spotlight from the world stage to a small hamlet in Indiana, to Ukiah in California, or to Jonestown in the Guyana jungle, we see the rise and fall of the Reverend Jim Jones, a small-town political wheeler-dealer turned cult leader and utopian social reformer. Like Hitler or Stalin, he developed a paranoid, megalomanic trend, collected a band of enthusiastic followers and led them ultimately, like a flock of lemmings, to their destruction and self-destruction. Jim Jones had all the hallmarks of a right-hemispheric personality, listening to hallucinatory voices whose message he interpreted in terms of his own self-seeking, narcissistic needs. He, too, showed evidence of a latent homosexual trend and of sadomasochistic tendencies. Like Hitler, he too chose suicide once his grandiose ideas collided with the hard and fast facts of social and political reality. Yet, unlike Hitler, his "final solution" was Flavoraid, laced with cyanide, and he died in his jungle hide-out with a heap of 900 corpses of men, women, and children around him. Like Hitler, his emotional impact on his followers who shared his hopes and delusional trend derived from the powerful appeal of his right-hemispheric communications to the right hemispheres of their recipients. This is how he became a mini-Hitler of the Guyana jungle.

What are the lessons of clinical case histories of this order and of their ominous affinity for the blood-stained pages of world history? They bring home to us once more the pressing need to reform the methods of selecting leaders in the civilized and not-so-civilized world. Unfortunately, neuroscience, at the present stage, can make only a very modest contribution to this problem. The psychologist Jerre Levy (1974), who has advanced an intriguing genetic theory of cerebral lateralization, suggests that a small minority of (right-hemispheric) left handers has always been a source of leadership in human societies. They were the planners, the innovators, the forerunners of charismatic personalities of our time. Her ideas are closely related to Julian Jaynes' (1976) thesis of the Bicameral Mind. It will be recalled that according to Jaynes the right hemisphere is essentially the mouthpiece of the gods, the source of divine inspiration, of "hallucinatory kings" who helped to cement the group together. It was the source of commands taking the place of personal volition.

By the same token, Dr. Levy suggests that it is the average run of left-hemispheric right handers from whom the majority of more pragmatically endowed followers is recruited. They possess the requisite sensory-motor skills, the practical know-how, to carry out the leader's divinely or otherwise inspired strategies of survival. Thus the proper mix, or frequency distribution of left handers versus right handers in a given group has a distinct survival advantage. The need for just such a frequency distribution accounts for its prevalence ever since the development of language and the lateralization of brain functions in man.

Be that as it may, the examples discussed in this chapter do not recommend the selection of right-hemispheric individuals for positions of highest leadership in our culture. The "divine commands" emanating from the right hemisphere may be too readily overruled by the demonic forces issuing from the lower centers. What, then, are the wider implications of what appears to be the potential for a built-in triangular conflict and cooperation in the modern mind? The question will be addressed in the third part of this book.

III

IMPLICATIONS

The heart has its reasons, but reason does not know them.

Pascal

Would-be critics should realize that my material is derived from the lives and labors of exceptional, creative personalities, not just from clinical case histories, laboratory tests or animal experiments.

J. E. Quote from *Epilogue*

14

DEXTRAVERTS VERSUS SINISTRAVERTS

Two Versions of Being Human?

One of the incidental and unexpected spin-offs of the present study is a new way of viewing and classifying people. It provides the steppingstones toward a typology based on a person's prevailing right versus left hemispheric orientation; that is, on two contrasting cognitive styles and existential modes of being. It points to two distinct personality types with either intuitively recognizable profiles of experimentally verifiable parameters.

TWO PSYCHOLOGICAL TYPES AND THEIR NEURAL MATRIX

Yet we have to keep in mind that the proposed dextraverted versus sinistraverted types are by no means congruent with right-versus left-handedness familiar to popular psychology. Nor do the two types occur in pure culture. They are ideal prototypes, as was indicated in the introductory chapter. They are fixed, abstract reference points in our argument, but no living entities of flesh and blood. We must realize, furthermore, that dextraverts and sinistraverts, as they are conceived here, represent extremes, at opposite ends of a continuum, with all shades and gradations existing between them. With this caveat their diagnosis can be based on evaluating clusters of a person's right versus left hemispheric skills, e.g. handedness; the three R's; the three I's; facility in spatial orientation, musical ability, etc., and on allotting to each function numerical values on a scale from 1 to 10. This would make it possible to express the degree of dextraversion versus sinistraversion in mathematical terms.

Incidentally, the same is true for other typologies: for William James's dichotomy of tough-minded versus tender-minded individuals; for Nietzsche's Apollonian versus Dionysian or, for that matter, for Gerald Holton's New Dionysian or New Apollonian types (1978); for Wilhelm Ostwald's distinction between classical versus romantic scientists, philosophers, or artists. Even Hans Eysenck's extroverts versus introverts are statistical constructs derived from elaborate factorial analysis with due allowance made for intermediary types, neuroticism, etc. Again, C.G. Jung's armchair typology is based on ingenious permutations of such variables as introversion and extraversion, coupled with intuition, feeling, and sensation.

By contrast, such biological classifications as Kretchmer's pyknic versus asthenic or athletic constitutional makeup, or Sheldon's ectomorphic, endormorphic, or mesomorphic types are based on more stable anatomical foundations, but cannot do justice to the fluidity of personality patterns and to the plasticity of the human brain.

There is another caveat called for at this point. In a left-handed artist, poet, or composer, we have to assume that it is the left not the right hemisphere, which presides over his three I's that are at the roots of his creativity. We should therefore typecast him as a sinistravert, despite the fact that, as a mirror image of the right-hander, his creativity is chiefly controlled by the left side of his brain. (It is the left hemisphere which, in his case, happens to be the minor or nondominant hemisphere).

Another problem is the ever-changing pattern of personality in the perspective of time. Life itself refuses to be tied down to geometrically fixed reference points. Our two contrasting prototypes have no permanent existence of their own. They are in a constant flux, defying attempts to capture them in a still picture, as it were, like moments of a symphonic piece frozen on a page of the musical score, or a Laban notation arresting a dance figure in midflight for the convenience of a left hemispheric observer.

On an earlier page I described Beethoven as a right hemispheric genius. But even at the peak of his creative periods his work amounted to an ideal blend of right hemispheric inspiration and left hemispheric organization, craftsmanship, and discipline. The same is true for Wolfgang Amadeus Mozart and his abrupt shifts from tomfoolery in his "Baesle letters," to Papageno's glorified baby talk or to the grandeur of his *Requiem* or the finale of *Don Giovanni*. Mozart too was a right hemispheric genius; but without the cooperation of the left side of his brain he would never have reached the perfection of the finished product.

Freud's genius, I stated, was preponderantly left hemispheric. Yet his genius would perhaps have never gotten off the ground without the intuition, inspiration, and imagination provided by the right side of the brain. The reverse is true for C.G. Jung. He was a preponderantly right-brained genius; but in the absence of the intellectual discipline and tempering effects of the left side of his brain, his life's work would have remained a magnificent failure. Much the same considerations, though not on a comparable scale, apply to Mrs. Eileen Garrett, Jim Jones, or even to Adolf Hitler, or for that matter, to most ordinary mortals. Exceptions are the few human guinea pigs whose right or left hemispheres respectively have been knocked out by such interventions as the Wada test or various psychotropic drugs.

Leonardo da Vinci or Einstein are other variations on the theme. Leonardo's record showed recurrent shifts from a prevailing right to a prevailing left hemispheric position, though there can be no doubt that during his peak periods as an artist or scientist neither his right nor his left hemisphere was in exclusive control or on leave of absence. On the other hand, we have seen the emergence, the triumph, and the eclipse of Einstein's genius, suggesting alternations of right versus left hemispheric preponderance over a lifetime.

Turning from here to the late 20th century political scene, a hypothetically unbiased observer of Jimmy Carter's, versus James Earl Carter's—dual personalities, is likely to be impressed with the conflict between their respective existential positions: one inspired by his maternal, the other by his paternal role model: a stern, authoritarian, left hemispheric father, and a loving, idealistic, right hemispheric mother, coupled with the failure to arrive at a reconciliation of the two. If this is true, it would account for the much debated zigzag course of Carter's political decision making. It is in turn suggestive of erratic shifts or pendulum swings from left to right hemispheric controls. By contrast, President Nixon's preponderant left hemispheric orientation was barely tempered by his Quaker background and religious upbringing. His pragmatic decision-making processes were rarely deflected by esoteric musings, moralistic scruples, or second guessing. On the other hand, the relaxed, amiable, intuitive personality of President Reagan is suggestive of a prevailing right hemispheric orientation. His past acting career, his flair for the spoken rather than for the written word, point in the same direction.

An ominous example of single-minded fanatical religious orthodoxy is the case of the Ayatollah Khomeini. His edicts banning music, the arts, and easy going pleasures from the spiritual diet of his countrymen are clearly designed to counterbalance an excessive *trend towards undisciplined right hemispheric laissez-faire* which has long been a bane of many people in the Moslem orbit. Khomeini's extreme position is in effect a left hemispheric overreaction, or reaction formation against, an equally maladjusted right hemispheric extreme. At the same time, his unbending commitment to the principle of talion, of an eye for an eye, of a tooth for a tooth, or rather of a wrong for a wrong, is a reminder of the survival of an atavistic, paleomammalian, reptilian version of proto-justice in man's mental organization. Hitler's or Jim Jones's example do not augur well for the survival value of such a principle in today's world.

Back to the more moderate clime of right versus left hemispheric dichotomy, it could be stated that Eastern philosophies and cultural patterns are essentially right hemispheric, in contrast to the essentially left hemispheric technological and scientific orientation of the Western world. This is in effect a position taken by Aldous

Huxley, Theodore Roszak, Allan Watts, Robert Ornstein, Julian Jaynes, and others on the contemporary scene.

Yet the cleavage between East and West should be taken with a grain of salt. Eastern philosophy, too, talks about a split between man's strivings and spiritual aspirations. The 7 Chakras of the Kundalini Yoga posit a hierarchical organization of human nature reaching from the crown of the head to the bottom of the spinal column. In effect, it proposes a split in the vertical. The Buddhist cleavage between Yin and Yang is a grand metaphor pointing in the same direction, though its redeeming feature is the quest for the reconciliation of the opposites, culminating in the Balance and Harmony of Taoist or Confucian philosophies.

Christianity, with its emphasis on the polarity of God and the devil, has done little to heal the split. It has been sharpened and conceptualized by Descartes, though men like Dante, Leonardo da Vinci, Goethe, Nietzsche, or Jung have tried their best to arrive at a more balanced position. It is only a new generation of social critics, seekers, and researchers who have discovered the split in the horizontal and tried to develop techniques for its resolution in life and lab.

Lifecycle and Hemispheric Orientation

Reverting to the individual, the part played by the life cycle in the vicissitudes of hemispheric orientation is of particular importance. The preschool child in Western society has not as yet been affected by the inexorable process of left hemispheric control, training, and education. His or her babbling and cooing shows no evidence of lateralization of function. A left hemispheric lesion suffered by a child of four or five does not impair the development of speech: the right hemisphere readily steps in for the left, and the child usually grows up into a normal left-hander. Meanwhile, a normal preschool child is still struggling with the intricacies of Chomsky's transformational grammar and syntax. Linguistic competence is roughly on the level of the right hemisphere. The child is given to agrammatic or telegraphic speech. Vocabulary is limited to the more familiar verbs and nouns (see Table I, Chapter 1). Yet Piaget emphasized as far back as 1924, that the child should not be considered a miniature adult; he is qualitatively different from the adult. "It (the child) operates primarily on images and must, in order to communicate, resort to roundabout methods evoking, by means of symbols and myths, the feelings that guide it." (1924, p. 59-60).

By the same token, the child readily responds to music, rhythm, lullabies, nursery rhymes, and pantomime. Kindergarten and nursery school teachers have, of course, always been aware of and attuned to this. Intuitively, or by trial and error, they hit upon an educational approach congenial to the right hemisphere. At the same time, early childhood has been described as the golden age of creativity. Chomsky noted that the child is creative when he is able to connect words into sentences he or she never heard before, though I have elsewhere pointed out that a telepathic element may likewise be involved in such a performance. If so, such an ability would merely highlight an added facet of the child's creativity.

The preschool child's prodigious drawing ability has been studied by numerous observers, both in this country and abroad, from the French psychologist G.H. Luquet to V. Löwenfeld (1970), J.H. Di Leo (1977) and to Howard Gardner (1980) in this country. The child is capable of catching a view of reality that most grownups have lost. The sculptor Brancusi has expressed it in a hyperbole: "Once we are past infancy, we are already as good as dead;" and Pablo Picasso declared with a mixture of pride and modesty: "I used to draw like Raphael, but it has taken me a whole lifetime to draw like a child."

Howard Gardner, the principal investigator of Project Zero at Harvard, notes that youngsters scarcely out of diapers use a richness of color and expression, and a sense of composition that bear "at least a superficial kinship to works by Klee, Miró, or Picasso." He also notes the child's knack for originality and poetic self-expression. It is illustrated by an observation in my daughter. At age three, delighted with the scenery of a summer's day, she dictated a poem to her mother: "The birdies sing like a big piano and the flowers make a merry face." The metaphors were those of the right hemisphere. But the poetry was all her own.

However, with the growing mastery of language and the

acquisition of the three R's, hemispheric control and lateralization gradually pass to the dominant, left side of the brain. The child learns to use all the symbolic means of communication, a new socially sanctioned cognitive style. Baby talk is discouraged; conformity reinforced; the songs of Blakean Innocence muted; drawing becomes realistic or is abandoned; the child artist is "brainwashed" by what critics like Ivan Illich (1971), Marshall MacLuhan (1964), Postman and Weingarten (1969), and others have described as subversive or corruptive teaching activities by educators of the old school.

It should be mentioned by way of a footnote only, that telepathic abilities which are part of the child's early, nonverbal means of communication with mother and mother surrogates (Ehrenwald, 1978) are likewise discouraged and "repressed" by growing left hemispheric controls. As a matter of basic principle, children's mental organization has apparently not yet undergone the process of lateralization and/or blocking by the dominant left hemisphere; hence the impression of a prevailing right hemispheric preponderance.

We have seen that the same is true for such geniuses as Einstein, Leonardo da Vinci, Mozart, or Beethoven. Whether or not similar considerations apply to the female gender is still a matter of controversy. Some investigators have found evidence of a lesser degree of lateralization—and left hemispheric control—in women. If this is true, it would confirm the popular notion of "female intuition" as a gender trait. Indeed, the mother's intuitive, if not telepathic responsiveness during the symbiotic stage to her baby's needs may well have a distinct survival advantage. The psychologist Paul Bakan (1971) suggests that women have "more hemispheric integration than men and that this may account for the observed cognitive and affective differences between the sexes."

Whether or not the conspicuous absence of women in the worldwide Pantheon of card-carrying geniuses is due to the lesser contribution of left hemispheric values is likely to remain a matter of controversy. Intuition alone is apparently not enough. It must be complemented by the perseverence, the slow, grinding labor and discipline—the *"stick-to-ition"*—of the left cerebral hemisphere, the product of "lateralization and its discontents."

The Table below summarizes salient features of hemispheric interactions in the child, the grownup and the potential genius. While even the infant shows signs of hemispheric differentiation, especially between sad and happy affect, the preschool child is undifferentiated in the cognitive sphere but well integrated on a global level. It can be described as *primary* integration. The grownup has a greater degree of differentiation and lateralization but often at the cost of what is described as *secondary* integration—including subcortical levels. In turn, genius achieves the fullest measure of integration of all levels, even in the face of a high degree of differentiation. Nevertheless, he too rarely maintains peak performance for any length of time.

Thus genius is by no means structure, but process. "Secondary" integration in genius involves an existential shift, a peak experience

Table 2

Brain functions	Child	Adult	Potential genius
Specialized?	Undifferen-tiated	Differen-tiated	Differen-tiated
Lateraliza-tion	Minimal	Marked	Marked
Integration	Primary, Adequate, "ambivert"	Secondary, limited	High, *ad hoc* maximal "ambivert"

Table II shows hemispheric functions in (1) the preschool child, (2) the adult, and (3) the potential genius. In the child the two sides of the brain are not as yet differentiated and work in unison. They are differentiated in the adult and the potential genius. So is laterilization of functions. Integration of functions may be primary and secondary: marked primary integration in the child, limited secondary integration in the adult, including subcortical (e.g. limbic) centers. The potential genius approaches highest integration and orchestration of functions of all levels. He or she is "ambivert." Yet even here, peaks of integration are reached *as hoc* only, geared to the task at hand.

leading to a creative resolution of the existing interhemispheric tension and its attending inner conflict. Indeed, it may well be that the proverbial turmoil, suffering and despair that marks the inner experience of genius are the well-nigh inescapable birth pangs of the act of creation—and of its happy consummation in the work of art.

How Can They Be Identified?

Yet age, lifecycle, and gender are not the only factors detracting from the purity and stability of the contrasting dextraverted and sinistraverted types. I noted that they rarely run true to the ideal prototype. More often than not, their component parts merely amount to a clinical syndrome or gestalt made up of a person's cognitive style or a cluster of such specific items as high or low linguistic competence, proficiency in the three R's, especially mathematics, in musical ability, spatial orientation, face recognition, or analytic thinking versus holistic gestalt perception, and so on and so forth.

This is why the largely clinical delineation of the two personality types is in need of further amplification and corroboration by reference to more specific indicators or personality tests. Such tests have specifically been called for by Roger Sperry (1982). They are still in their infancy and have a long way to go before they are generally accepted. As noted in Chapter 1, monitoring the electrical activity of the brain can provide a clue to what happens in either the right or the left hemisphere at a given moment. More significant indicators of habitual hemispheric functioning can be obtained from the dichotic listening test. Another test involves tachystoscopic stimuli aimed at the right or left side of a subject's visual field. Together with Zaidel's scleral contact lense procedure (1975) it too can afford useful information about prevailing right or left hemispheric orientation. More recent revolutionary studies of positron emission tomography, and the neurological work-up proposed by Elliott Ross (1981) may be valuable added procedures.

More direct clinical information can be gleaned from observing what opthalmologists call the individual's "conjugate lateral eye movements." According to psychologist J. Duke (1968), Gur and

Gur (1980), and others, a flick of the eyes to the right or the left indicates prevailing activity of the contralateral cerebral hemisphere. This permits classifying individuals as either "right-lookers" or "left-lookers." Significantly, P. Bakan (1971) and others have found that habitual right-lookers have a greater tendency toward analytic thinking than left-lookers. They are likely to be dextraverts. Left-lookers are more prone to relational, nonanalytic thinking: they are more artistic and musical and show a greater susceptibility to hypnosis as well as to the production of alpha waves than right-lookers. They are likely to be sinistraverts. On the other hand, right-lookers are better at diverse specialized, typically left hemispheric skills.

Closely related to these observations are reports by Bogen, Galin and Ornstein, Budzynski and others suggesting that different professional groups show a prevalance of different patterns of electrical brain activity. Such findings have led to the distinction between right and left brained professional groups, that is, between dextraverts versus sinistraverts, as described here. Not surprisingly, they are recruited from among lawyers or accountants on the one hand and creative artists or architects on the other.

Whether or not the "Two Versions of Being Human" proposed here are of genetic or cultural origin is an open question. We know that, by and large, each hemisphere controls movement and sensation projected toward the other side of the body. Right-lookers are under the control of specific cortical (and lower) centers on the left side, and vice versa. On the most elementary level, they control directional impulses toward the contralateral side. Thus the natural directional impulse of the right-hander is to write from left to right; this is, in fact, an innate tendency in the vast majority of the population. By contrast, the natural tendency of the "lefty" is mirror writing, that is, thrusting his left hand from right to left. However, children in our culture have for countless generations been trained to favor the right hand and to write from left to right. This is of course not the case in other cultures. The ancient Greeks used a boustrophedon type of script, a term derived from the alternating pattern in which cows had drawn the plow to make their furrows from left to right and from right to left. Hebrew or Arabic writing, directed as it is from right to left; Chinese or Japanese scripts, the *kanji* and the *kana*, are variations on the same theme.

Lateralization of writing under the control of the left hemisphere is thus by no means "wired" into our brain circuits. Indeed, New York ophthalmologist Arthur Linksz (1973) has suggested that for Jewish children taught to read in both Hebrew and English public schools, it is not unnatural to read the Bible in Hebrew from left to right and the translation printed on the same page from right to left. He notes that such a training may be partly responsible for an individual's ability "to see things from more than one point of view" (p. 177).

The Importance of Being Bi-Hemispheric

It is important to note that such incidental or habitual shifts of prevailing directional impulses seem to go hand in hand with the facility for shifting one's attention to corresponding higher, cognitive, creative, or existential derivatives of the original impulse. They may be channeled into emotional attitudes and may culminate in diverse spiritual, religious, or philosophical positions and "ultimate concerns." Yet once they are identified as derivatives of the directional impulse from which they were derived, they too can serve as diagnostic clues to a person's prevailing dextraversion or sinistraversion.

It is interesting to note that there is a pathological counterpart to these exalted and sublimated derivatives of the underlying directional impulse. My Vienna patient with a left sided hemiplegia described in Chapter 1 is a case in point. He developed a violent revulsion to (and physical *a-version* from) the "bad," paralyzed side of his body. Such reactions are often seen in lesions of the right hemisphere, especially in men. It will also be recalled that at times a creative artist of the stature of Chirico, Franz Kafka, or Pablo Picasso may exhibit a similar, though purely psychological tendency to repudiate his or her right hemispheric brainchildren: paintings produced at a past state of their development, or the whole output of a life time (see Chapter 10).

The ultimate precipitating factors behind such fluctuations—or existential shifts—are obscure. They are perhaps unamenable to mere causal-reductive interpretations. But the ability to change movement into meaning, to transmute raw directional impulses into an array of multifarious psychological derivatives may well be one of the major accomplishments of *homo sapiens*. It transcends the human being's original biological endowment and opens up new dimensions of freedom from the individual's genetic programming. They may be rungs on the evolutionary ladder to genius.

To sum up, the diagnosis of the two contrasting personality types proposed here can be derived from both direct clinical observations and from such physiological indices as monitoring electrical brain activity, the dichotic listening test, the tachystoscopic stimulation of the right or left side of a subject's visual field, or from determining whether he is a habitual "right- or left-looker." We have to realize, furthermore, that the higher, transmuted or sublimated derivatives of the underlying right or left oriented directional impulses may manifest themselves in corresponding emotional attitudes, value judgments or existential positions of the individual. Moving from the individual to a broader perspective, the same cleavage between what has been described as the essentially right hemispheric spiritual cultures of the Far East, and the essentially left hemispheric, technological civilization of the West, can be discerned.

But the concept of dextraversion versus sinistraversion, as it is proposed here, is largely based on a hypothetical neurological model, with either genetic or cultural factors tipping the balance in favor of one or the other. In ordinary life—and even in genius—the two versions of being human are embedded in a composite picture made up of diverse personality traits, attitudes, inclinations and learned sensory-motor skills. Some of them are readily recognizable as derivatives of their original neurological prototypes, clustered around the central theme. They range from the gift of the composer to the grace of the ballet dancer, the prowess of the athlete, to the acumen of the mathematician, the computer programmer, or the idiot savant.

We must also realize, however, that the two cerebral

hemispheres, and indeed our whole neural organization, are merely the instruments of being human. Who or what is the ultimate decision maker as to which side of the brain should be dominant and call the tune, or relinquish control to the other at a given moment, is still an unanswered and perhaps unanswerable question.

15

RIGHT VERSUS LEFT
HEMISPHERIC CYCLES IN
HISTORY

From Vico and Herder to Michelet, Spengler, or Isaiah Berlin, the study of cycles in history has in itself been a recurrent cyclical event. But is it appropriate for a book on the anatomy of genius to include a discussion of right hemispheric, sinistravert, versus left hemisphreic, dextravert, cycles of ideologies and strategies of adaptation? I submit that it is, when the dichotomy of right versus left hemispheric dominance is one of the implications of the argument presented, and when even writers of advertising copy for automobiles jump on the bandwagon, insisting that there are cars geared to the left versus the right side of the brain.

But the very flippancy of such hypes should serve as a reminder to spell out what is meant by right hemispheric (or sinistravert) versus left hemispheric (or dextravert) cycles in the historic perspective, or for that matter, in the lifespan of the individual. In either case, it refers to the apparent dominance of hemispheric directional impulses and their derivatives in meaning, value, cognitive style, mentality, or the special skills and interests of those involved. The pendulum-swings from one side to the other are then instrumental in developing a variety of distinctive programs, strategies, and blueprints of action in the individual or the group. It may culminate in adopting a new mental set, mentality, or specific existential position, and it may be conducive to what I have described as existential shifts, including "altered states of consciousness," as well as alterations in style, mode, or patterns of behavior and conduct, suggesting ebbs and tides in right versus left hemispheric dominance.

It will be noted that existential shifts are here discussed in the same breath as right versus left hemispheric dominance, and no attempt is made to probe into causal relationships, that is, to ask which came first, the chicken or the egg? The reason is that the question is ill-conceived from the holistic point of view, or can at least, be shelved as irrelevant as far as a practical course of action is concerned.

It should also be noted that existential shifts—and existential positions—possess a many-layered, hierarchical structure. On the highest level are ideologies, or bodies of doctrine, sociopolitical theories, and "systems of firmly held beliefs and ideas," as Webster's dictionary puts it. On a lower level are programs, blueprints, or strategies, the knack for the use of tools or machines, the ability to cope with increasingly complex social and physical realities, including the manipulation of such extension of cerebral functioning as robots, computer software and hardware.

In the present context, it will suffice to focus on ideologies, blue-prints, and other "maps of the mind" because they are the most sensitive indicators of major or minor changes rippling the surface, or of volcanic or seismic upheavals erupting from below. At the same time, ideologies may carry all the hallmarks of their right or left hemispheric origin and sharpen our insight into their operation.

Right Hemispheric Ideologies

Right hemispheric ideologies are in effect programs suffused with the ambiguities of symbol, myth, and metaphor. They bear the stamp of Vico's "poetic period." They have many character-istics of Freud's primary processes, while their stubborn hold over the minds of their advocates suggests a precarious affinity with paranoid ideation. Nevertheless, or perhaps for this very reason, they usually amount to a consistent, closely knit, self sealing system of thought and imagery. They carry considerable conviction for their holder and have a marked configurational or gestalt quality, with a tendency to "closure" of the gestalt. On a different hierarchical level, they are reminiscent of the stubborn viability of embryonic tissue, or suggestive of the holographic model of cerebral functioning proposed by Karl Pribram (1971).

Seen in historic perspective, ideologies have always shown a remarkable tenacity and staying power. They are hard to kill, but may incite to killing dissenters or opponents. Endless successions of religious wars, the witch craze of the Middle Ages and the Renaissance; Fascism, Communism, National Socialism, and the recent revival of diverse fundamentalist beliefs (Christian, Moslem, Judiac) are cases in point.

Since right hemispheric ideologies are usually based on intuition or preconceived ideas rather than on experience and logical analysis, they are hard to prove—or to disprove: they are not falsifiable, as Karl Popper put it. Still, there can be no doubt about their potential spiritual value or even biological survival advantage. They help to cement cohesion of family, tribal, ethnic, or national groups; they safeguard their sense of identity in time and space. But there can also be little doubt about the destructive power of ideologies that lack the balancing, tempering influences emanating from the left cerebral hemisphere. What we described as Hitler's reptilian brain on the rampage, or the mass hysteria of murders and suicides in the Reverend Jim Jones's flock in Guyana, were graphic illustrations.

Such destructive and self-destructive extremes of right hemispheric ideologies are usually dismissed as madness or symptoms of paranoia or paranoid schizophrenia. But it will be recalled that right to the moment of Hitler's fall from power and the collapse of his paranoid "project," he was seen by his compatriots as a political genius, a second Barbarossa, a redeemer of the German nation, offering them reflected glory and vicarious participation in the greatness of his personality.

With all this, Hitler's Manichaean world, sharply divided as it was into white and black, good and evil, German and Jew, is another outcropping of typically unbalanced right hemispheric ideologies, a closed, self-sealing system of thought, protected by the delusional ideation of an uncompromising paranoid mind—a holophrenic turned schizophrenic, if you will.

LEFT HEMISPHERIC IDEOLOGIES

Left hemispheric ideologies are more in the nature of strategies for action than mere theoretical constructs. The left hemiphere is concerned with monitoring social and physical reality, with analyzing, processing, verbalizing ideas, and programming them for execution. Put in psychoanalytic terms, the left hemisphere is the executive agent of the ego, in charge of reality testing, of synthetic and integrative functioning and, perhaps, the habitat of the Kohutian self. If the specialty of the right hemisphere is eidetic imagery, metaphor, myth, and symbolic transcription of intrapsychic states, the left hemisphere develops strategies for coming to grips with the outside world, of coping with the here and now, with learning from the past and preparing for the future.

Thus its repertoire ranges from the silent incubation of things to say and to do, to transforming thoughts into strings of words and sentences, sermons, memos, or lawyer's briefs, to cookbook recipes and medical prescriptions. It presides over decision making, political action, corporate organization charts, blueprints for mechanical drawings, bridges, and skyscrapers, advertising copy, laundry lists, and telephone books. On a still higher level of cerebration its business is the penning of a musical score, the formulation of scientific hypotheses, of philosophical systems, generalizations, or Kuhnian paradigms.

Like right hemispheric ideologies, their left hemispheric counterparts too show a veritable passion for wholeness, for closure of gestalten. They aim at arriving at overarching conceptual schemes, reflecting the sought-for global unity of the self; they reach for an all-encompassing system of thought or mode of experience. The strictly monotheistic Judeo-Christian religion, as opposed to diverse polytheistic creeds; the 7th century's as well as today's "reborn" fundamentalist Islam; the Marxist-Leninist world of dialectical materialism illustrate the point on the spiritual plane. It is duplicated on the level of military action by Alexander the Great's, or Napoleon's, or even Hitler's quest for global planetary conquest.

On the highest level of abstraction, we have the arcane world of mathematics, of Euclidian and non-Euclidian geometries; we have the ceaseless search of theoretical physics for rival but pragmatically workable models of reality. Indeed, the crucial difference between the two types of hemispheric ideology is that left hemispheric propositions are amenable to experimental testing and verification, in contrast to right hemispheric propositions which are rarely testable.

Still, right hemispheric constructs—or castles in the air—have given rise to western man's shining cathedrals, symphonic, epic, and literary masterpieces and their supporting casts of craftsmen, guilds, bureaucratic and governmental institutions. They spawned the pluralistic world of the creative artist, rivaling nature herself in producing viable wholes of projected imagery, of "melodies heard and unheard," of visual and tangible shapes made of amorphous clumps of clay or stone. In effect, there may be a greater affinity than meets the eye between Leonardo's unfinished canvasses, bronzes, or drawings of machinery, between Schubert's Unfinished Symphony, and Einstein's equally unfinished Unified Field Theory, to say nothing of nature's own experiment of Evolution.

RIGHT VERSUS LEFT HEMISPHERIC IDEOLOGIES AND THE GENERATION GAP

We have seen that passion for wholeness, for archetypal mandalas, for completion of the circle, for rounding of the square, is one of the salient features which both right hemispheric ideologies and left hemispheric programs have in common. But it may be confounded by the stubborn tendency of either hemisphere to reassert its identity and to "do its own thing," sometimes at the cost of the truly integrated or synergistic performance.

If so, the result is the pendulum-swing in the opposite direction:

conflict—personal, interpersonal, or generational. A familiar example is the gap between the parental generation and offspring. Such a gap had perhaps always been a standard fixture in the generational cycle though it may have been virtually absent in stagnating ancient Egypt or Byzantium. In the living memory of most readers it may have been brought home by a major change in the American climate in the wake of World War II and after the Vietnam debacle. It brought a rude awakening from the complacency of a generation steeped in the successes of the Protestant work ethic, safely ensconced in the prosperity and power of a chiefly left hemispheric civilization. It was an awakening to a growing crisis of authority in both private and public life.

There was, furthermore, the belated arrival in this country of Nietzsche's message of the death of God, followed by the demythologization of the Bible; by the debunking of a whole pantheon of heroic figures, past and present, by the erosion of patriotism, of "law and order," of traditional value in the arts and sciences, including conventional codes of behavior, sexual mores, and ethical absolutes. Even grammar and syntax, functional literacy, the art of articulate verbal communication (like "you know...") were getting lost in the shuffle. The correlation of this collective existential shift with the eclipse of left hemispheric dominance is unmistakable.

Yet at the same time, a new set of right hemispheric values, of the counterculture, came to the fore. The flower children, followed by the hippies and Yippies were reaching out for the lost innocence of a past age. "Make love, not war" became the slogan. Transcendental meditation, the relaxation response, the teachings of Don Juan, and diverse pop psychologies added to the erosion of the compulsive left hemispheric mentality of a perfectionist older generation. They also led to the ascent of a set of new, *imperfectionist,* right hemispheric programs and ideologies in their offspring. Zen exercises, *Koans* interminable chanting accompanied by the roll of bongo drums were used to put traditional ego and superego controls out of commission. They were aided by tranquillizing drugs, uppers and downers, marijuana, LSD, and ultimately by the freaking out of misfits—the fractional suicide—with hard drugs.

It would be wrong, however, to underrate the creative potential unleashed by this essentially right hemispheric pendulum swing of the new Dionysians. They were discussed in the Picasso chapter and touched upon elsewhere in this book. Expressionistic, nonrepresentational art, I have noted, was in effect the harbinger of emancipation from left hemispheric controls. It was anticipated by Dadaism in the 20s, followed by jazz, blues, rock and roll, punk rock and the dance-in-America movement, to say nothing of the bacchanalia and episodes of collective acting out in Woodstock, sports stadiums, and discos.

The wider repercussions of such right hemispheric trends were partly obscured by the pluralistic organization of American society; by the numbing effect of the culture of poverty which had other things beside the left hemisphere to rebel against, and by certain more traditionbound ethnic and religious minority groups. Another more radical countervailing principle was injected by a group of fundamentalist sects and far-out rightist factions seeking to recapture a legendary utopian past, a bucolic world untroubled by harsh economic realities, bureaucratic imperatives, federal deficits, and international complexities. It may be no coincidence that the trend culminated in the election of an intuitive, relaxed, amiable right hemispheric ex-actor and ex-sportscaster, President Ronald Reagan. As noted earlier, he was certainly the diametrical opposite of President Nixon's cold, calculating, compulsive left hemispheric personality—while President Jimmy Carter's uneasy mix of an alternating right and left hemispheric personality makeup placed him somewhere midway between the two.

Be that as it may, it is a remarkable fact that a similar drift towards the re-emergence and reinstatement of right hemispheric influences can be discerned in other, developing, preindustrialized countries. The bloody fundamentalist revolution of the mullahs and backward masses against the Shah of Iran and his feverish attempt at modernization and secularization of his country is a case in point, even though his downfall may have been aided by international power plays and diverse socioeconomical factors.

According to V. S. Naipaul (1981), similar considerations apply to the more temperate Islamic revolution in Pakistan where a fundamentalist clergy seeks to establish a "purified" theocratic state, doing away with all alien influences and their attendent "corruption on earth." Even in the late 20th century Israel, a fanatic religious minority tries to set the clock back (or forward?) to the past, or a fervently hoped-for future messianic time, not unlike that envisaged by their Muslim cousins. The resurgence of fundamentalism in this country is another dramatic illustration. That our home grown fundamentalists try to exorcise the devil of the counterculture with an even more radical dose of the same medicine, is one of the major paradoxes of the contemporary American scene. At the same time they are running the risk of triggering the release of pent-up destructive forces from lower, subcortical, if not reptilian, centers.

But we have to recall that in everyday life the respective contributions of right and left hemispheric, cortical as well as subcortical, centers tend to be fairly well-coordinated, integrated, if not synergistic; they operate in terms of what MacLean described as the *triune* brain. Only in such borderline conditions as split-brain patients, in cases like Adolf Hitler or Jim Jones at one end, or of genius at the other end of the scale, can we observe the "ideal" prototype in pure culture. It is the broken surface of a crystal which best reveals its hidden structure. By the same token, it is the generation gap which lays bare the deeper layers in the order of historic events.

But is such a cleavage an unalterable fixture in the chain of successive generations, a preordained heartbeat (or brainbeat) of history? The answer is no. There have always been attempts to heal the rift between reason and emotion, between the head and the heart, between dextraversion and sinistraversion, if you like. Jung has described the reconciliation of the opposites as the litmus test of maturity and individuation. Abraham Maslow (1963) considered it the consummation of man's or woman's self-actualization. It may be one of the achievements of genius. It has been the goal of Zen; of the alchemists of the past age; of Renaissance men like Alberti, Leonardo or Michelangelo. In a similar vein, C. P. Snow, René Dubos, Jacob Bronowski, Philip Morrison, Douglas Hofstadter and many others have extolled the integration of all human potential as the foremost objective of modern education. It has been a goal pursued by such American psychiatrists of my generation as Karl Menninger, Jules Masserman, Silvano Arieti, or Kurt Eissler.

Evidently, a more detailed review of the recurrent pendulum swings of right versus left hemispheric mentality, and of their bihemispheric reconciliation, would be a task going far beyond the competence of the present writer. It is respectfully passed to the historian, the social scientist, or the theologian.

In the meantime, we have to turn our attention closer to home: to the part played by interhemispheric conflict in the origin of neuroses.

16

NEUROSIS AND INTERHEMISPHERIC CONFLICT

One more theory of neurosis? The temptation is hard to resist. Apparent conflict between left versus right hemispheric preponderance in some of the heroic or not so heroic figures reviewed here is unmistakable. Whether or not it should then be described in terms of neurosis is largely a matter of semantics.

Yet it should not be surprising that evidence of much the same patterns of conflict can occasionally be found under less exalted conditions in both neurotics and non-neurotics. Here are a few clinical vignettes:

CLINICAL VIGNETTES

Ron D. was a brilliant college student, the son of a driving, compulsive businessman father and an artistically inclined mother. He had a limp following an accident at the age of eleven. He was valedictorian of his class, keenly interested in the humanities, but complied with his father's wish to study science and engineering. He wrote short stories and sonnets, composed music, and was a gifted piano player. He was interested in psychical research, Eastern mysticism, and experimented with psychedelic drugs.

Ron's training in the exact sciences and experimental psychology soon put a damper on his esoteric interests. He became closely associated with one of his Skinnerian professors, wrote his Ph.D. thesis on computer technology, married at twenty-two, and soon found a well-paying job in his field. This was the time when he first sought treatment with me. He complained of anxieties, general malaise, marital difficulties, and expressed doubts about his sexual identity. Psychotherapy was conducted along psychoanalytic lines, with emphasis on his wavering between identification with his demanding, tough-minded father and his ineffectual, idealistic, but doting mother. Inferiority feelings connected with his limp and repressed homosexual undercurrents completed the picture. Working with his dreams and free associations helped to bring his oedipal conflict into the open; he lost his fear of latent homosexuality, started a series of extramarital affairs and became an increasingly successful executive in his company. Only his continued promiscuity and occasional indulgence in drugs or alcohol were indicative of remaining personality difficulties. An added focus on existential aspects of his problems did not seem to improve matters much further. On reaching a plateau, we decided to discontinue treatment.

There is nothing of unusual interest in this condensed account of Ron's treatment, stretching, with several minor and major interruptions, over the years 1951-1953. Yet viewed in retrospect, it shows one glaring omission in my therapeutic approach: I failed to recognize, or to make allowance for, problems arising from what can now be readily identified as his right versus left hemispheric orientation. I noted that Ron was a gifted, creative child. But his education soon stifled his creativity and spontaneity. It placed the usual emphasis on rote learning and memory training; on content instead of process. It certainly helped to develop his gifts for analytic thinking, mathematics, and the hard sciences. Early influences from his father reinforced his knack for the three R's and penalized his bent for the three I's. His postgraduate training did the rest in "subverting" his lingering propensities for creative self-expression. Ultimately, he himself came to regard his youthful interests in music, the arts, and poetry as aberrations, incompatible with his role as a hardnosed businessman, scientist, and womanizer. Put in psychoanalytic terms, Ron had repressed his passive-feminine propensities and overcompensated for them by an excessive show of masculine prowess. Oedipal conflicts, castration anxieties, and a latent sadomasochistic trend were at the root of his neurosis.

But Ron's case history, as it is presented here, suggests a rival interpretation, or at least one supplementary to the Freudian model. It does not detract from the validity of basic psychoanalytic principles, but it introduces a new neuropsychiatric perspective and reference point for a better understanding of his case. It suggests that Ron's passive-feminine identification roughly coincided with his methodically discouraged and suppressed right hemispheric potentials. By the same token, his identification with father ran parallel with the strict discipline and superego demands his left hemisphere had stood for. In the absence of a successful resolution of this interhemispheric conflict Ron had hit upon two ways of alleviating the situation: he resorted to occasional indulgence in drugs and alcohol; and he developed a pattern of extramarital affairs which at the same time met his need to deny his still lingering homosexual trend and allay doubts about his masculinity.

To repeat, such a reading does not amount to the unveiling of a new theory of neurosis. It merely adds a hitherto neglected neuropsychiatric dimension to its understanding. Nevertheless, we shall presently see that it has significant therapeutic implications for patients whose problems go beyond the classical Freudian formula of intrapsychic conflict between ego and id, between ego and superego, a clash between instincts and societal demands. It calls for what can be described as hemispheric integration therapy.

My next case, Teddy U., aged forty-five, is a musician who started his career as a saxophone player. An immigrant from Germany, he made his way into the lucrative field of musical commercials, both as a performer and composer. His financial success soon overshadowed his artistic interests, yet left him unfulfilled and with the feeling that he was wasting his talents and betraying his ego ideal: " I feel both guilty and failing to pay my debts...what the

Germans call *Schuld; guilt* and *debt* rolled into one." However, his conflict over sacrificing music for the sake of mammon was only part of the picture. He became an alcoholic and was plagued by the temptation of homosexual adventures. It may well be argued that it is problems of this order that lay at the core of Teddy's neurosis.

But deeper probing revealed an unconscious identification of his artistic aspirations with his repressed, right hemispheric, feminine identity. Interpretation along these lines helped him to integrate his repudiated feminine aspects with the rest of his personality and thereby relieve his guilt complex.

The following vignette is illustrative of an existential shift from a prevailing left to a prevailing right hemispheric orientation. It was touched off by a major traumatic experience of the person involved. At the same time, it ushered in an internal reorganization of his defenses, it mobilized his recuperative powers and helped to restore his "vital balance," as Carl Menninger put it (1963).

My next example is not a patient, but a student of mine, a man of thirty-two. This is his report:

> After the sudden death of my wife I noticed a dramatic change in my patterns of thinking. Before she died, I had been heavily involved in mathematics, training myself to become a statistician. I seemed to be quite talented in that area. Since her death I have not been able to concentrate on mathematics in the way I once could. At first I thought this was only a temporary disruption due to grief. However, even after recovering from my grief, the change has persisted. On the other hand, I find that in some more intuitive ways I am more capable now than I was before. I do occasional writing on religious topics, and the writing I have done since the tragedy is far superior to anything I have written earlier. Today, instead of becoming a statistician, I am pursuing a career as a psychotherapist, something I never would have felt comfortable doing before.

He is now functioning on a new, ego-syntonic base line with no evidence of interhemispheric conflict.

Two considerations have to be kept in mind at this point. First, interhemispheric conflict is more a learned condition than a biological fact of life. Although it does not usually manifest itself on the conscious level, it is primarily geared to cognitive, ideological, intellectual aspects. Secondly, "cognitive" types of psychotherapy proceeding along these lines are bound to employ such intellectual tools as words and concepts as their principal means of communication. Their remedial effects are therefore predicated on the *leverage* of concepts and words in the patient's mental organization. In a patient of high intelligence the leverage effect is likely to be considerable. But it may be nil in a person of low verbal intelligence; he will be unaffected by the most ingenious interpretation, psychoanalytic or otherwise. The cases of Ron D. and Teddy U. are illustrations of the leverage effect of ideas in persons habitually geared to functioning on the cognitive plane.

The case of Elsie L. is an altogether different order. She is the only child of Russian immigrant parents who discovered her talent for dancing at an early age. Her ambitious, compulsive mother placed her in a ballet school at eight, and Elsie soon became a prize pupil of the school. At fourteen she was given the opportunity for solo performances, and critics praised her lyrical style, her spontaneity, and gymnastic abilities. Yet Elsie's delight in self-expression through dancing was soon dampened by the gruelling demands and discipline of her training. She had introjected her mother's rigorous standards of excellence and came to share her compulsive need for achievement. By contrast, the father was an easy-going type, given to gambling and occasional alcoholic binges. On the surface, Elsie adopted her mother's contemptuous attitude towards him, but deep down she was ambivalent towards him and men in general.

At fifteen she developed anxieties, diverse compulsive rituals involving personal grooming, and bizarre food fads. She became increasingly concerned about putting on weight, insisted on more and more restricted diets. At the same time she went on occasional eating binges, stuffing herself with "junk" food. At fifteen, 5 feet, 4 inches tall, she weighed 101 pounds but lost some 12 pounds within a few months. She avoided the company of her classmates, withdrew from her peers and her family, and became increasingly debilitated. The clinical picture suggested *anorexia nervosa*.

Psychoanalytic probing revealed a marked obsessive-compulsive trend with oedipal conflicts superimposed on severe oral regression in an emotionally immature girl. She had average verbal intelligence, was poor in academic subjects, with limited ability for verbal communication, but had an intuitive flair for music, and relied chiefly on body language for self-expression. Treatment was largely supportive and directive, but did touch on her elaborate defensive maneuvers and her hostility to men—including her therapist. Special emphasis was placed on Elsie's rebellion against the "introjected" mother, reinforced by the harsh discipline of her training. Her need to escape from the sexual role and from the frailties and iniquities of the "flesh" was only hinted at.

Elsie responded to treatment with symptomatic improvement of the most ominous symptom: her self-starvation. She put on weight, but remained aloof and withdrawn, and her compulsive-obsessive rituals persisted. She dropped out of school, stopped therapy, and refused referral to a female therapist.

Elsie's case shows the limitations of analytic psychotherapy in patients of this type. The pathology of *anorexia nervosa* is still obscure. But the conflict arising from her prevailing right hemispheric orientation, versus her left hemispheric superego demands and discipline was obviously of minor importance in its origin. In any case, the leverage effect of insight and interpretation was negligible; it helped the therapist's understanding but not the patient. No doubt, Elsie rebelled against the compulsive standards emanating from her mother and yearned for the freer life-style her father had stood for. But the root of her disorder was beyond the scope of juggling with concepts, or manipulating the transference relationship, or of attempts to bring about better hemispheric integration.

Yet there are numerous cases in my files who responded favorably to such an approach. There is a plastic surgeon whose dream as a child was to become a famous sculptor. His parents steered him into the medical profession and persuaded him to forego his artistic aspirations. He had a moderate obsessive-compulsive trend and did his best to live up to the demands of his arduous professional training. He went into private practice, frustrated and angry with his operating routine and his family life. In therapy he was encouraged to reactivate his disowned artistic interests. He took time out for belated training as a sculptor and became a more than gifted amateur. He discovered that art, for him, was more effective therapeutic expedient than psychological treatment and succeeded in

striking a satisfactory balance between his right versus left hemispheric orientation. In all this his obsessive-compulsive trend
turned out to be an added advantage.

I have come across numerous examples pointing to similar problems of interhemispheric conflict and attempts at their resolution in
both patients and nonpatients. Bob D. is a homosexual in his thirties. He is suffering from various obsessive symptoms and bizarre
compulsive rituals, suggestive of borderline schizophrenia. Yet he
is a successful painter specializing in portraits of society ladies,
presumably inspired by his identification with and sympathetic
understanding of women. He was a high school dropout and had
only a brief period of professional training. He became a member
of the international jet set, on the French Riviera. His flair for
ingratiating himself with important people certainly helped him in
his career. He has an agent, a financial manager, and has never
learned how to balance his checkbook. Despite his erratic ways and
general disorganization, his paintings are done in a meticulous neo-
realistic style, show a remarkable sense of balance, and an exquisite
sense of color and texture of materials. Evidently, for him art
became a means of self-healing: a creative alternative to psychosis.
I have pointed out elsewhere (1960) that, in a similar vein,
homosexual acting out may serve as an alternative to schizophrenic
breakdown. Whether and how far here, too, the right hemisphere is
instrumental in such a course of events, will be for future research
to decide.

Here is another example. A noted radiologist and college teacher
in his fifties had been given to several minor depressive mood
swings in the course of his life. He was frustrated by what he came
to regard a sterile, uninspiring scientific career. Yet he was a gifted
painter and found growing fulfillment in his art and in the critical
acclaim extended to his work. He liked to tease his psychiatric col-
leagues with his success in do-it-yourself occupational therapy.

There is reason to believe that the legions of amateur musicians,
painters, poets, and artists in our society—and indeed in western
society in general—have hit upon the same avenue of escape from
the tyranny of an overly specialized, overbearing left hemisphere,
and find solace in existential shifts through creative self-expression
in the luxury of art for art's sake. Indeed, civilization, with all its
built-in discontents, has been quite inventive in developing anti-

dotes against some of the ills of its own making: from church services to revival meetings, from theaters, movies, and rock concerts to diverse mindless media events, to art therapy, and occasionally helpful mental health clinics. Even the most cursory look at western social institutions shows that they too are geared to meeting the conflicting needs of human nature symbolized by the three R's versus the three I's. They even try to cater to the need for their reconciliation in some of their avant garde institutions such as Esalen, Arica, or assorted religious retreats or communes.

It is readily understood that hemispheric conflict may spill over and become a problem in family relationships. This is illustrated by a married couple in whom the husband, a gifted mechanic, a man of few words and poor academic record, found himself at odds with an intellectually ambitious wife who looked down at his lack of education. Good-natured but irascible, he sought solace in alcohol, while his wife developed psychosomatic symptoms. In this case, the battle lines were clearly drawn between his essentially right hemispheric orientation and her essentially left hemispheric pretensions.

Such a glimpse into the origins of their interpersonal conflict helped to relieve the situation. The therapist tried to explain to the wife the merits of her husband's right hemispheric personality makeup, and to bring home to the husband his wife's equally legitimate system of values. Marital therapy, pursued along these lines, steered the spouses into a more wholesome complementary relationship and ameliorated the existing pathology.

It stands to reason that brief clinical vignettes of this order cannot do justice to the complexities of a given case. Above all, they gloss over the usual involvement of both neurobiological and psychodynamic factors in real life. Paradoxically, this is best illustrated by shifting our spotlight to one of the most poignant descriptions of neurosis in world literature: to Shakespeare's "case history" of Hamlet.

CURSORY LOOK AT SHAKESPEARE, GOETHE ET AL.

Freud, Ernest Jones, Kurt Eissler, and others have thrown the case of the melancholy prince and his inability to take action into sharp relief. He was unable to avenge the murder of his father by his uncle, the treacherous Claudius, because Hamlet himself had at the back of his mind incestuous wishes to posses his mother and fantasies of killing his father. Thus his procrastination had its roots in his oedipal conflict. He could not obey the command of his murdered father and kill Claudius because Claudius had in effect acted out Hamlet's own repressed incestuous wishes.

However, most Shakespeare scholars are still inclined to interpret Hamlet's puzzling inaction in more cognitive, pre-Freudian terms. They attribute it to his alienation and detachment, to his "conscience"—the Elizabethan equivalent of "consciousness"—that "makes cowards of us all." It had left his "native hue of resolution sicklied o'er with the pale cast of thought" and indeed rendered him unable to do what had to be done.

Viewed in the present context, such a reading does not necessarily conflict with the Freudian interpretation but is complementary to it. It foreshadows the thesis that Hamlet's obsessive ruminations had sapped his energies, stifled his spontaneity and forced him to trade talk for the relieving thrust of action. Put in our terms, it was his left cerebral hemisphere that put a damper on the right side. To be more exact, it could be stated that the emotional conflict of one of the most celebrated neurotics in history who had been analyzed free of charge by the most prominent analysts of our time, had been fed from two sources: from his unresolved oedipal conflict on the one hand, and from the conflict between his two cerebral hemispheres on the other. This state of affairs seems to account for both the intriguingly modern aspects of his character and for the flatness, sterility, and the absence of creative qualities of his personality. Apparently, the playwright chose to preserve all creativeness and daring—from *acting* (in both senses of the word) to poaching and womanizing—for himself, and unloaded scruples, anxiety, and *Weltschmerz* on his melancholy brain child. He made him the mouthpiece of some of the greatest and most quoted soliloquies in world literature, but in so doing performed a kind of psychological lobotomy on the prince: he relieved him of the more vital functions of the right cerebral hemisphere and left him at the mercy of an articulate but obsessive and thought-ridden left hemisphere. No wonder that Hamlet tried to escape from his predicament into a psychotic break—or to what he himself had thought to be a mere self-inflicted counterfeit insanity: Ganser's syndrome.

Nevertheless, Hamlet's case can be viewed as a classical example of a both structurally and dynamically determined and overdetermined model of neurosis. As such, it is another fringe benefit of Shakespeare's genius bequeathed to posterity.

Like Shakespeare's, it is impossible to compress the towering genius of Johann Wolfgang Goethe into a brief clinical or literary vignette. His genius ranged from the tender shoots of lyrical poetry to the profundities of *Faust, Part One* and *Two,* to one of the first German novels; to studies on optics; the morphology of plants, and comparative anatomy. Add to this a more than amateurish gift for painting, drawing and music, and the burden of public office. Yet his full measure of wordly success notwithstanding, he was not spared the ordeal of neurotic conflict (Eissler, 1961). "Only those familiar with the agony of longing, know how much I suffer," he exclaimed in one of his poems. Hinting at the existence of a typical inter-hemispheric conflict, he complained that his philosophical bent ruined his poetry.

In a happier mood, he gladly acknowledged the dual sources of his native endowments:

> From father came my body frame,
> My sense of obligation
> From mother dear my zest for life
> And knack for fabulation.*

The fact is that he was a paragon of a bi-hemispheric genius who succeeded in weaving together the disparate strands of his personality into a holistic tapestry of artistic and intellectual achievement which ranks him alongside Dante, Shakespeare and Leonardo da Vinci among the greatest geniuses of the western world.

CAN ANALYTICAL AND NEURODYNAMIC READINGS BE RECONCILED?

What, then, is the available evidence that can be legitimately attributed to conflict between the two cerebral hemispheres? The

* Author's translation.

psychohistories of geniuses and near-geniuses reviewed in the preceding chapters have provided at least a few tentative clues in this direction. In some cases the waxing and waning of left versus right hemispheric preponderance was unmistakable. Even in the global mind of genius, a steady and harmonious cooperation of the two sides of the brain is the exception rather than the rule. Goethe may have been functioning on such an exalted plane much of the time. The same is true for Leonardo da Vinci, Michelangelo, Freud, or Einstein, though neither of them had entirely escaped occasional neurotic difficulties, bi-hemispheric or otherwise.

We have seen that Beethoven, the right hemispheric genius, was subject to violent fits of temper, giving vent to smoldering rebellion against left hemispheric superego constraints. They were suggestive of the right side of the brain trying to rid itself of the tutelage of the left, while at the same time he was obliged to rely on the latter's contribution to his acts of creation. An added factor may have been ripple effects from the storm centers in lower levels of his central nervous system.

Similar considerations apply to Nietzsche's conflicts between the professorial, if you like, Apollonian, aspects of his personality, versus his ecstatic, Dionysian, Zarathustran aspects, or to the polarity between Jung's number One and number Two personalities. Evidently, Shakespeare's genius defies compression into a simplistic formula. But it can be conjectured that the 300 to 350 characters conjured up in his plays were likewise all "secondary" personalities caught and refracted by the magic prism of his own primary personality.

By contrast, Hitler's or Jim Jones's pathology was due to such a multiciplicity of factors, psychodynamic, psychiatric, sociopolitical and situational, that any contributions of interhemispheric conflict to the overall picture may have been of much lesser importance. Again, the lack of information about Cortes, to say nothing of Montezuma, precludes any speculation along these lines. Mozart? His creative self-expression and the very exuberance of his genius had acted as miraculous safeguards against pathology.

Mrs. Eileen Garrett and her secondary personalities are a case apart. Here, too, their emergence was predicated on the abeyance of the left hemisphere, lulled to sleep, as it were, under conditions of mental dissociation. It is true that Mrs. Garrett was not a genius and that her *dramatis personae* were more caricatures than authentic productions of the playwright's or dramatist's creative imagination. Nevertheless, they are closely akin to the genuine article and show all the hallmarks of right hemispheric origin. What is puzzling in her case—and, for that matter, in such cases of multiple personality as the *Three Faces of Eve, The Case of Bridie Murphy,* or *Sybil*—is the very number of *dramatis personae* spawned in their dissociated state. Still, we have seen that *Uvani, Abdul Latif, Tahoteh,* and *Ramah* were all aspects of Mrs. Garrett's own personality, meeting deep-seated emotional needs, neurotic or otherwise. They may or may not have included genuine paranormal elements in their utterances and their emergence may have been possessed of a restitutive self-healing quality as far as the medium is concerned. But if we are right in attributing their emergence to an existential shift to right hemispheric functioning, we are soon running out of hemispheres to accommodate them in the same location. In cases like Sybil and her 16 subpersonalities, it would certainly call for rather crowded quarters. The right hemisphere is apparently capable of accommodating quite a number of "transients," in addition to its permanent occupants.

Yet it is necessary to sound a note of caution at this point. We know today that attempts at "localizing" diverse cognitive or executive functions in specific areas of the brain are based on false premises. Speech disturbances following lesions in Broca's or Wernicke's areas merely indicate that they are *instrumental* in facilitating efferent and afferent language functions. Similarly, the right hemisphere is merely *instrumental* in processing the three I's: intuition, inspiration, and imagination, including the retrieval and mobilization of dormant memory traces, ideas, and imagery, and weaving them into scenarios of elaborate hallucinatory or dream-like experiences. In the last analysis, it is the pressure of the individual's needs and instinctual drives which is responsible for the final outcome: the more pressing the needs, the more dramatic and variegated the script. Yet since such scenarios inevitably fall short of fulfillment, they have to resort to more and more *dramatis personae,* to make up in numbers for what they lack in experiential quality. The result is the emergence of *multiple* personalities—as in the cases of Mrs. Garrett, of the *Three Faces of Eve,* of the 16 subpersonalities of Dr. Wilbur's *Sybil,* or of Pablo Picasso.

More recent studies of brain waves, using so-called evoked potentials, have shown that each secondary personality produces a characteristic pattern or signature of its own, regardless of cerebral localization (Putnam, 1982). They thus tend to support my argument.

That the left hemisphere is usually trying to counterbalance the right hemisphere—or the individual's unbridled flights of fancy—is another matter. If so, the stage is set for neurotic conflict in both the psychoanalytical and neuropsychological terms of the work. And here again it is usually confined to the patient's unconscious.

"Repression" or Inhibition of Hemispheric Dominance?

It will be noted that so far our evidence pointing to the ups and downs of conflict and cooperation between the two hemispheres has been based on two groups of observations: geniuses and neurotics. Both represent extremes or borderline cases of the human condition, and this presumably is the reason why they help to throw both problems and potentialities of interhemispheric balance into sharper perspective.

But we have seen in the introductory chapter that there is a large body of observations, both clinical and experimental, pointing in the same direction.

The psychologists J.F. and G.M. Bogen (1969), pioneers in modern split brain research, specifically noted that the left brain may directly suppress certain kinds of right hemisphere activity, or "prevent access to the left hemisphere of the products of right hemisphere action". The psychiatrist Daniel Galin (1974) noted that there may be reciprocity between the two sides of the brain. Or else, they may operate "in alternation;" that is, take turns, depending on situational demands. The psychologists S.J. Dimond and J.G. Beaumont (1974), another team of pioneers in the field, remark that "the two hemispheres work together in a way similar to a marriage: each partner has his or her specialization; there is a division of labor, and division of responsibilities. There may be dominance of one partner over the other, and either conflict and tension or harmonious interaction may result" (p.50).

In an important series of brain wave studies, Galin and Ornstein (1972), Galin (1974), and others have found that "the EEGs of normal subjects performing verbal and spatial tasks to determine whether there are differences in activity between the two hemispheres, produced relatively higher alpha amplitude (a measure of idling) over the right hemisphere during verbal tasks, and relatively more alpha over the left hemisphere during the spatial tasks" (p. 573).

From experimental observations along these lines, Galin arrives at the proposition that one hemisphere may actually turn off or "repress" the other hemisphere, and that "in normal, intact people mental events in the right hemisphere can be disconnected from the left hemisphere (to) continue a life of their own." He concludes his argument with the bold hypothesis that there should exist a neurophysiological mechanism for at least some instances of repression and an anatomical locus for the unconscious mental contents."

Although Galin himself disclaims the intention of attempting to "neurologize" psychiatric concepts, his formulations clearly set the stage for a new approach to neuroses as expressions on the behavioral level of conflict, lasting or transient, between the two cerebral hemispheres. This precisely has been the main thrust of the case histories discussed on an earlier page.

Colorado psychologist T. H. Budzynski approaches the problem along similar lines (1979). He suggests that the right, or minor, hemisphere may express frustration by channeling it into hysteric or psychosomatic disorders. More than that: he has tried to change or "reprogram" maladjusted tendencies of the right brain by sidestepping the influence of the left hemisphere, for instance, by putting the patient into a twilight state, and by talking to him "in the language of the right hemisphere." To do so he used techniques of "twilight learning" by means of taped messages fed into the subject's ear or by applying sensory overload to the left hemisphere to block its effect on the right. He found that such reprogramming of right hemisphere functions may result "in the alleviation or elimination of some of the more recalcitrant psychological and psychosomatic disorders" (p. 139).

Evidently, such attempts at re-evaluating psychodynamics and influencing the operation of the two cerebral hemispheres has far-reaching implications for both the theory and practice of psycho-therapy. Such familiar Freudian concepts as the unconscious; as primary versus secondary process functioning, as ego defenses; repression, or reaction formation are infused with new meaning and should become subject to experimental testing and verification. To be more specific, the unconscious no longer appears as a repository of repressed instinctual drives or of ego-alien primary process functioning. It is a combination of such repudiated mental content with the effective blocking by the left hemisphere of right hemispheric programs, patterns of behavior, and cognitive styles.

Elsewhere I pointed to a growing body of parapsychological observations which suggest that the right hemisphere is also involved in the processing of telepathy and related psi phenomena, especially of those of the need-determined type (1978). Here, again, their intrusion into consciousness is blocked—or repressed—by the pragmatic, here-and-now oriented left hemisphere. Repression is thus a dual process, aimed at biological impulses as well as culturally repudiated ego-alien material. In a similar vein, Freudian ego defenses are closely akin to, if not identical with, more elabo-rate left hemispheric maneuvers of denial, projection or reaction formation against undesirable patterns and programs originating from the right hemisphere. If this is true, it tends to support Lacan's thesis of the ego being itself the carrier of neurosis.

SOME DIAGNOSTIC AND THERAPEUTIC IMPLICATIONS

Perhaps the most significant implication of the present approach is the transformation of right or left hemispheric directional impulses into their higher emotional, cognitive or value-oriented derivatives discussed in the preceding chapters. Such a process can easily be recognized as a neurophysiological counterpart of the Freudian concept of sublimation. Yet what is here transmuted into higher psychic activity is not a welter of repressed instinctual drives but the pressure of directional motor impulses originating from the contralateral cerebral hemisphere and/or lower centers.

This dawning insight should be a welcome aid in promoting the theraputic alliance between therapist and patient. Both will be in a better position to overcome still-lingering left hemispheric blocks in their work. They will be able to do so by combining cognitive analytic know-how with an intuitive right hemispheric approach. That such an approach in effect duplicates Freud's original prescription is one more testimony to his clinical intuitions—even though such Freudian concepts as sublimation, repression, or cathartic release are now being called other names.

Who or what is responsible for the alchemy of metamorphosing motion into meaning, into symbolic message or neurotic manifestation, is an open question. But the work of Nobel Laureate John Eccles and the philosopher Karl Popper (1977) suggest that, here again, the left hemisphere plays a decisive role. It presides over the awareness of the conscious self, as well as over will and volitional action; in short, over most of the executive functions of the ego. By contrast, the right hemisphere is geared to automatic functions or preconscious mental activity.

If this is true, neuroanalysis may hold the promise of providing a new neurophysiological underpinning for some hitherto highly speculative psychodynamic principles. In so doing it may help to resolve a problem that had eluded Freud from the beginning to the end of his career. It will be recalled that our attempt in chapter 5 at throwing new light on Freud's conflict over his left versus right hemispheric orientation has led to the same conclusion.

17

WHAT GAIN HAS THE WORKER FROM HIS TOIL?

A critical reader may well ask at this point whether all the ingenuity and effort that went into exploring the implications of modern split-brain research, and especially of the psychology of genius, is worth the candle after all? What gain has the worker from his toil, as the Psalmist put it? The answer is that there are at least four aspects of human affairs that are brought into sharper perspective by our findings. The first is the anatomy and natural history of genius itself. The second is a new look at education and at today's cult of illiteracy, or, by indirection, the cult of the right hemisphere. The third aspect are the pros and cons of knowledge and insight for the survival of the individual and the group. The fourth are some of the ultimate concerns of the human condition as they are dramatized by the great parables of the Judeo-Christian tradition: the Fall of Man; the dual nature of Jesus; Plato's fable of the Charioteer; and the myth of Prometheus who snatched fire and the blessings of technology from the gods.

GENIUS RESTATED

While some of the preceding chapters have sought to take a closer look at the workshop of genius, and to speculate about its *modus operandi*, I am afraid they will be of little help to the would-be genius seeking a do-it-yourself home study course on how to become one. We have seen that, operationally speaking, genius leans heavily on the innate endowments of the right hemisphere. It is the wellspring of the three I's, intuition, inspiration, and imagination, even though it has also to rely on the cooperation, the talents, the linguistic skills, the analytic powers, the perseverance and discipline of the left side of the brain. It should be noted, furthermore, that some of these are likewise innate qualities, but are reinforced by cultural conditioning and learning. They have resulted from the lateralization of specialized functions, a process which, we are told, goes back as far as Neanderthal man some 50,000 years ago.

The right hemisphere's innate endowment calls for a few more comments at this point. It is a concatenation of the brain's programs as described by J.Z. Young of the University College of London (1978). Programs, according to Young, "are inherited plans for action, written in languages of the DNA code." They are "transmitted and translated during development throughout life to produce the living individual, able to react appropriately with the world" (p. 10). But the programs and languages encoded in the right hemisphere are not those of articulate human speech or writing brought into focus in Broca's or Wernicke's areas in the left hemisphere. They are superimposed on our prenatal, prehuman evolutionary inheritance, "stretching back through natural selection over countless generations," as Professor Young puts it. They are essentially unconscious, automatic, like the operation of instinct, and, like diverse autonomic regulatory processes, usually inaccessible to deliberate volition. They are in effect closer to nature than the programs encoded in the left hemisphere. It is this quality which surrounds them with an aura of strangeness, of the uncanny, but occasionally also of the sublime, the holy, the divine.

At the same time their archaic origin, reaching back to the evolutionary past of the species, imparts to them properties bordering on the miraculous. They are feats of adaptation, of "fitness," of the "wisdom of the body," characteristic of living organisms in general. Indeed, the information carried in the molecular structure of the DNA of each individual cell is far superior to all of the left hemispheric know-how of a Ph.D. in biochemistry or molecular biology. This is what, in the last analysis, accounts for the prodigious feats of intuition and what we have called the innate endowment of the right hemisphere. It is the repository, on the human level, of the navigational skills of the homing pigeon; of the spawning salmon; of the timetable of. the hermit crab; of a flock of migratory birds; it is attuned to the Ecclesiastes' seasons, mindful that "there is a time to mourn and a time to dance, a time to be born and a time to die." It is the sounding board of the music of the spheres; of the beat of African drums; of the cadenzas of a violin concerto or the liquified architecture of a Bach oratorio. But we have seen that under stress or in moments of crisis, the right hemisphere may also be laid open to the ferocity of Sagan's *Dragons of Eden* and of the killer instincts welling up from McLean's reptilian brain.

In the end, the creative act emerges from the orchestration of the three levels of the central nervous system and, by indirecton, of the personality as a *whole*. Usually the process proceeds in two steps, but we are told that Mozart's musical inspiration sprang from his brain in all its glory and in full bloom as though the score was dictated by his muse ready to be penned by the composer and to be performed before a delighted audience. By contrast, Beethoven caught the dominant theme of his compositions in an embryonic form. He would jot it down on a scrap of paper or in his conversation book, but it would still be in need of further technical, left-hemispheric elaboration, amplification, and filling in of harmonic or contrapuntal detail. Thus Beethoven's act of creation proceeded in two stages while Mozart's was telescoped into one.

It is interesting to note at this point that gifted psychics, especially those engaged in telepathic or clairvoyant perception, (e.g. Ingo Swann, 1981), likewise tend to obtain the first impression of their target "in a flash." This has to be followed by several steps of secondary elaboration on a cognitive or analytic level, testifying to the involvement of the left side of the brain.

Reverting to the creative artist, Flaubert's prolonged struggle to achieve the matchless perfection of his prose has become legendary, while Picasso's studio must have been the theater of unremitting battles in which right versus left hemispheric influences were variously weighted in favor of greater originality and spontaneity versus meticulous craftsmanship and attention to detail.

We may also recall that borderline personalities or paranoiacs like Hitler or Jim Jones, dominated as they were by lower, limbic or reptilian centers and lacking the saving grace of higher cortical levels, were doomed to lose whatever truly creative or intellectual potentials with which they may have originally been endowed.

On the other hand, we have noted that mystics, psychics, mediums—their harmless counterparts—represent the right-hemispheric mentality in pure culture, as it were. Theirs is the voice of prophecy, divination, or poetry; they are the repositories of the wisdom of the body, of the past experience of the species. They walk through the pageant of history at their own risk but they do so without endangering the lives of their contemporaries. Their gaze is fixed on the past, even though they may try to predict the future. It is for the genius to try to change it.

Seen in this light, genius duplicates the creative thrust of evolution even though only the rare case of a viable mutation is likely to reach the top—and survive. And here again it may be this very contingency which fills the innovator with the joy of discovery and accomplishment: the reward for the hardships, the suffering, the existential anxiety with which he had to contend on his way. Yet the existential joy of being a genius has apparently escaped the attention of most investigators. "Why do you labor so hard, O Leonardo?" asked Leonardo in his diary. But his zest for living has been recorded by some of his contemporaries. Goethe's poetry and Mozart's music knew all about it. Lusty *joi de vivre* has imbued some of Shakespeare's sonnets. Even Beethoven penned an *Ode to Joy* in his Ninth Symphony, while Nietzsche recorded his "highs" on the venom of the tarantula—or the spirochete—in some of his ecstatic lines in *Zarathustra*. Whether the balance of existential "highs" versus existential anxiety comes out in genius' favor in the end, only genius can tell.

The Cult of Education Versus the Cult of Illiteracy

We have seen that prior to the recent rediscovery and reaffirmation of the virtues of the right side of the brain, the left hemisphere had exercised undisputed sway over our mental life. It was the dominant hemisphere in more than one sense of the word. Education was in effect left hemispheric education. It was the time-tested instrument for the transmission and processing of information, of cultural values as well as of specialized skills in literate societies, the principal vehicle of the spoken and written word. Indeed, there can be no doubt that the cultivation of learning and intellectual pursuits had proved their positive survival value over countless generations. This is why education has become one of the cherished goals of every group aspiring for self-improvement and for the better things of life. It is still so regarded in the developing countries of our day, presumably because they do not as yet have enough of it. But we have also seen that in the western world there is a growing disenchantment with learning and scholarship, particularly with some of the most celebrated scientific and technological accomplishments of the left hemisphere. The hero of the past age has been the culture-hero, the manipulator of symbols, the master of the written word: Prometheus, Thoth, Zoroaster, Hermes Trismegistus, Quetzalcoatl. But in the West he is now being displaced by the hero of the counterculture: the mystic, the consciousness-raiser, the drug enthusiast.

The trend is not new. Jean-Jacques Rousseau, himself a culture hero of sorts, was the first to raise doubts about the merits of the intellect, and pleaded for the return to nature, to the innocence of the child, to the virtues of the "noble savage." Nietzsche's re-evaluation of all values pointed in the same direction. The philosopher Ludwig Klages, one of his followers, specifically stressed the adversary relationship between the intellect (*Geist*), and the soul (*Seele*), the representative of *homo natura*, of a holistic mode of existence. He pitted intuition and instinct against analytic reason. The Spanish philosopher and novelist Miguel de Unamuno described the same polarity in dramatic terms: "Reason annihilates, and imagination completes, integrates or totalizes; reason by itself alone, kills, and it is imagination that gives life" (1956, p. 25).

We have seen in an earlier chapter that the distortions and anti-intellectual excesses of such a philosophy have culminated in Hitler's right hemispheric raptures and ravings. Modern and postmodern spokesmen of the counterculture, or progressive education, express the same sentiments in a lower key. They indict traditional education for being mainly concerned with dispensing information, insisting on classroom drill, on reinforcing left hemispheric values, authority, and superego demands, but stifling the emotional needs, the spontaneity and creativity of the child. Champions of the new (or not so new) wave like A.S. Neill of Summerhill fame (1960) or Ivan Illich (1971, 1976) of Guernavaca, Mexico, are pleading for the release of youth from the drudgery of rote learning in conventional schools, from the dreary hours chained to the school bench where they are taught what they don't want to learn. Neill, Illich, and their followers want to shift the emphasis to "incidental learning:" to the ways the infant picks up his or her mother tongue, including grammar and syntax, without even trying, and develops "coping skills" through interacting with the environment during apprenticeship to life itself.

Paradoxically, the most vocal spokesmen for a "children's liberation movement" were themselves well past the *Sturm und Drang* of adolescence. Ivan Illich, a maverick Catholic priest, founder of a "university without walls" in Guernavaca, published his revolutionary volume *Deschooling Society* well in middle age. The Scottish schoolmaster A.S. Neill launched his celebrated experiment in progressive education and student government in *Summerhill* (1960), England, when he was in his late thirties. He was a friend of Wilhelm Reich, had close affinities with Herbert Marcuse, and leaned heavily on early Freudian concepts.

Still, the personal histories of both Illich and Neill show that they themselves never lost the spirit of rebellion against authority, conformity, and sexual repression which may have been the bane of their formative years. We are told that Neill had learning difficulties while in secondary school. He obviously spoke from his own experience when he stated that most of the schoolwork that adolescents do is simply a waste of time: "It robs youth of its right to play and play and play" (p. 27). He quotes Nijinsky's failure to pass his school exams in St. Petersburg and notes: "We do not know how much creation is killed in the classroom with its emphasis on learning."

Ashley Montague, the noted anthropologist, declared himself an avowed Summerhillian (1970). He saw the greatest virtue of Neill's experiment in his emphasis on love and freedom for the child. His most serious objection to traditional education is that "for the most part (it) succeeds in achieving the frustration of the individual's uniqueness and creativity" (p. 51). Paul Goodman (1970), the social critic, strikes a similar chord. He notes in the same volume that "the greatest waste of ability occurs because a playful, hunting, sexy, dreaming, combative, passionate, artistic, manipulative, destructive, jealous, magnanimous, selfish and disinterested animal is continuously thwarted by social organization, perhaps especially by schooling." It will be noted that Ivan Illich's clarion call for the *Deschooling of Society* is animated by the same spirit of social criticism. Yet it should also be recalled that long before Neill or Illich, another venerable rebel, Mark Twain, called education "an organized fight of the grownups against the youth."

But I submit that after more than five decades of controversy the battle lines should be drawn between the right and the left hemisphere, rather than along generational boundaries. The issue cannot be resolved in the arena of social or political partisanships, but by making due allowance for the basics of our mental organization. Specifically, two fundamental facts have to be borne in mind (1) Originally, the child is an essentially right hemispheric creature, or at least one that has not as yet come under the sway of the dominant left hemisphere, as ordained by our essentially left hemispheric society; (2) As the preschool child moves into adolescence and adulthood, the developing cleavage between two contrasting personality types—the dextraverts versus the sinistraverts—becomes gradually discernible.

It is this cleavage to which our schools should adjust, instead of imposing a uniform, prefabricated curriculum on all comers. The fact is that the cleavage goes hand in hand with the propensity of typical dextraverts for enlisting their talents for an essentially pragmatic, science, technology, or mathematically oriented syllabus, while sinistraverts are drawn towards the humanities, the arts, letters, music, dance, and sports activities, or use their flair for social relationships, for the trades, or service-related jobs. Clearly, this is an area in which a new approach to psychological aptitude-testing can make a valuable contribution; it should develop tests distinguishing between dextraverts and sinistraverts.

TOWARDS A NEW BI-HEMISPHERIC CURRICULUM

Once this is understood, the deck is cleared for designing a curriculum tailor-made for the two principal classes or personality-types of students. Such a curriculum will avoid coercing pupils into a mold that runs counter to their innate endowments, in which they cannot perform well and in which they are bound to be bored, frustrated, and to become ultimately rebellious. It will reduce conflict in the classroom, "battle fatigue" among teachers, and make students more willing to learn—according to their right or left hemispheric predilections. In the worst case, it will replace artificial, school-grown illiteracy with elective, unadulterated, sinistravert illiteracy. It will also give the youngsters a chance to recover from their battle fatigue and to pick up their three R's at a later time.

Those more gifted, or falling between the two personality types, should, of course, be given the opportunity to extend their curriculum beyond their special area of interest and to develop as yet dormant potentials. Yet those wanting to "drop out" should be given the chance to switch to vocational training. It is true that society has an interest in producing well-rounded personalities, ambiverts, even geniuses, equally competent in left as well as right hemispheric fields of endeavor. But society has certainly no interest in producing—and financing—academic failures, social misfits, and rebels who lack the wherewithal to benefit from standard left hemispheric education. They are those whose only alternatives would be delinquency, drugs, or escape into the never-never land of esoteric right hemispheric cults or imported pseudoreligions.

It is interesting to note that academic failure, passive or active defiance of authority, depersonalized sex, and the drug culture tend to run together. They form a syndrome in which the fiasco of the left hemisphere is compounded by regression to sterile self-absorption and escape into right hemispheric reveries and fantasy life. More often than not, the use of psychedelic drugs leads to a vicious cycle in which society's attempts at restoring left hemispheric dominance are being thwarted by pharmacological means. By trial and error, the would-be truant from life hits upon the drug best suited to reduce or deaden the activities of the more highly differentiated (and therefore more vulnerable) cortical areas of the left, versus the less highly differentiated, and therefore less vulnerable, cortical areas of the right side of the brain.

The point is illustrated by Michael Rossman's (1970) enthusiastic approval of Neill's Summerhill experiment in the same volume: "America's young," he writes, "are learning to undo the crippling effect of the Authority Complex through a many-levelled system of education that, on a large scale, resembles Neill's experiment in freedom" (p. 143). It includes "varieties of psychedelic experience" but also the deliberate option to "think proudly of themselves as *freaks*—a term reflected in the acid motto: *'Freak Freely!'"* (*sic!*) And he goes on to say, "to freak freely is to fully let out, to fully live in the energies repressed by our society. All the media of alternative education in America now partake in this process of young people learning to love the beauty of their dark selves."

Evidently, few will endorse Rossman's prescription as a remedy for the malaise of American youth. But his is merely an extreme statement of views also expressed by Wilhelm Reich, Fritz Perls, Herbert Marcuse, Ivan Illich, A.S. Neill, Charles Reich (1970) or Theodore Roszak (1972), and other "neo Dionysian" critics of our time. The malaise is there for everyone to see. Yet if Karl Marx has called religion the "opiate of the people," opium (or psychedelic drugs) are certainly no remedy for the ills of either Marxist or capitalist society. The ills call for constructive social action, including judicious educational reforms dictated, among other considerations, by the rationale proposed here. As hinted in earlier chapters, they include sympathetic understanding, guidance and cultivation of the child's right hemispheric creative potentials, while at the same time avoiding premature coercive pressures to reinforce the still prevailing trend towards one-sided left hemispheric dominance.

But the new dispensation also calls for such novel educational approaches as those proposed by Budzynski (1976), F.X. Barron (1969), E.P.Torrance (1963), S.I. Parnes (1967), Howard Gardner (1979), G.A.Castillo (1974), and many others. In case of need, Budzynski's "twilight learning" and diverse forms of psychotherapy and group psychotherapy, existential or otherwise, guided by the rationale proposed here, may be called upon to help release blocked creative potentials and to restore a more harmonious balance between the two hemispheres. Music therapy, poetry therapy, the "healing dance" of the !Kung of the Kalahari desert, or "drawing on the right side of the brain" (Betty Edwards 1980) belong in the same category. So does Akhton Ahsen's (1977) eidetic psychotherapy, seeking to circumvent left hemispheric interference with an essentially right hemispheric use of imagery and its intuitive evaluation by therapist and patient.

Another means of largely right brained communication as a therapeutic resource was discovered by millions of cat and dog lovers and owners of other pets, not by experts in mental health. They derive a considerable degree of emotional gratification from companionship with their pets. It involves communication—from one right hemisphere to another, as it were—which is usually blocked by man's and woman's prevailing left hemispheric routine. "Pet-therapy" along these lines is a hitherto neglected remedial resource and in need of further study and development.

Clearly, attempts along these lines have advanced little beyond trial and error. But they are part of man's determination to take his destiny into his own hands, to stop the degradation of his physical environment, to improve the genetic pool of the species through genetic engineering, and to open up new frontiers of cosmic exploration. Yet I submit that a methodical educational approach aimed at reconciling our psychological and neurobiological dichotomies is of at least equal importance for our very survival as *homo sapiens*. The question is whether the "knowledge" of "man—and woman— the *knower*" can indeed be harnessed in the best interests of the individual and his society.

18

LATERALIZATION AND THE FALL OF MAN

Neuropsychologists, from A.R. Luria (1973), Roger Sperry (1969), Norman Geschwind (1978), or Jerre Levy (1974), have stressed the biological survival value of the duplication of the hemispheres, of both their symmetries and asymmetries; of their sharing as well as division of labor. The adaptive cultural advantage of their cooperation and of the lateralization of functions is equally important. We have seen that the two can learn to operate either in concert or in sequential, alternating or relay patterns. It is an ability best illustrated by the virtuosity of the pianist or violinist. But it is by no means confined to the genius or performing artist. This is borne out by countless examples of what I described as the existential shift, associated with a corresponding shift from right to left hemispheric dominance, and vice versa.

251

THE MERITS OF SHIFTING GEARS AND LINGUISTIC PLURALISM

It should be noted, however, that such shifting of gears does not necessarily involve the switch from the three R's to the three I's, or even to higher existential modes of functioning. On a more elementary level, it may merely amount to a fine-tuned shift of directional impulses involving what is described as conjugate lateral eye movements. In a preceding chapter I quoted opthalmologist Arthur Linksz's observation that Jewish children receiving concurrent Hebrew and English instruction at an early age learn to shift gears from right to left oriented eye movements as a daily routine.

He argues that as a result they develop a special knack "for looking at things from both sides." It is a facility that may well spill over to a certain dialectical turn of mind and outlook on the world. In the extreme case, it may be conducive to Rothenberg's Janusian thinking. This, incidentally, is a doubtful blessing since it may prevent a Talmudically inclined Hamlet from taking decisive action. But it may also have had a hand in provoking the world's ambivalent, if not frankly hostile, response to the *So-Called Jewish Spirit* (Ehrenwald, 1936).

We have to realize, however, that this is by no means an exclusively Jewish specialty. An early bilingual or polyglot upbringing in a multicultural setting, e.g. of children in Irish, Dutch, Polish, French Canadian, or Hungarian families, or in mixed metropolitan neighborhoods, may likewise contribute to the ease of shifting gears from one side of the brain—or at least from one set of linguistic programs—to the other. The same is true for training in Latin, in various branches of higher mathematics, trigonometry and Euclidian versus diverse non-Euclidian geometries, or diverse computer languages, or for the psychiatrist's recurrent exposure to the many and varied worlds experienced by his patients. It may also pay dividends in the education of Japanese, Chinese, or Arabic students mastering both their idiomatic and Western script. A more recent as yet unpublished study by Edward Moss, a psychologist at the State University of New York at Purchase involving bilingual and multilingual subjects, points in the same direction.

Interesting Japanese studies, recently reviewed by F.L. Benderly (1981), have compared neurological aspects of the Japanese *kana* versus the *kanji* system of writing; the former is phonetic, the latter idiographic. They found that the two rival systems are processed in the right, versus the left, side of the brain respectively. In the same review, Benderly reports observations of a group of Hopi Indian children. They suggest that when Hopi children are speaking their native tongue, the right hemisphere seems to be activated, and vice versa. However, the case is complicated by the finding that, by and large, "socially subordinate individuals show a greater right hemispheric involvement than socially dominant individuals"—which may or may not include Hopi children.

On the other hand, Martin Albert and Lorain Obler (1978), of the Boston Veterans' Administration Center, have found that Yiddish-English bilinguals exhibit a generally better balance between the two sides of the brain, thus tending to support Dr. Linksz' observations. The same authors also suggest that "knowledge of multiple languages has anatomical consequences." The studies of Wallace E. Lambert and his associates at McGill University (1976) make the same point. They found that bilingual education confers greater flexibility and faster cognitive development in Canadian children brought up in bilingual French-English cultural settings. But we have also learned from B.L.Whorf, Sapir, and other students of comparative linguistics that language has a profound influence upon a person's perception of reality, behavior, and outlook on the world. This is particularly true for Jews brought up in bilingual and bicultural traditions. To be more specific, we have to realize that the early bookish training of the"people of the book" may have been conducive to a precocious lateralization of the three R's—to something like a *lateralisatio praecox*.

It is a cultural conditioning that goes back thousands of years, and though we have no reason to believe that competence in the three R's can be transmitted by genes, we know that Jewish scholarship has been highly regarded by Jews throughout history: so much so, that for countless generations, young Talmudic scholars had a distinct reproductive advantage over other educationally inferior suitors. Jewish brides—or rather their parents—all over the Diaspora and especially in the *shtetls* of Eastern Europe often preferred their daughters to marry penniless rabbinical students as against well-heeled moneylenders, merchants, or artisans.

The result was predictable: it brought about a selective breeding advantage, or "fitness," both for the group and for individuals brought up according to Linksz' specification. They were a breed fluent in bilingual reading and writing skills coupled with a facility for shifting readily from left to right or right to left hemispheric orientation, spurred by intellectual curiosity, a thirst for knowledge and a flair for Rothenberg's Janusian thinking (see Chapter 4). It was one of the fringe benefits of the mating game studied by the geneticist and social scientist. It will be noted that such a reproductive advantage of the literate versus the illiterate Jewish male is in stark contrast to the rule of celibacy imposed on the Catholic monk. It deprived generations of the intellectual elite of the Middle Ages of a chance to hand down their intellectual patrimony to their offspring.

Three Allegories of the Human Condition: The Tree of Knowledge and the Rise of the Left Hemisphere

Making the best of both the innate and the acquired potentials of the two cerebral hemispheres is undoubtedly one of man's crowning achievements. Still, he was apparently always dimly aware that the acquisition of insight, knowledge, and specialized skills was by no means an unmixed blessing. We have seen that the lateralization of functions had its formidable practical awards. It was instrumental in spawning a prodigious array of cultures and civilization on our planet. But we have also seen that Freud or Rousseau or Nietzsche were not the only thinkers to question their value for human happiness and comfort. Indeed, the question—and the questioning— goes back to the very dawn of man's intellectual awakening. It was brought into focus in several major allegories from the mythic past, above all in the intriguing narrative of Adam's and Eve's Fall from Grace in the Garden of Eden.

Much ingenuity has gone into unravelling the hidden symbolism of this story. Viewed from the psychoanalytic angle, its sexual connotation is unmistakable. It is a parable of the oedipal (and oral) crime, culminating in the forbidden "carnal knowledge" of man and woman, in open defiance and symbolic killing of the father. It is followed by the expulsion from paradise and the abiding feeling of guilt. Jewish tradition, as laid down in the Soncino Edition of the Pentateuch, stresses the deadly sin of reaching out for omniscience and putting mortals in a position of defying a Divine command. In a similar vein, the Catholic *Jerusalem Bible* emphasizes the sin of Pride, "the claim of complete moral independence by which man refuses to recognize his status as a 'created being'." "Knowledge," the commentary suggests, "is a privilege of God alone" (p. 17).

As far as knowledge in the biblical sense is concerned, the Oxford Dictionary describes it as a Hebraism which has been taken over by modern Western languages. It indicates perceiving by means of the senses, and ultimately by the mind. Translated into modern language, the serpent is the voice of cunning, of defiance, heresy, and Promethean rebellion against the father figure, a call to snatch not fire, but divine knowledge from the gods—even at the price of losing the paradisical state of childish innocence.

Early Christian Gnosticism, as it emerges from the Gnostic Gospels found in Nag Hammadi (Elaine Pagels, 1981), had an altogether different conception of "knowledge," one wholly purged of intellectual left hemispheric presumptions, pride, and aspirations. Gnostic insight is purely spiritual, intuitive, if not mystical communion of the self with the Creator and with the world at large. "On this basis, (Gnostics), like artists...express their own insight—their own gnosis—by creating new myths, poems, rituals, dialogues with Christ, revelations, and accounts of their visions." (Pagels, p. 23). By the same token, the Gnostic Gospel of Mary Magdalene "depicts her not only as a visionary, but as an apostle who excels above all the rest. She is the 'woman who knew the All'"—in short, she was, from all we know, distinctly right hemispheric.

No wonder that orthodox left-hemispheric doctrine rejected such a position as outright heresy. Indeed, it held that with the loss of innocence and with the dawn of insight, men and women came face to face with sin, guilt, shame, and the realization of the inevitability of death. Even the mating of man and wife was turned into carnal "knowledge" with all its associated irrational taboos. Seen in this light, the narrative of Adam's Fall symbolizes man's separation from the animal kingdom where the lion could mount the lioness without carnal *knowledge* of his mate. At the same time, it is a scenario dramatizing a revolutionary shift from the original undifferentiated, right hemispheric mode of existence to a preponderantly left hemispheric orientation of "man—and woman—the knower," the master of the magic of the spoken and written word. Significantly, according to modern estimates, this shift coincides with what historians describe as the protoliterate period, that is, 3200–2850 B.C., the date when early Sumerian or Babylonian traditions were first transcribed into the script of the Old Testament. If this is true, the Jewish calendar dates the creation of the world roughly from the birth of the written word some time in the fourth millennium B.C. The fourth Evangelist was even more specific when he stated, "In the beginning was the *word*."

At the same time, the dismay expressed by the priestly authors of the original text seems to prefigure modern man's misgivings about this new revolutionary turn of events. Poets, churchpeople, prophets, and philosophers, from Hesiod or Ovid to Milton, Rousseau, Nietzsche, Ivan Illich, and A.S. Neill have ever since bemoaned the loss of the Golden Age and Adam and Eve's expulsion from paradise. It is a theme reverberating in the personal memories of every man and woman in all literate societies.

What, then, is the significance of this state of affairs?

I submit that the universality of the theme of the Golden Age and of the disparagement of knowledge is due to the intuitive insight into its awesome consequences. It is the burden of assuming personal identity, of going through the world with open eyes, aware of the need for existential choices at every step and of death at the end of the road. It is a predicament neither animals nor children in their paradisiac state are aware of. In the last analysis, it is the consequence of the dichotomy of our emerging right versus left hemispheric orientation—of lateralization and its discontents.

•　•　•

TWO FACES OF JESUS AND THE WHOLENESS OF MAN

The life and death of the historic Jesus is a second major allegory of the human condition. Its reverberations, after two millennia, are still with us, like the cosmic radiation in the wake of the Big Bang after the billions of years postulated by the astronomers. Jesus of Nazareth, as he emerges from the studies of such modern historians as Hans Küng, Schillenbeekxs, Michael Grant (1977) and others, reflects the dual nature of man like other more-than-life-size figures in the annals of civilization. According to Grant, the dominant theme of Jesus' teaching was the coming of the Kingdom of God. It was a utopia in which man would regain his original state of goodness and innocence. This is why he declared: "unless you turn around and become like children you will never enter the Kingdom of God" (*Matthew*, 18:3). It is a realm "independent of spatial and temporal relationships...implicitly indwelling in the hearts of men and women in a spiritual fashion" (Grant, p. 21). No wonder that the Pharisees, the Doctors of Law, the Scribes, scoffed at his words. They were too right hemispheric for their taste. Instead of putting forward his teachings in scholarly texts, Jesus spoke in metaphors and parables. Bible scholars counted 65 of them in the four Gospels. The Dutch theologian Schillenbeekxs talks about the dual nature of Christ in terms of a Christology from *below* versus *above*. By the same token, it would be just as fitting to supplement his thesis with a Christology from the *left* versus the *right* hemisphere.

A further indication of Jesus' prevailing right hemispheric orientation is his apodictic certainty of being the mouthpiece of the Lord—of what Julian Jaynes called the hallucinatory voices of the gods—his conviction of having to fulfill an ancient prophecy. The power of healing, of exorcising demons, were added features of his Messianic syndrome. They remained part of the same syndrome among his followers and disciples up to our day.

But one of the most striking signs of Christ's intuitive gifts is his hitherto little understood claim of being at once the *Son of God* and the *Son of Man*. Viewed in the present context, it is a poignant expression of his wavering between his left-hemispheric, earthly, secular identity, ready to give unto Caesar what is Caesar's, and his higher, right-hemispheric aspirations driving him with irresistable force to his commitment to the Kingdom of God.

Still, in the end, Jesus opted unequivocally for the existential shift to the right hemisphere and to essentially right-hemispheric values: for childlike innocence, for nonviolence, for the hope of arresting aggression by turning the other cheek, that is, by a gesture of surrender to the enemy, anticipating by two millennia a recipe written by the ethologists of our day. It is a recipe which, according to modern opinion, may be detrimental to the individual but adaptive for the group. If this is true, it would, in effect, furnish a new ethological rationale for the story of Christ's Passion on the cross. At the same time, his claim of being the son of Man seems to be an allusion to his this-worldly, left hemispheric commitments and to bring him back to his family roots in the land of his forefathers. This is how for many he has become the paragon of the wholeness of man. Not surprisingly, Nietzsche, the champion of the Dionysian aspects of the right hemisphere, saw in Christ the representative of the slave-morality and abject surrender to the dominance of the left side of the brain.

But it is not by coincidence that the doctrine—or allegory—of the two faces of Christ seems to be a perfect fit to the longstanding existential dilemma of ordinary men and women in the Christian orbit. Ever since the waning of the Middle Ages, the Christian faithful felt committed to religious teachings which were incompatible with the growing body of scientific findings. He or she had to live with the deepening schism between faith and unyielding and stubborn facts of worldly life.

As a general rule their response consisted of recurrent existential shifts from the demands of workaday life to prayer and worship in church or synagogue. Yet it stands to reason that for a sensitive spirit the transition from one world to the other was fraught with anxiety. For others, however, it had apparently become part of a well-ordered, disciplined, god-fearing routine: a mode of existence which replaced the stresses of recurrent existential shifts with a safe, bi-hemispheric, de-problematized, *co-existentialist* position. It may well be that such a position holds the key to the good life for the faithful believer, Christian, Jewish, Moslem or otherwise.

•   •   •

PLATO'S TWO HORSES AND THE MYSTERIOUS CHARIOTEER

Plato's celebrated fable of the Charioteer and his two winged horses is another grand allegory dramatizing the condition of Western man. This is how I retold it in the closing chapter of an earlier book (1978): The white horse on the right of the Charioteer represents the noble side of the soul: the dark horse on the left symbolizes man's savage instinctual drives, his animal nature. It stands for what Freud labelled as the id, while the Charioteer, and his precarious control over the two horses, represented the virtually powerless ego.

But I also proposed a new reading of both Plato's and Freud's metaphors. The two winged horses, I suggested, stand for the left and the right hemispheres locked in a ceaseless struggle with the raw, untrammelled forces dwelling in man's primitive phylogenetically oldest neural centers, in what neuroanatomists and their popularizers dubbed the reptilian brain.

This reading of Plato's fable leads to another question: if the two horses stand for the two cerebral hemispheres with their difference in cognitive styles, goals, motivational patterns, and behavioral repertoire, who is the mysterious Charioteer? Who holds the reins? Who is the ultimate decision maker? Who sets the destination of the ride or, to drop the metaphor, who or what is it that bestows on the operations of the brain—on its computerized circuitry, electronic feedback loops, or Pribram's holographic wave patterns—the element of freedom suggested by Plato's Charioteer or by the exploits of genius? In what way, if any, is the genius able to transcend his innate programming, to make the best of his genes and to preside over the seemingly random existential shifts from one level of functioning or from one cerebral hemisphere to another? How is genius able to draw on the innate resources of the two hemispheres and to shift gears automatically from one side to the other according to the demands of the task on hand, to orchestrate the diverse parts and hierarchical levels of the brain, creating beauty, harmony, novelty, or intended dissonance—even absurdity—in the process? The question gains added poignancy when we realize that the shifts seem to duplicate in the individual case the random occurrence of creative innovation in the fits and starts of the evolutionary process itself.

The answer to the question admittedly leads to the very limits of scientific inquiry. Materialists or logical positivists may dispute its very presumption of freedom. They may insist that the genius, like everyone else, is a product of his circumstances and of his age. They may point to the pitiful lack of control over his life, shared with ordinary mortals. Prometheus, the mythical prototype of genius, has dared to rebel against the laws laid down by Zeus, the father of the gods. But in the end, he too was chained to the rock of physical and psychic determinism pervading organic and inorganic nature alike.

But a closer look at the artistic or scientific exploits of genius reveals a distinct, though admittedly narrow, range of freedom in which he is able to make the break from the rigid, causal-reductive frame of reference of classical, pre-relativistic, pre-probabilistic physics. Einstein, tied down to his desk at the dreary patent office in Bern, was able to give free rein to the kaleidoscopic play of associations and bi-sociations crowding his mind, to make them fall in line with his Janusian thinking, to select this or that field equation, tensor calculus, or differential geometry as the intellectual tools with which to construct his special and general theory of relativity.

Beethoven, misanthropic, colicky, deaf, and tongue-tied, solved his problems of harmony or counterpoint in his unprecedented trailblazing way, and he chose the third *Leonore Overture* to replace earlier versions in accordance with his own inspired musical judgment. Yet while, mathematically speaking, this was at best a binary or triadic decision, Beethoven picked from a universe of virtually unlimited choices the decision to replace the traditional form of the *minuet* with the *scherzo* in his early symphonies. Evidently, the work of genius is predicated on a ceaseless procession of minor and major decision makings of this order. Leonardo da Vinci, a displaced person arriving in Milan from Florence, stooped to penning a self-demeaning job application with the Duke Lodovico di Sforza. But when he was pouring over mechanical drawings in his diaries, or when caught in the frenzy of painting his *Last Supper* in the church of Santa Maria delle Grazie, he was the sovereign ruler over his right- or left- or bi-hemispheric output. Then and there, he indeed succeeded in making the best of his genes and imparting the highest leverage effect on his ideas. He moved beyond the limitations of his genetic programming.

There is an inexhaustible record of creativity and human resourcefulness along these lines. They seem to duplicate the fits and starts, the trials and errors that went into the making of the evolutionary process itself. But they have injected a brand new ingredient: the element of meaning, purpose, and planning into the mix. Writers, wordsmiths, and think-smiths, the makers of shapes, images, or musical sounds, the inventors of novel technologies, social or religious reformers and innovators have always been engaged in major, minor, or minuscule acts of decision making. They included doing and undoing, learning and relearning, guessing and second-guessing, weeding and pruning, phrasing and rephrasing, typing and retyping—that is, skills which neither the legendary typewriter monkeys of evolutionary theory, nor the most sophisticated electronic office machines nor even nature herself has contrived to use.

Indeed, unless we are prepared to grant to these skills honorary citizenship in the natural domain, they would have to be relegated to something like extraterritorial status in the overall scheme of things.

This, then, is the area of freedom, serving as the privileged proving ground for genius and, by indirection, for the genius of the human species. Genius, under favorable circumstances, is capable of transcending his genetic or cultural programming and early childhood conditioning. He is able to make the best of his innate endowments and capable of defying determinism in the process. At the same time, the minor epidemics of genius in ancient Greece, in the Renaissance, in the Low Countries of the 17th century—and the star-studded record of contemporary science on both sides of the Atlantic—show that his example can become contagious: it can mobilize latent potential for peak performance and peak experiences in his or her contemporaries as well as in generations to come.

Thus genius is poised at the growing edge of civilization. Where he goes, his generation and succeeding generations are likely to go. This is why the genius is both the most precious and potentially the most dangerous representative of our species, as illustrated by Christ and Anti-Christ, by Jesus and Adolf Hitler, brought into focus in the preceding pages. Genius dramatizes both the beckoning rewards and the awesome perils of the human enterprise. He exemplifies man's struggle to assert human freedom in the face of all odds piled up against him.

EPILOGUE

Strictly speaking, this is not so much an epilogue as a postscript with a few afterthoughts attempting to pick up loose ends and to answer questions which may have occurred to the reader of this book.

Question 1: You said your book is not meant to be a home-study course in how to become a genius. Still, can you give a hint as to how the two cerebral hemispheres can be made to work together in harmony and not at odds with one another? And how to activate one or the other side of the brain at a given moment?

Answer: We have to stimulate and train *ambidextrous* sensory-motor skills from early childhood. This includes manual dexterities, gymnastic exercises, playing of musical instruments, etc. I am ambidextrous and can write and draw with both hands "in unison," designing symmetrical patterns when the spirit moves me. This helped to coordinate my right and left hemispheric directional impulses when engaged in a given task. But I noted that the same facility tends to spill over to assorted psychomotor derivatives of the directional impulse, e.g., attention, value judgment, point of view, etc.

The following palindrome is a "magic" formula that can be used as an exercise in reading backward and foreward, as well as upward and downward. It perhaps goes back to kabalist tradition.

S A T O R
A R E P O
T E N E T
O P E R A
R O T A S

Familiar examples of (unintentional) right hemispheric exercises are Zen *Koans*: diverse forms of the relaxation response, meditation, various yoga practices, self-hypnosis, auto-suggestion, etc. They all tend to activate the right and to deactivate the left side of the brain. The same is true for sequences of nonsense syllables and such homemade mantras as:

No sense, no thought, no words,
No goals, no ends, no hurts,
No will, no task, no mind,
No rules, no laws, no bind...

It may be no coincidence that modern scientists like to lace their strictly left-hemispheric discourse with quotes or epigraphs taken from *Alice in Wonderland*. Einstein amused himself and his friends by composing humorous jingles—and relaxed by playing classical music on his violin. Young Wolfgang Amadeus Mozart's scatological letters to his girl cousin show the same existential contrast to the beauty of his musical output.

Other means of shifting the emphasis from left to right hemispheric functioning were mentioned in the text. However, this is only one-half of the story. Right-hemispheric exercises should alternate with pendulum swings to the left side. This can be accomplished by deliberate shifts to specific left-hemispheric intellectual tasks, e.g., counting backwards from 100 by sevens, doing the multiplication table in one's head from 3 times 3 to problems of increasing complexity. Alternatively, the subject may turn to specific problem-solving related to his ordinary workaday concerns. This should, in turn, be followed by reverting to the "no-mind" exercises described above. On the other side of the coin are exercises of the type proposed by Douglas Hofstadter (1982) in the columns of the Scientific American.

You will note that these recommended double-barreled procedures merely duplicate the traditional cleavage between work and play, between discipline and laissez-faire, between the Yin and Yang of the East. The difference is that here, for once, the procedure is based on a specific rationale outlined here, though it is still in need of experimental verification, e.g., by the EEG, evoked potentials or "metabolic mapping" of the brain.

Question 2: How do you arrive at the diagnosis of the two contrasting right-versus left-hemispheric personality types proposed in the book?

Answer: Some of the physiological indicators were mentioned in Chapters 1 and 14. They range from monitoring the alpha activity of the two sides of the brain to the "dichotic listening test," the tachystoscopic stimulation of the right and left halves respectively of a subject's visual field, to observing his "conjugate lateral eye movements" and ascertaining whether he is a "right looker" or a "left looker." Other tests along these lines are still in the exploratory stage.

However, the available test results are by no means concordant or "covariant." They deal with diverse specialized functions and subfunctions of the right or left hemisphere respectively and have not as yet provided a coherent picture. In the end, it is the global, essentially right hemispheric gestalt perception (or "face" recognition) controlled by the right side of the brain which tips the balance for diagnosing the dextravert versus the sinistravert personality type.

Question 3: How does the thesis of a person's right- versus left-hemispheric orientation, and of a potential conflict between the two sides of the brain, affect the basic Freudian dichotomy between the Ego and the Id, between conscious and unconscious, between reason and instinctual drive?

Answer: Psychoanalytic theory is based on the cleavage between the individual's innate biological endowments, his instinctual drives, and his higher intellectual and cultural aspirations. Neurotic conflict arises from the tension between the two or three spheres of the mental apparatus: Ego, Superego, and Id. It is a conflict between cortical and subcortical structures operating in the vertical. Post-Freudian and neo-Freudian analysts focus more specifically on ego psychology, on cultural aspects, on "object relationship theory," on new dimensions of the "self." They have added a wealth of clinical and speculative detail to the original Freudian scheme without, however, detracting from the crucial importance of instinctual drives emanating from the Id in the working of the human mind. Classical Freudian theory still hews to an essentially vertical scheme of psychodynamics.

The present approach does not try to belittle the part played by instinctual drives and their derivatives in our mental makeup. But it shifts the emphasis to a play of forces *in the horizontal:* to the dynamic interaction of the two cerebral hemispheres. At the same time it suggests that a significant part of neurotic conflict arises from the tension and tug of war between the two sides of the brain.

It will be noted that such a reading of neurotic conflict is amenable to direct clinical observation—even potential experimental verification (e.g., EEG or biochemical studies)—and does away with the need to invoke metaphorical interventions from a disembodied Freudian Ego, Superego, or Id. Nevertheless, or rather for this reason, the approach proposed here remains committed to an essentially biological theory of mental functioning. Nor is it an entirely "Id-less" scheme of psychodynamics. It makes due allowance for the part played by subcortial—visceral, limbic or hypothalamic—structures as the potential sites of the Freudian Id.

Question 4: What, then, is the nature of the forces involved in the interaction of the two hemispheres?

Answer: The forces involved fall wholly in the domain of the neurophysiologist. They are amenable to direct clinical observation or laboratory studies and no longer need to invoke the semi-mythological concepts of early Freudian metapsychology. A typical example is the directional motor impulse emanating from well-defined areas in the left or right brain cortex and/or lower centers. Excitation of these areas leads to motor action in the contralateral arm or leg, with a thrusting movement in the opposite direction. Its sensory, afferent counterpart are visual, auditory, or cutaneous perceptions or hallucinatory experiences which are likewise projected to the opposite side. Sensory-motor transactions of this order are, of course, the primary concern of the neurologist.

I have emphasized however, that we have to make allowance for a graded scale of psychological equivalents or *derivatives* of these elementary sensory-motor transactions. In Chapter 1, I described a patient suffering from left-sided hemiplegia who produced an extreme rightward rotation of his head and neck, with his torso and eyes likewise turning away, or *"averting,"* from the paralyzed left side of his body. This initial poststroke phase of "a-version" was followed by hallucinatory changes of his body image, coupled with a violent rejection and repudiation of the left side. It had assumed a literally *"sinister"* quality.

A similar but purely emotional symbolic repudiation of the left side was illustrated by another patient who developed a hysterical hemianesthesia, or numbness, of the left side of his body, a "hemi-depersonalization," as it were. At the same time, he perceived the ugly, sinister, unesthetic side as the *"Jewish"* aspect of his personality. There are numerous cases in the psychiatric literature and in my files that show psychological equivalents or derivatives of sensory-motor directional impulses or projections of the same order. They are closely akin to the derivatives, emotional equivalents, metaphorical expressions, and "sublimations" of instinctual drives postulated by psychoanalytic theory whose origins can likewise be traced to disturbances in the projective areas of the right or left brain cortex, rather than to mythical constructs of Freudian metapsychology.

Nevertheless, here again the part played by diverse lower, subcortical centers that are usually associated with the Freudian Id, is still in need of further exploration and conceptual clarification. So is the part played by the "Self"—or Plato's mysterious Charioteer.

Question 5: What is the origin of the consciousness of self and of the executive functions of the Ego in the scheme of mental organization outlined here?

Answer: The contributions of Eccles and Popper (1976), and of a long line of their neurological forerunners, offers significant clues on this score. They suggest that in the right hander both Ego functions are controlled by the left hemisphere, as are most motor and sensory aspects of speech. By contrast, the operations of the right hemisphere are largely automatic, preconscious, or unconscious. (Some authors claim that the left hemisphere operates in the way of a digital computer, while the right hemisphere functions more like an analog computer.)

There is also a wealth of evidence pointing to the tendency of one hemisphere engaged in a given specialized task to inhibit the operations of its opposite number. Much of the time, they may work together in perfect harmony and "concert."

Question 6: What is the relationship of the mutually inhibiting functions of the two sides of the brain to the Freudian concept of repression?

Answer: It will be recalled that the operations of the right hemisphere are essentially nonverbal or preverbal. This is why they largely coincide with the sphere of the Freudian preconscious. Some of them remain just as remote from conscious awareness and control as the wholly automatic machinery of autonomic, or visceral, regulatory functions. The difference between them and the Freudian unconscious lies in the fact that they have always been confined to the unconscious sphere and were never "repressed" or

pushed below the threshold by a censor or superego bent on warding off the intrusion into the Ego of repudiated material. If this is
true, the left hemisphere emerges as the fount and origin of the
Kohutian self—of the monitoring functions of the Ego—as well as
of some of the censoring, repressing, or inhibiting functions of the
Freudian Superego. It is the repository of learned or culturally
acquired behavioral attitudes and value judgments which, in the
course of their gradual automatization, have passed under the control of the right hemisphere.

By the same token, sublimation appears as an automatic or
semiautomatic transformation of directional or projective impulses
into their derivatives. It results from a shift of movement into
message and meaning: from projected pain or pleasure, badness or
goodness, into affective experience, value judgments, or belief system. In the process, right hemispheric sensory input may be "sublimated" into the realm of the divine, the sacred, the beatific; or it
may be subject to *reverse sublimation,* to profanization or demoni-
zation, as it were. Either way, right hemispheric experience all too
often evokes the feeling of the sinister, the uncanny, the ego-alien.
It is then subjected to what I described as *cultural,* in contrast to the
familiar Freudian represssion.

Question 7: What are the therapeutic implications of the present
study?

Answer: There is a richly orchestrated scale of concerted, synergistic actions, alternating with tension, conflict, and reciprocal
inhibition between the two hemispheres. Yet apart from a few
clinical vignettes described in Chapter 15, their relevance to psychotherapy is still a matter of speculation. What seems to be clear at
this point is that detached, left-brained intellectual dextraverts are
the best subjects for classical analysis. They are geared to verbal
communication, "cognitive," or insight therapy, to logical
exposition. By contrast, right-brained sinistraverts, artistic and
intuitive types, are more suggestible, more readily hypnotizable and
less easily influenced by mere intellectual reasoning than their left-
brained counterparts. The right-hemispheric patient is more

attuned to the therapist's tone of voice, to his overall demeanor, to prosódy, to his "vibes" than to the intellectual content of his message. He is more comfortable in the dialogue of one right hemisphere with the other. In either case, free association is specifically geared to both the patient's and therapist's right hemisphere.

In other respects, my approach merely provides a new rationale for doing what therapists have been doing all along. Freudian psychoanalysis tries to engage both horizontal and vertical levels of personality at the same time. Alfred Adler's *Individual Psychology* frankly denies the reality of the unconscious or the Id; it is an "Idless" psychoanalysis, as it were, and confines its interest and therapeutic interventions to the Ego level. By contrast, the biologically oriented psychiatrist stresses the limitations of the psychological approach and relies chiefly on psychotropic drugs with specific subcortical structures as his target. He aims his magic bullet at the Freudian Id.

In effect, Freud himself had realized early that the Id could not be reached or altered by the psychoanalyst. He had to be satisfied to deal with the derivatives of instinctual drives or with the defenses against them. In the end he avoided treating psychotic patients and predicted that one day drugs would be added to the psychiatrist's armamentarium. This is where such modern psychoactive agents as Thorazine, Haldol, or Lithium come into the picture.

Thus the foremost therapeutic tool available to the post-Freudian psychotherapists remains a judicious blend of communications, verbal and nonverbal, geared to the patient's right or left hemisphere respectively, depending on his or her prevailing sinistravert or dextravert orientation. Still, such interventions as hypnosis, cathartic release, focusing on dreams, twilight learning, or transcendental meditation specially attuned to the right side of the brain, are the best means by which to filter its message down to deeper levels of the patient's personality.

Question 8: What is the relevance of the argument presented here to parapsychology, that is, to the exploration of such psychic or "psi" phenomena as telepathy, clairvoyance, psychokinesis, or precognition?

Answer: I pointed out in earlier publications (1978) that one of the functions of the left hemisphere, aided by the reticular formation, by various perceptual defenses, "lateral inhibition" and synaptic barriers, is to protect the individual from excessive stimulation from sensory overload and, last but not least, from the influx into consciousness of biologically indifferent or undesirable psi phenomena. This is why "extrasensory" stimuli that happen to pass through the organism's protective screen—known as the Bergsonian filter—carry the hallmarks of their processing in the *right hemisphere*. Except in relatively rare dramatic incidents, they are preconscious or remain altogether below the threshold of consciousness. By the same token, they are not amenable to deliberate volition. This is particularly true for Rhine's card-calling or dice-throwing tests, that is, laboratory incidents which can be described as *flaw*-determined because they are due to haphazard *flaws* in the operation of the Bergsonian filter. By contrast, the major, spontaneous, dramatic incidents are usually *need*-determined

Other clues pointing to the right-hemispheric origin of the phenomena is the ambiguous, symbolic, metaphorical, dreamlike quality of telepathic impressions. They show characteristic distortions in space and time and an affinity to Freud's primary process functioning. As a result, they may strike the observer as absurd, irrational, ego-alien. He may experience them as nefarious, sinister, demonic, or else as awe-inspiring, holy, divine. Unfortunately, they also tend to defy all attempts to provide statistical proof of their occurrence to meet the requirements of the scientific method and the criteria of the typical left-hemispheric skeptic.

It is wholly consistent with this state of affairs that psi phenomena—and the very attempts at their scientific investigation—should elicit highly emotional hostile reactions from otherwise fair-minded, left-hemispheric critics. Evidently, the very possibility of their occurrence is incompatible with the skeptic's tacitly implied scientific paradigms, cognitive style, internal model and, indeed, with the whole mode of existence prevailing in our dominant left-hemispheric civilization. It is apparently difficult to transcend a preprogrammed, built-in bias towards either left- or right-hemispheric belief systems and value judgments. But to do just that is perhaps one of man's most noble objectives. It has been the business of genius and of the culture hero of all ages. Indeed, it may be the "genius" of *homo sapiens*.

Question 9: What are the implications of the functional differences between the two hemispheres on the current controversy about IQ and IQ tests?

Answer: The question raises an issue that is likely to lead to a new approach to testing. It will stop throwing apples and oranges into the same basket: it will try to separate presumptively right-versus left-hemispheric responses in the light of modern split-brain research. We have to realize that the traditional approach had been chiefly concerned with testing the three R's while neglecting, or paying less attention to, the three I's, or to such specific functions of the right hemisphere as modulation of voice, emotional gesturing, face recognition, musical abilities, and the like. On the other hand, most projective tests do not "measure" intelligence and are difficult to express in quantifiable terms. Wholly "culture free" tests are still subject to controversy.

I noted that, as a result, Beethoven would have probably barely scored above the moronic level, while a competent left-hemispheric pedant, or a member of the Mensa Society, would be certified as a card-carrying genius. If this is true, the explosive issue of cultural bias in mental testing (against Blacks and other minorities) simply boils down to the modern bias in favor of the left hemisphere and left-hemispheric values, and the corresponding flouting of its junior partner. We must recall that most IQ tests were developed by essentially left-hemispheric psychologists, geared to gauging the left-hemispheric potentials of their subjects. In so doing, they were bound to gloss over or ignore the contributions of such right-hemispheric cortical areas as were recently mapped out by Elliott Ross and his associates. Traditional methods extol cognitive, verbal abilities, propositional language, linear reasoning. They are still laboring to devise quantifiable approaches to right-hemispheric performance. They duly note the semantic meaning of an eloquent preacher's perorations, but turn a deaf ear to the musical cadences of his delivery. Cicero extolled oratory as the perpetual motion of the soul, but they would only register the vibrations of Martin Luther King's voice box. The dean of a divinity school so inclined would flunk Jesus Christ out of the Seminary—for poor academic performance.

The problem is how to overcome *hemispheric* rather than *cultural* bias. The problem is how to develop and streamline two complementary batteries of tests, one geared to the left, the other geared to the right-cerebral hemisphere, so as to do justice to the three R's as well as to the three I's, regardless of ethnic background or formal education.

Question 10: Are there gender differences in brain function, and is it because of such presumed differences that you did not include a female genius in your book?

Answer: The recurrent feminist complaint about ignoring or belittling women's share in major left-hemispheric contributions to our culture merely reflects the still existing tendency to belittle the creative potential of the right side of the brain. Yet "female" intuition and sensitiveness may just as well be considered superior to "male" rationality or mechanical ability. Genius is neither the result of male versus female structural organization or programming, nor is it due to a particular mix of this or that group of gonadic hormones. The brain itself is not a machine with fixed anatomical or functional characteristics. Whatever differences have been observed are due to a greater facility in women for a flexible integration of brain functions. In effect, it goes hand-in-hand with a lesser tendency to lateralization and an increased ability for recovery after organic injury to the brain. Such a difference actually points to a relatively higher native endowment of the right hemisphere in women which should, in turn, increase their potential for geniushood. I noted, however, that genius is not just a function of anatomical structure, genes, or hormonal influences. Genius is process. It is correlated to the individual's life cycle, to the Spenglerian life cycle of the culture in which he or she is immersed, to the values held by society, here and now. Above all, it is dependent on what the individual—Husserl's "transcendental ego," Eccles and Popper's "Self," or Plato's Charioteer—is doing or determined to do with his or her native endowment. Given the opportunity and the approval of society, there should no longer be any question of a male or female *genie*—or genius—emerging from the mix in the alchemist's bottle; nor will the pantheon of culture heroes be separated into two wings: *Reserved for Men,* or *Reserved for Women only*.

Question 11: Are your "three I's"-the triad of Intuition, Inspiration and Imagination-more than appealing figures of speech or attention getting devices? Are they based on demonstrable component parts of the creative process?

Answer: The question would call for a summary of the whole book. Put in a capsule: Intuition is the automatic processing by the right hemisphere of information needed for rapid problem solving and closure of gestalten, visual, auditory or otherwise. Inspiration is a traditional term pointing to the extermal, ego-alien, even divine origin of creative expression and self-expression that has been initiated by right hemispheric programming in the first place. Imagination—scientific, artistic or otherwise—points to the visual origin of a vast body of imagery or preconceptual, preverbal, metaphorical thinking that goes into the making of scientific discoveries or diverse works of art or flashes of intuitive insight. Their reality is borne out by both clinical and documentary evidence, case studies and a growing number of experimental findings.

Question 12: You have talked a lot about the workshop of genius, about his or her modus operandi. But where does genius come from? What is its origin?

Answer: Genius often seems to come out of the blue; Leonardo, Shakespeare, Einstein. Some geniuses appear to alight from a family tree in generational order: the Bachs, the Della Robbias, the Breughels. Others emerge as a seemingly disconnected cluster of individuals congregating in the Golden age of Greece, Islam, of Biblical prophecy, of the Renaissance or seventeenth-century Dutch painting. They may be beneficiaries of favorable external socio-economic circumstances, of the silent incubation of talent lying dormant in their forebears or of laboriously acquired special skills of gifted parents.

But it is needless to say that mere combination or recombination of genes, of chromosomal matter, right or left hemispheric, is not enough. Leonardo's father was a notary of sterling character, his mother a servant girl, Kepler the offspring of a drunk innkeeper, Faraday the son of a village blacksmith, Freud the child of a struggling small business man, while his mother's only claim to fame was her "Golden Sigi."

How then did the masterpieces of Leonardo, the Shakespeare plays, the Maxwell-Faraday equations or Goedel's theorems come about? Genius is apparently capable of changing or picking the set of cards which was handed down to him by his genetic endowment, to assume control of the uncontrollable. By hook or crook, the genius alters or breaks the rules, or invents new rules, of the game he or she was programmed to play. This is how the genius becomes the trickster, the anarchist, the religious reformer, the creator of new shapes or sounds or paradigms, a culture hero, a composer or de-composer—Prometheus, Moses, Beethoven, Marx, Schoenberg, Picasso. This is how he or she becomes the mover and shaker of the evolutionary process, the antidote to Monod's chance and necessity, the charioteer of Plato's vehicle of randomness in the universe. It is this irreducible man made principle of order, duplicating the structure of crystals, of the double helix, of the rhythm of the seasons, or the pulse of the heart which makes the individual the master of the purportedly programmed and strictly deterministic evolutionary process. It is a mastery which in a diluted form is perhaps the essence of the genius of the human race itself.

Question 13:   Are you aware of recent criticism levelled against some popularizers of the results of split-brain research?

Answer: Yes, and I have raised my own objections in the preceding pages. The fact is that results derived from pathological cases, from speech disorders or trouble with the three R's do not warrant such claims. But would-be critics should realize that my material is derived from the lives and labors of exceptional, creative personalities, not from clinical case histories, laboratory tests or animal experiments. In order to get the whole picture of the human condition you must be prepared to shift attention from the deficits of split-brain patients to the accomplishments of "global minds" reviewed in the foregoing chapters, and to extrapolate from genius to more pedestrian areas of human affairs. Surely, it would be wrong to sensationalize such an extended approach. But neither should lingering left-hemispheric bias against the three I's, stultify the quest for the unity of our bi-hemispheric mental organization.

REFERENCES

Ahesen, A. *Psycheye*. New York: Brandon House, 1977.

Anderson, E. *The Letters of Mozart and his Family*. London: Macmillan, 1938.

Arieti, S. *Creativity, The Magic Synthesis*. New York: Basic Books, 1976.

Arnheim, R. *The Genesis of a Painting, Picasso's Guernica*. Berkeley: University of California Press, 1962.

Bakan, P. *Hypnotizability, Laterality of the Eye Movements and Functional Brain Asymmetry, Perceptual and Motor Skills*. 1969, *28*, 927–932.

Bakan, P. The Eyes Have It. *Psychology Today*, 1971, *4*, 64–69.

Balmary, M. *Psychoanalyzing Psychoanalysis*. Baltimore: Johns Hopkins University Press, 1981.

Barr, A. H. *Picasso, Fifty Years of his Art*. New York: Museum of Modern Art, 1946.

Barron, F. X. *Creative Person and Creative Process*. New York: Holt, Rinehart & Winston, 1969.

Baumer, F. *Kafka*. New York: R. Ungar, 1971.

Benderly, B. L. The Multilingual Mind. *Psychology Today*, 1981, *3*, 9–12.

Berger, J. *The Success and Failure of Picasso*. New York: Pantheon Books, 1965.

Bertram, E. *Nietzsche: Versuch einer Mythologie.* Berlin: Bondi Verlag, 1918.

Biancolli, L. *The Mozart Handbook.* Cleveland and New York: World Publishing Co., 1954.

Binion, R. Hitler's Concept of Lebensraum, the Psychological Basis. *History of Childhood Quarterly,* 187–215. (1973)

Boeck, W., & Sabartes, J. *Pablo Picasso.* New York: Abrams, 1957.

Bogen, J. F., & Bogen, G. M. The Other Side of the Brain III. *The Corpus Callosum and Creativity Bulletin,* Los Angeles: Neurological Society, 1969, *34,* 191–220, 73–105.

Brain, R. *Some Reflections of Genius and other Essays.* Philadelphia and Montreal: Lippincott, 1960.

Brod, M. *Franz Kafka, A Biography.* New York: Schocken Books, 1970.

Broughton, R. S. Psi and the Two Halves of the Brain. *Journal of the Society for Psychical Research,* New York, *48,* 765, 133–147, 1978.

Buckminister-Fuller, R. *Synergetics,* New York: Macmillan, 1975.

Budzynski, T. H. Brain Lateralization and Biofeedback. In *Proceedings of an International Conference on Brain and Mind in Parapsychology, Parapsychology Foundation,* New York: 1979.

Bullock, A. *Hitler: A Study in Tyranny.* New York: Harper Torch Books, 1962.

Burland, C. H. *The Gods of Mexico.* London: Eyre & Spottiswood, 1967.

Bychowski, G. *Diktatoren.* Munchen: Szezeny Verlag, 1965.

Camus, A. *The Myth of Sisyphus.* New York: Knopf, 1964.

Cassirer, E. *The Myth of the State.* New Haven: Yale University Press, 1946.

Castillo, G. A. *Left-handed Teaching: Lessons in Affective Education.* New York: Praeger, 1974.

Clark, K. On the Relation of Leonardo's Science and His Art. In Phillipson (Ed.), *Leonardo da Vinci.* New York: Braziller, 1966.

Clark, R. W. *Einstein, The Life and Times.* New York: Avon Books, 1971.

Clark, R. W. *Freud.* New York: Doubleday, 1980.

Collis, M. *Cortes and Montezuma.* New York: Avon Books, 1954.

Crick, F. H. C. Thinking about the Brain. In *The Brain.* Scientific American Books, 1979.

Critchley, M. Observations on Anosodiaphoria. *Encephale 46,* 540–546.

Critchley, M., & Henson, R. A. (Eds.). *Music and Brain.* Springfield, Ill.: London: Heineman & Thomas, 1977.

Davidson, E. *The Making of Adolf Hitler.* New York: Macmillan, 1977.

Diaz del Castillo, B. *The Discovery and Conquest of Mexico.* New York: Evergreen Books, 1956.

DiLeon, J. H. *Child Development*. New York: Brunner & Mazel, 1977.

Dimond, S. J., & Beaumont, J. G. Handedness and Hemispheric Function. In *Hemispheric Function in the Brain*. London: Elek Science, 1974.

Duke, J. Lateral Eye Movements Behavior. *Journal of General Psychiatry* 1968, *78*, 1, 189–196.

Duncan, D. D. *Picasso's Picassos*. New York: Harper & Rowe, 1962.

Eccles, J. *The Understanding of the Brain*. New York: McGraw Hill, 1977.

Eccles, J., & Popper, K. *The Self and Its Brain*. New York and London: Springer International, 1977.

Edwards, B. *Drawing on the Right Side of the Brain*. Los Angeles: S. J. Tarcher, 1980.

Ehrenwald, J. Anosognosie und Depersonalisation: Ein Beitrag zur Psychologie der linkseitigen Hemiplegie. *Nervenarzt 4*, 12, 45–48, (1931).

Ehrenwald, J. *Telepathy and Medical Psychology*. New York: W. W. Norton, 1948.

Ehrenwald, J. The Symbiotic Matrix of Paranoid Delusions and the Homosexual Alternative. *American Journal of Psychoanalysis 20*, 1, 49–65.

Ehrenwald, J. *Neurosis in the Family, A Study of Psychiatric Epidemiology*. New York: Harper & Row, 1963, chapter VIII.

Ehrenwald, J. The Visual Distortion Test, A Study in Experimental Psychiatry. *Psychiatric Quarterly*, July 1966, *40*.

Ehrenwald, J. *Psychotherapy: Myth and Method, An Integrative Approach*. New York: Grune & Stratton, 1966.

Ehrenwald, J. On the So-called Jewish Spirit. In *The Jews of Czechoslovakia*. The Society for the History of Jews from Czechoslovakia, New York, 1971, 455–468.

Ehrenwald, J. *The ESP Experience: A Psychiatric Validation*. New York: Basic Books, 1978.

Ehrenwald, J. Einstein Skeptical of ESP? Postcript to a correspondence. *Journal of Parapsychology*, 1978, *42*, 2, 137–142.

Einstein, A. *The World As I See It*. New York: Philosophical Library, 1934.

Einstein, A. Autobiographical Notes. In *Albert Einstein, Philosopher-Scientist*. Evanston, Ill.: Library of Living Philosophers, 1949.

Einstein, A. How I Created the Theory of Relativity. *Physics Today*, *35.8, pp. 45–47*, 1982.

Eisenbud, J. *Paranormal Foreknowledge*. New York: Human Sciences Press, 1981.

Eissler, K. *Goethe: A Psychoanalytic Interpretation*. Wayne University Press, 1961.

Eissler, K. *Leonardo da Vinci*. New York: International Universities Press, 1961.

Ellenberger, H. *The Discovery of the Unconscious*. New York: Basic Books, 1970.

Ellerman, C. P. Nietzsche's Madness; Tragic Wisdom. *Imago*, 1970, *27*, 338–357.

Eysenck, H. *Handbook of Abnormal Psychology*. New York: Basic Books, 1961.

Farrell, K. On Freud's Study of Leonardo. In Phillipson (Ed.), *Leonardo*. New York: Braziller, 1966.

Fisher, R. Visions, Hallucinations, Consciousness, Hemispheres, Symbols. *Journal of Altered States of Consciousness*, 1974, *1*, 2, 145–152.

French, A. P. The Story of General Relativity. In *Einstein, A Centenary Volume*. Cambridge: Harvard University Press, 1979.

Freud, S. *Die Traumdeutung*, in Gesammelte Schriften. Internat. Psychoanal. Verlag, Leipzig, 1900, Wien, Zurich.

Freud, S. Eine Kindheitserinnerung des Leonardo da Vinci. *Gesammelte Schriften IX*. Leipzig, Wien, Zurich: Internationaler Psychoanaltischer Verlag, 1910.

Freud, S. Das Ich und Das Es. *Gesammelte Schriften*. Leipzig, Wien, Zurich: Internationaler Psychoanalytischer Verlag, 1925.

Freud, S. *The Origins of Psychoanalysis*. New York: Basic Books, 1954.

Fromm, E. *Escape From Freedom*. New York: Rinehart Co., 1941.

Fromm, E. *The Forgotten Language*. New York: Grove Press, 1951.

Fromm, E. *Anatomy of Human Destructiveness*. New York, Chicago, San Francisco, 1973.

Galin, D. Implications for Psychiatry in Left and Right Cerebral Specialization. *Archives of General Psychiatry*, 1974, *31*, 552–583.

Galin, D., & Orinstein, R. Lateral Specialization of Cognitive Mode, An EEG Study. *Psychophysiology*, 1972, 412–418.

Gardner, H. *Artful Scribbles*. New York: Basic Books, 1980.

Garrett, E. *My Life as a Search for the Meaning of Mediumship*. London: Rider & Co., 1939.

Gazzaniga, M. S. *The Bisected Brain*. New York: Appleton Century Crofts, 1970.

Gazzaniga, M. S., & LeDoux, J. E. *The Integrated Mind*. New York: Plenum Press, 1978.

Gedo, J. E. Nietzsche and the Psychology of Genius. *Imago*, 1978, *35*, 1-2, 77–91.

Geschwind, N. The Anatomical Basis of Hemispheric Differentiation, In Diamond & Beaumont (Eds.), *Hemisphere Function in the Human*

Brain. London: Elek Science, 1978.

Gilot, F., & Lake, C. *Life with Picasso*. New York: Signet Books, NAL 1964.

Goodman, P. In *Summerhill*. New York: Hart Publishing Co., 1970.

Grant, M. *Jesus*. New York: Scribner, 1977.

Gur, R. C. & Gur, R. E. Handedness, Sex, and Eyedness as Moderating Variables in the Relation between Hypnotic Susceptibility and Functional Brain Asymmetry. *Journal of Abnormal Psychology*, 1974, *83*, p. 635–643.

Hadamar, J. *The Psychology of Invention in the Mathematical Field*. New York: Dover, 1945.

Hampden-Turner, C. *Maps of the Mind*. New York: Macmillan, 1981.

Haring, C. H. *The Spanish Empire in America*. New York: Harcourt Brace & World, 1963.

Hayman, R. *Franz Kafka*. New York: Oxford University Press, 1982.

Herren, J. (Ed.). *Neuropsychology of Left Handedness*. New York: Academic Press, 1980.

Hildesheimer, W. *Mozart*. New York: Frarrar, Straus & Giroux, 1982.

Hoffman, B. *Albert Einstein, Creator and Rebel*. New York: New American Library, 1972.

Hofstadter, D. R. *Godel, Escher, Bach*. New York: Basic Books, 1979.

Holton, G. *The Scientific Imagination: Case Studies*. Cambridge: Harvard University Press, 1978.

Hoppe, E. D. Split Brain and Psychoanalysis. In *Psychoanalytic Quarterly*, 1977, *46*, 220–244.

Illich, I. *Deschooling Society*. New York: Harper & Row, 1971.

Jaspers, K. *Nietzsche: Eine Einfuehrung*. Berlin, Leipzig: DeGruyter, 1936.

Jaynes, J. *The Origins of Consciousness in the Breakdown of the Bicameral Mind*. Boston: Houghton Mifflin, 1976.

Jones, E. *Freud*, Vol.I-III. New York: Basic Books, 1953.

Jung, C. G. *Psychologische Typen*. Zurich: Rascher Verlag, 1921.

Jung, C. G. *Memories, Dreams Reflections*. A. Jaffe (Ed.), New York: Pantheon Books, 1962.

Jung, C. G., & Pauli, W. *Naturerklaerung und Psyche*. Zurich: Rascher Verlag, 1952.

Kafka, F. *Dearest Father*. New York: Schocken Books, 1954.

Kaiser, H. Franz Kafka's Inferno. Eine Psychologische Deutung seiner Straf Phantasie, Vienna: Intern. PsychoanalVerlag, *Imago*, Feb. 1931.

Kanzer, M. Freud and his Literary Doubles. *Imago*, 1976, *33*, 3, 231–243.

Kaufmann, W. *Nietzsche*. Princeton: Princeton University Press, 1974.

Kemp, M. *Leonardo da Vinci*. Cambridge: Harvard University Press,

Koestler, A. *The Act of Creation.* New York: Macmillan, 1964.

Kris, E. *Psychoanalytic Exploration in Art.* New York: International Universities Press, 1952.

Kubie, L. *Neurotic Distortions of the Creative Process.* Kansas: Kansas University Press, 1958.

Lambert, W. E. The Effects of Billingualism, etc. Paper presented to the Conference on the Plattsburgh Campus of the State of N.Y., March 12-13, 1976.

Lange-Eichbaum, W. *Nietzsche: Krankheit und Wirkung.* Hamburg: Lattenbauer, 1946.

Langer, W. C. *The Mind of Adolf Hitler.* New York: Basic Books, 1972.

Laor, *Abrechnung mit dem Abendland.* Vienna, Sensen Verlag, 1962.

Levy, J. Psychological Implications of Bilateral Asymmetry. In Dimond & Beaumont (Eds.), *Hemisphere Functions in the Human Brain.* London: Elek Science, 1974.

Levy, J., & Gur, R. C. Individual Differences in Psychoneurological Organization. In Herren (Ed.), *Neuropsychology of Left Handedness.* New York: Academic Press, 1980.

Linksz, A. *On Writing, Reading and Dyslexia.* New York: Grune & Stratton, 1973.

Lippman, E. A. Theory and Practice in Schumann's Aesthetics. *Journal of the American Musicological Society,* 1969, *17,* 3, 310–345.

Loewenfeld, V., & Brittain, W.L. *Creative and Mental Growth.* New York: Macmillan, 1970.

Luria, A. R. *The Working Brain.* New York: Basic Books, 1973.

McCurdy, B. *The Notebooks of Leonardo da Vinci.* New York: Reynal & Hitchcock, 1939.

McGregor Burns, J. *The Vineyard of Liberty.* New York: Knopf, 1981.

McLean, P. D. On the Evolution of Three Mentalities. In Arieti & Chzanowski (Eds.), *New Dimensions in Psychiatry.* New York: J. Wiley, 1977.

McLuhan, M. *Understanding Media.* New York: McGraw Hill, Signet Books, 1964.

Madariaga, de S. *Hernan Cortes, Conqueror or Mexico.* Chicago: Regnery Co., 1955.

Malinowski, B. *Magic, Science and Religion.* New York: Doubleday Anchor Books, 1954.

Marek, G. R. *Beethoven: Biography of a Genius.* New York: Crowell, 1969.

Marinoni, A. In Reti (Ed.). *The Unknown Leonardo.* New York: McGraw Hill 1974.

Maser, W. *Hitler: Legend, Myth and Reality.* New York, San Francisco, London: Evanston, 1973.

Maslow, A. Presidential Address, *Boston New England and Psychological Association,* 1963.

Meccaci, L. *Brain and History.* New York: Brunner/Mazel, 1979.

Mills, J. *Six Years with God: Life Inside Reverend Jim Jones' Peoples' Temple.* New York: A & W Publishers, 1978.

Montague, A. In *Summerhill.* New York: Hart Publishing Co., 1970.

Muir, E. In R. Gray (Ed.). *Kafka, A collection of Critical Essays.* Englewood Cliffs, N.J.: Prentice Hall, 1969.

Naipaul, V. S. *Among the Believers.* New York: A. A. Knopf, 1981.

Neill, A. S. In *Summerhill.* New York: Hart Publishing Co., 1960.

Nietzsche, F. *Ecce Homo.* A. Messer (Ed.), Leipzig: Kroener Verlag, 1930.

Nietzsche, F. *Thus Spoke Zarathustra.* Leipzig: Kroener Verlag, 1930.

Nietzsche, F. *The Birth of Tragedy from the Spirit of Music.* Liepzig: Kroener Verlag, 1930.

Nietzsche, F. *The Will to Power.* Leipzig: Kroener Verlag, 1930.

Nietzsche, F. The Dawn of Day. In Kaufman (Ed.), *The Portable Nietzsche.* New York: Viking, 1954.

Obler, M. & Albert, M. The Bilingual Brain. In The Multilingual Mind. *Psychology Today,* 1981, 1978, 3.

Oppenheimer, R. J. On Albert Einstein. In French (Ed.), *Einstein, A centenary Volume.* Cambridge: Harvard University Press, 1979.

Ornstein, R. *The Psychology of Consciousness.* San Francisco: Freeman, 1972.

Pagels, E. *The Gnostic Gospel.* New York: Random House, 1979.

Pais, A. *Subtle is the Lord, The Science and the Life of Albert Einstein.* New York: Oxford University Press 1982.

Papini, G. *Visita a Picasso.* Firenze: Libro Nero, Vallecchi Editore, [Italy]. 1951.

Parnes, S. J. *Creative Behavior Workshop.* New York: Scribner's Sons, 1967.

Payne, R. *Leonardo.* New York: Doubleday, 1978.

Pedretti, C. *Leonardo: A Study in Chronology and Style.* Cambridge: Harvard University Press, 1972.

Penfield, W. *The Mystery of the Mind.* Princeton: Princeton University Press, 1975.

Penrose, R. *Picasso: His Life and Work.* New York: Harper & Row, 1958.

Piaget, J. *Six Psychological Studies.* New York: Vintage Books, 1968.

Podach, E. F. *The Madness of Nietzsche.* New York; Putnam, 1931.

Postman, N., & Weingarten, C. *Teaching as a Subversive Activity.* New York: Delta books, 1969.

Prescott, W. H. *History of the Conquest of Mexico.* New York: Modern Library, 1856.

Pribram, K. *Languages of the Brain.* Englewood Cliffs: Prentice Hall, 1971.

Pribram, K., & Gill, M. *Freud's Project Reassessed.* New York: Basic Books, 1976.

Progoff, L. *The Image of an Oracle.* New York: Helix Press, 1964.

Putnam, F. Traces of Eve's Faces. *Psychology Today, 16*(10), 88, October 1982.

Rank, O. *Der Kuenstler.* Wien: Imago Buecher, Internationaler Psychoanalytischer Verlag, 1912.

Rauschning, H. *Gesprache mit Hitler.* Zurich, 1940.

Reich, C. *The Greening of America.* New York: Bantam, 1970.

Reti, L. *The Unknown Leonardo.* New York: McGraw Hill, 1974.

Rhine, J. B. *Frontiers of the Mind.* London: Farber & Farber, 1938.

Richter, J. P. *The Literary Work of Leonardo da Vinci.* London: Oxford University Press, 1939.

Rosen, C. Rediscovering Haydn. In *New York Review of Books*, June 4, 1979, *26*, 10, 11.

Ross, E.D. Localization of Lesions in the Right Hemisphere Associated with Disorders of Affective Language. The Aprosodies. In A. Kertesz (Ed.), *Localization in Neuropsychology.* New York: Academic Press, 1981.

Ross, E.D., & Mesulam, M.M. Dominant Language Functions of the Right Hemisphere? Prosody and Emotional Gesturing. *Archives of Neurology*, 1979, *36*, 144–148.

Rossman, M. In *Summerhill.* New York: Hart Publishing Co., 1970.

Roszak, T. *Where the Wasteland Ends.* New York: Doubleday, 1972.

Rothenberg, A. Einstein's Creative Thinking and the General Theory of Relativity: A Documentary Report. *American Journal of Psychiatry*, 1979, *136*, 1. 38–43.

Rubin, W. *Picasso in Retrospect.* New York: Museum of Modern Art, 1980.

Sabartés, J. *Picasso, An Intimate Portrait.* Englewood Cliffs: Prentice Hall, 1948.

Santillana, G. Man Without Letters. In Phillipson (Ed.).*Leonardo da Vinci.* New York: Braziller, 1966.

Schenk, E. *Mozart: Eine Biographie.* Wien, Leipzig, Zurich: Amalthea

Verlag, 1955.

Schenk, L., & Bear, D. Multiple Personality and Related Dissociative Phenomena in Patients with Temporal Lobe Epilepsy. *American Journal of Psychiatry*, Oct. 10, 1981, *138*, 1311–1316.

Shapiro, M. Leonardo and Freud, An Art-Historical Study. *Journal of the History of Ideas*, 1956, *17*, 147–178.

Slochower, H. Franz Kafka, Pre-Fascist Exile. In *A Franz Kafka Miscellany*. New York: Twice a Year Press, 1940.

Snow, C.P. *The Two Cultures and the Scientific Revolution*. New York: Cambridge University Press, 1959.

Solomon, M. *Beethoven*. New York: Macmillan, 1977.

Soustelle, J. *The Daily Life of the Aztecs*. New York: Macmillan, 1962.

Speer, A. *Inside the Third Reich*. New York: Macmillan, 1970.

Sperry, R. Hemisphere Deconnection and Unity in Conscious Experiences. *American Psychologist*, 1968, *23*, 723–733.

Sperry, R. Some Effects of Disconnecting the Cerebral Hemispheres. *Science*, 1982, *217*, 1223–1225.

Stein, G. *Picasso*. Boston: Beacon Press, 1938, 1959.

Sterba, E. & Sterba, R. *Beethoven and his Nephew*. New York: Pantheon, 1954.

Stern, M. Freud's Scientific Personality. *Newsletter, New York Psychoanalytic Society and Institute*, February 1980, *17*(1), 1–2.

Stierlin, H. *Adolf Hitler: A Family Perspective*. New York: Psychohistory Press, 1976.

Sullivan, J.W.N. *Beethoven, His Spiritual Development*. New York: Vintage Books, Random House, 1960.

Sulloway, F. *Freud: Biologist of the Mind*. New York: Basic Books, 1979.

Toland, J. *Hitler*. New York: Doubleday, 1977.

Torrance, E.P. *Education and the Creative Potential*. Minneapolis: University of Minnesota Press, 1963.

Toynbee, A.J. *A Study of History*. Oxford University Press, 1947.

Trevor-Roper, H.R. *The Last Days of Hitler*. New York: Collier Books, 1968.

Unamuno, M. de. *Three Exemplary Novels*. A. del Rio (Ed.). New York: Grove Press, 1956.

Unger, M. *Beethoven's Handschrift*. Bonn: Beethoven Haus, 1926.

Vaillant, G.C. *The Aztecs of Mexico*. Harmondworth, England: Penguin Books, 1956.

Weinstein, E.A., & Kahn, R.L. *Denial of Illness, Symbolic and Physiological Aspects*. Springfield, IL: C. Thomas, 1956.

Wexler, B.E. Cerebral Laterality and Psychiatry. *American Journal of Psychiatry*, 1980, *137*(3), 279–291.

Young, J.F. *Programs of the Brain*. Oxford: Oxford University Press, Oxford, 1978.

Zaidel, E. *Vision Research*, *15*, 283, 1975.

GLOSSARY

ANOSOGNOSIA: Imperception of illness or existing defect, e.g. in leftsided hemiplegia.

APHASIA: Inability to speak or to comprehend the meaning of sentences, e.g. in lesions in Broca's or Wernicke's region.

BAESLE: Mozart's "little girl-cousin."

CORPUS CALLOSUM: A massive bundle of fibers connecting the two halves of the brain.

DERIVATIVES OF DIRECTIONAL IMPULSE: The transformation of movement into meaning, e.g. a-version versus in-clination; turning against, versus turning towards; *Ab-neigung* versus *Zu-neigung* in German.

DEXTRAVERSION: A person's prevailing tendency to left hemisphereic functioning. Not identical with handedness.

DIRECTIONAL IMPULSE: The projection of movement and perception onto the opposit (contra-lateral) side of the body.

DOCTRINAL COMPLIANCE: A person's tendency to comply with another person (experimenter's, therapist's, hypotist's or mentor's) emotionally charged wishes, expectations or doctrines.

DOPPELGANGER: One's double.

EXISTENTIAL SHIFT: The abrupt global reshuffling and reorganization of a person's psychological and physiological programming, including his or her behavioral repertoire. It may or may not include an associated shift of cerebral dominance as indicated by changes of electrical brain activity.

GENIUS: The optimal combination of innate right hemispheric and general native endowment with special culturally acquired and transmitted left hemispheric skills. They are fuelled by energies sublimated from lower centers and deployed to society's best advantage. The resulting product of genius is "poised at the growing edge of our civilization."

HOLOPHRENIC: A person with a closely knit, strictly logical though deviant system of thought, clinically not subject to deterioration.

IMAGINATION: Mental imagery evoked and adapted from the past, or the emergence of novel creative ideas from the unconscious.

INSPIRATION: An exalted or creative experience attributed to an external divine or transcendental source.

INTUITION: In the present context, the unconscious, automatic processing of information, usually attributed to the right cerebral hemisphere.

LATERALIZATION: Localization of a special mental function in one side of the brain.

PET-THERAPY: Using chiefly right hemispheric means of communication with household pets as a remedial resource, e.g. tone of voice, emotional gesturing, stroking or petting.

PHALLOPHAGIC: Cannibalizing the phallus.

PREPONDERANCE, HEMISPHERIC: A functional composite made up of derivatives from left or right hemispheric directional impulses.

PROSODY: The affective component of speech aided by emotional gesturing and its comprehension. It is localized in the right hemisphere and corresponds with left hemispheric language areas.

PSYCHIC: A person having or claiming to have such paranormal or psi experiences as telepathy, clairvoyance, precognition or psychokinesis.

REPTILIAN BRAIN: According to Sherrington and MacLean, one of the most primitive subcortical structures of the brain.

SECONDARY PERSONALITIES: The dramatic emergence, staging and acting out of one or more closely knit systems of thoughts, memories and phantasies with the loss of a strictly personalized sense of self.

SINISTRAVERSION: A person's tendency to right hemispheric functioning, e.g. intuitively; not identical with handedness.

INDEX

Abdul Latif, 165, 169, 170
Aberration, 73-81
Achilles, 182
Adam and Eve, 254
Adler, Alfred, 39, 77, 270
Agamemnon, 182
aggression, 258
Ahsen, Akhton, 250
Albert, Martin, 253
alchemy, 99
alienation, 15
alpha rhythms, 9, 10
Amenda, 28
analysis, Freudian, 73
anasognosia, 12, 13
anatomists, 5
Anderson, Emily, 108
Andreas-Salome, Lou, 49
anorexia nervosa, 158, 229
Anti-Christ, the, 42, 261
Apollonian mode, 16
Apollonian spirit, 41, 235

aprosodiac patients, 9
aprosodias, 15
Aragon, Luigi of, Cardinal, 66
Archbishop of Salzburg, the, 106
archetypes, Jungian, 49
Archimedes, 55, 114
Arieti, Silvano, 4, 30, 35, 224
Aristotle, 16
Arnheim, Rudolf, 138
art therapy, 99
Auschwitz, 197
Aztec society, 181, 182, 183

Babi Yar, 198
Bach, Johann Sebastian, 69, 111, 243, 274
Baesle Briefe, the, 108, 111, 205
Bakan, Paul, 209, 212
Balmary, Marie, 71
Barbarosa, 218
Barcelona, 135

290

Barr, Alfred, 142
Barron, F. X., 249
Baucis, 98
Bauer, Felice, 150
Baumer, Frany, 154
Bear, David, 67
Beaumont, J. G., 237
Beauvoir, Simone de, 161
Beethoven, Karl, 26, 28, 30
Beethoven, Ludwig van, 4, 23-35,
    36, 57, 59, 60, 106, 131, 146,
    161, 205, 209, 243, 244, 260,
    272, 275
  antihero, the, 30
  creativity of, 30
  "family romance" of, 24
Beethoven, Maria Magdalena, 27,
    28
Benderly, F. L., 253
Berenson, Bernard, 54
Berger, John, 141, 146
Bergsonian filter, 128, 271
Berlin, Isaiah, 216
Bertram, E., 44, 50
Biancolli, L., 103
bi-Hemispheric, 213-224
Binion, R., 191
Blake, William, 157, 171
Bleuler, Eugen, 94
Blond Beast, the, 39, 195
body image, 167
  of Leonardo, 63
  of Picasso, 136, 138
Boeck, W., 142
Bogen, J. E. and E. M., 7, 8, 10,
    237
Bohr, Niels, 120, 126
Bollingen Tower, 100
Boltzmann, Ludwig, 73
Bonaparte, Marie, 75
borderline patients, 77
Borgia, Cesare, 66
Born, Max, 120
Brain, Russel, 4, 5
Brancusi, Constantin, 208

Brandes, Georg, 44
Braun, Eva, 197
Breuer, Joseph, 73, 76
Breughels, the, 274
Broca, Paul, 6, 7, 9, 197
Brod, Max, 145, 150, 155, 156
Bronowski, Jacob, 223
Broughton, R. S., 10, 11
Brown-Skinned Savage, the, 98
Buchenwald, 198
Budzynski, T. H., 10, 212, 238,
    249
Bullock, 193
"buostrophedon," 181
Burckhardt, Jakob, 45
Busch, Wilhelm, 122
Bychowski, Gustav, 191, 198

Caesar, Julius, 177, 189
Camus, Albert, 47, 154
Carlyle, Thomas, 172
Carnegie, Dale, 179
Carroll, Lewis, 122
Carter, James Earl, 206
Carter, Jimmy, 206, 222
Casanova, 178
Case of Bridie Murphy, The, 236
Cassirer, Ernst, 53
Castillo, G. A., 249
Castle, The, 153
Cezanne, Paul, 141
Charcot, Jean-Marie, 72
Charles V, 175, 186
Chomsky, Noam, 207, 208
Christianity, 207
Christology, 257
Churchill, Winston, 189, 190
clairvoyance, 10, 157, 168
Clark, Kenneth, 54, 59, 60
Clark, R. W., 122
Claudius, Emperor of Rome, 119,
    233
closure, 218, 219
cocaine, 72

Cockney, rhyming slang of, 109
cognitive style, 15, 18-19, 42, 114, 118, 172
collective unconscious, 78, 100
Collis, Maurice, 182
complementary relationships, 232
computers, 5
conflict, interpersonal, 232
Confucian philosophies, 207
conjugate lateral eye movements, 252
conscious, the, 85
consciousness, altered states of, 33, 42
contamination, 50
conversion hysteria, 11
Copernicus, 88
corpus callosum, 8
Cortes, Hernan 174-180, 189, 191, 235
  and Catalina, 178
  and Dona Juana, 179
  and Dona Maria, 179
counterculture, 69, 77
Crab Canon, the, 111
Creativity
  and Beethoven, 30
  and IQ, 34
  and homosexuality, 68
  and neuroticism, 4
Crick, F. H. C., 5
culturally repressed, return of the, 84
Curie, Madame Marie, 161
Curran, Pearl, 132, 171
cybernetics, 74

Dadaists, 143, 222
Dali, Salvador, 143, 155
Dante, 207, 234
Darwin, Charles, 72, 72, 88
Daumier, Honore, 148
Davidson, E., 192

da Vinci, Leonardo, 4, 24, 54-64, 71, 80, 114, 125, 133, 144, 161, 205, 207, 209, 220, 223, 234, 260, 274, 275
de Chirico, Girogio, 145, 213
Delacroix, Eugene, 137
Della Robbia family, 274
de Lovella, Pietro, 55
depersonalization, 15, 167
derealization, 15
Descartes, Rene, 207
d'Este, Isabella, 55
De Sohagun, 176
developmental stages, reptilian, paleo-mammalian, and neomammalian, 14
dextraversion, 111, 203-215, 270
Diaz, Bernal, 176
dichotic listening, 211
Di Leo, J. H., 208
Dimond, S. J., 237
Dionysian mode, 16
Dionysian spirit, 41, 53
Dionysians, the new, 222
directional impulses, 113, 212, 213, 239, 252, 263, 267, 269
directional motor impulse, 267
DNA code, 242
doctrinal compliance, 147, 163
Don Giovanni, 71
Don Juan, 178
Dostoevsky, Fyodor, 150
double within, the, 82
dreams, 74
DuBois-Reymond, Emil, 72
Dubos, Rene, 223
Duke, J., 211
Duncan, D. D., 142
Duran, Diego, 176
Durer, Albrecht, 144
dyslexia, 32

Eccles, Sir John, 5, 51, 82, 89, 188, 240, 268

Eddy, Mary Baker, 172
Edison, Thomas Alva, 5, 37, 119
education
    cult of, 244
    progressive, 246
Edwards, Betty, 250
ego, the, 74, 86, 268
    defenses of, 239
    tyranny of, 77
Ehrenwald, Jan, 13, 47, 69, 169, 209, 252
eidetic psychotherapy, 250
Einstein, Albert, 5, 37, 57, 114, 117-130, 161, 205, 209, 260, 274
    and Ilga K., 127,128
Eisenbud, Jule, 146
Eissler, Kurt, 4, 54, 55, 63, 66, 68, 224, 232, 234
electrical activity, 211
El Greco, D., 138
Ellenberger, Henri, 39, 41
Ellerman, C. P., 45
Erikson, Erik, 24
Ernst, Max, 147
Eros, 39
Esalen, 232
Escher, M. C., 111
ESP, 163
    experience, 80
    performance, 10
Euclid, 55, 119
    geometries of, 220
Eusepius, 141
Existential Shift, 30-32, 59, 74, 76, 78, 86, 122, 132, 142, 165, 217, 228, 231, 236, 251
    collective, 221
Eysenck, Hans, 4, 204

Fall of Man, the, 241, 251-261
Faraday, Michael, 124
Farrel, Brian, 63

Fauves, the, 132
Fenichel, Otto, 76
Ferenczi, Sandor, 11, 80
Fisher, Roland, 9
Flaubert, Gustave, 243
Flavoraid, 199
Fliess, Wilhelm, 73, 74, 75, 80, 84, 93, 97
Florestan, 141
Foerster-Nietzsche, Elizabeth, 39
Francis I, King of France, 66
Franco, Generalissimo, 137
Frazer, James J., 97
free association, 76, 77, 270
French, A. P., 120
Freud, Sigmund, 4, 16, 24, 35, 39, 54, 55, 61, 63, 67, 70-87, 88, 145, 217, 232, 240, 254, 259, 270
    and Jung, 93-97
    Project of, 74, 75, 99, 114, 149
    Schreber case of, 152
Fromm, Erich, 78, 153, 191
frontal lobes, 51
Fuller, Buckminster, 6
fundamentalist beliefs, 218
Futurists, 143

Galin, David, 9, 10, 212, 237, 238
Galton, Francis, 4
Ganser's syndrome, 234
Gardner, Howard, 34, 138, 208, 249
Garrett, Mrs. Eileen, 132, 157, 161-173, 205, 235, 236
Gast, 43
Gaugin, Paul, 141
Gazzaniga, M., 7, 34
Gedo, J. E., 37
general paresis, 44, 50
Genesis, 3

genius, 244, 261, 273
  and artists, 4
  "evil", 3
  exploits of, 259
  and madness, 4
  neurological approaches to, 5-6
  and obsessive personality, 4
  process, 210, 273
George, Stefan, 36
Geschwind, N., 34, 251
gestalt quality, 218
Ghandi, Mahatma, 24, 190
Gianni Schicchi, 148
"Gift of the Tarantula", 45, 48
Gill, Morton, 74
Gilot, Francoise, 136, 143
Giovanni the mirrormaker, 67
Gnosticism, 255
Goebbels, Joseph, 197
Goedel, Kurt, 111, 275
Goethe, Johann, 36, 114, 198,
  207, 234, 235, 244
Goethe prize, the, 81
Golden Age, theme of, 256
golden scarab, the, 91
Gondola Song, 44
Goodman, Paul, 247
Gospel of Mary Magdalene, 255
Goya, Francisco, 137
Grant, Michael, 257
Greeks, the ancient, 3
Guernica, 137
Gur, R. C. and R. E., 211, 212

Hadamard, J, 123
Haeckel, Ernst, 72
hallucinations, 9, 15
Hamlet, 232, 233, 252
  case as model of neurosis, 234
Hampden-Turner, Charles, 6, 175
Hannibal, 177
Haring, C. H., 176
hashish, 52

Hayman, Ronald, 159
"healing dance," the, 250
hearing cap, the, 83
Hebrew, instruction of, 252
Hegel, Georg W. F., 40
Heiligenstadt Testament, 32, 33
Heisenberg, Werner, 120, 127
  principle of indeterminacy, of,
  120, 126
Helmholtz, Hermann von, 72
hemianesthesia, 11
hemi-depersonalization, 267
hemispheric dichotomy, 125
hemispheric dominance, 59, 82
  right, 32
hemispheric integration therapy,
  227
hemispheric preponderance, 59
Herder, Johann G., 216
Hesiod, 256
Hesse, Hermann, 37, 119, 154
heureka experience, the, 75, 114
Hilbert, David, 119
Hildesheimer, W., 106, 108, 113
history, cycle in, 216
Hitler, Adolf, 191, 192-198, 205,
  206, 218, 222, 235, 244
  and Stalin, 199
  testament of, 194
Hoffmann, Banesh, 122
Hofstadter, Douglas, 111, 223, 265
Hogarth, William, 148
Holocaust, the, 123
holographic model, 218
holography, 74
Holophrenics, 171, 173, 219
Holton, Gerald, 121, 123, 124, 204
homosexuality, 62, 68, 199, 231
Hook, Robert, 126
Hopi Indian, 253
hubris, 51
Hugo, Victor, 4
Huitzilopochtli, 187
humanities, the, 247

Hunger Artist, A, 153, 157, 158
Huxley, Aldous, 207
Huxley, T. H., 72
hypnosis, 76
hysterical conversion symptoms, 11

id, the, 86, 259
Illich, Ivan, 246, 249, 256
Illiteracy, Cult of, 244
Imagination, 18, 171
Immortal Beloved, 27
imperfectionist programs, 221
In the Penal Colony, 152
Inca society, 181
"incidental learning", 246
Individuation, 99
information theory, 74
Ingres, J. A. D., 141
Inspiration, 18, 171
intelligence, 5
interhemispheric conflict, 225, 231
intuition, 18, 39, 171, 193, 195, 243
    Einstein's, 119, 120
    "female", 209
    Freud's, 73-81
    Nietzsche's, 38
Ixtilxochitl, 176

Jackson, Hughlings, 72
James, William, 204
Japanese, systems of writing of, 253
Jaspers, Karl, 43
Jaynes, Julian, 18, 53, 82, 163, 166, 174, 175, 181, 200, 207
Jerusalem Bible, the, 255
Jesus, 172, 241, 257-258
Jewish question, the, 195
Joan of Arc, 161, 173
Jones, Ernest, 76, 96, 97, 232

Jones, Reverend Jim, 188, 191, 199, 205, 206, 218, 222, 235, 244
Jordan, Pascual, 128
Joyce, James, 143
Judeo-Christian tradition, the, 241
Jung, Carl Gustav, 16, 70, 78, 80, 84, 88-101, 114, 119, 146, 158, 173, 204, 207, 222, 235
    and omnipotence, 94
    "personal myth" of, 89, 100

Kafka, Franz, 143, 145, 149-160, 171, 213
    intuitive flashes of, 158
Kafka, Herman, 149-, 152
Kaiser, Helmuth, 151
kana, 253
Kandinsky, Wassily, 147
kanji, 253
Kant, Immanuel, 40
Kanzer, Mark, 80, 81
Kaufman, W., 40, 43, 49, 52
Kemp, Martin, 54
Khomeini, Ayatolla, 191, 206
Kierkegaard, Soren, 155
Kingdom of God, 257
Klages, Ludwig, 245
Klee, Paul, 147, 208
Kleist, Heinrich von, 152
knowledge, 255
    "carnal" knowledge, 256
Koestler, Arthur, 166, 123, 124
Kretchmer, Ernst, 204
Kris, Ernest, 4, 34
Kubie, Lawrence, 4
Kuhn, Thomas, 147
Kundalini Yoga, 207
Kung, Hans, 257
Kung of the Kalahari, 250

labor, hemisphere's division of, 15, 237

Lacan, Jacques, 239
Lambert, Wallace E., 253
Lange-Eichbaum, W., 4, 50
Langer, W. C., 191
Laor, Eran, 40
lateral testing, 8
lateralisatio praecox, 253
lateralization, 14, 18-19, 161, 207,
   209, 242, 251-261, 273
   "and its discontents", 209, 256
Lautrec, Toulouse, 141
left hemispheric potential, 35
   tyranny of, 86, 231
left-lookers, 212, 214, 265
Leibnitz, Gottfried W., 40
Leo X, Pope, 66
Leonore Overture, 260
Les Demoiselles D'Avignon, 135,
   143
leverage effect, the, 229, 230, 261
Levine, David, 85, 87
Levy, Jerre, 200, 251
lifecycle, 207, 211
limbic lobe, 86
Linksz, Arthur, 213, 252, 253
Lippman, E., 142
lobotomy, 197
Lodovico il Moro, 58, 60, 66
logic, symbolic, 40
Lomazzo, Gian Paolo, 62
Lombroso, Cesare, 4, 50
Lorenzo il Magnifico, 66
Louis XIV, 182
Lowenfeld, W., 208
LSD, 52, 139, 221
Luquet, G. H., 208
Luria, A. R., 8, 251
Luther, Martin, 24

Maclean, P. D., 14, 188, 222
   reptilian brain of, 86, 259
Madariaga, S., 176, 179
madness, 43-47, 218

Magritte, Rene, 1, 55
Malinowski, Bronislaw, 196
mandalas, 99, 220
Mann, Thomas, 80
Marcuse, Herbert, 246, 249
Marek, G. R., 26, 31, 33
Margenau, Henry, 128
Maric, Mileva, 129
Marinoni, Augusto, 56, 58
marital therapy, 232
Martini, Monsignor, 110
Marx, Karl, 16, 249, 275
Maslow, Abraham, 223
Masserman, Jules, 224
Mathias, King of Hungary, 57
Maxwell-Faraday, equations of,
   275
Mayan society, 181
McCurdy, B., 56, 64
McLuhan, Marshall, 144, 209
Meir, Golda, 161
Melzi, Giovanni, 63, 66
Menninger, Karl, 224, 228
mental dissociation, 163
Messianic syndrome, 257
Mesulam, M. M., 8, 165
Metamorphosis, The, 152
metaphor, 12, 40, 41
metapsychology, 73, 83
Meyer, Konrad Ferdinand, 119
Meyer, Robert, 73
Michelangelo, 61, 79, 144, 223,
   235
Michelet, Jules, 216
Middle Ages, the, 4, 218, 258
Milton, John, 25, 6
Miro, Joan, 143, 208
Moebius, Paul, 4
Mohammed, 36, 172
Mona Lisa, 64
Monet, Claude, 141
Monod, Jacques, 275
Montague, Ashley, 246
Montezuma, 180-188, 189, 235

Morrison, Philip, 223
Moses, 275
Moss, Edward, 252
movement, 212
Mozart, Leopold, 26, 103-108
    sharing, pattern of, 104
    and symbiotic tie with son, 106
Mozart, Wolfgang Amadeus, 26,
    102-106, 134, 157, 205, 209,
    235, 243, 244, 264
Muir, Edwin, 154
Murphy, Patricia, 171
music therapy, 250
Mussolini, Benito, 191
mutation, 244
mysticism, 73

Naipaul, V. S., 222
Napolean, 29, 36, 177, 189, 190
Neill, A. S., 246, 249, 256
neuroanalysis, 240
neurosis
    overdetermined models of, 234
    structurally and dynamically
    determined models of, 234
neurotic contagion, 135, 136
neurotransmitters, 19
Newton, Isaac, 69, 117, 122, 123,
    124, 126
Nietzsche, Friedrich, 4, 36-53,
    60, 61, 72, 75, 119, 150, 157,
    171, 195, 204, 207, 235, 244,
    256, 258
    as Dionysos, 45
    general paresis of the insane, of
    44, 50
    madness, "inoculated with"
    43, 45, 47
    manic phase of, 45
    oracular propensities of, 47
    secondary personalities of, 49
    Zarathustra as double of, 49
nihilism, European, 41

Nijinsky, 246
Nixon, Richard M., 111, 206, 222
non-Euclidean geometries, 220
Nurenberg rallies, the, 196

Obler, Laurain, 253
"oceanic feeling", 73, 80, 83
Olmec society, 181
omens, 183
Oppenheimer, J. Robert, 125, 126
opposites, reconciliation of the,
    100, 160, 222
Ornstein, Robert, 9, 10, 207, 212,
    238
Ortega y Gasset, Jose, 47
Ostwald, Wilhelm, 204
Ouija board, the, 171
Ouvani, 163, 169, 176
Ovid, 256
Oxford Allegory, the, 64, 67

Pacioli, Luca, 56
Pagels, Elaine, 255
Pain and Pleasure, 64, 67
Pais, Abraham, 121, 126
Papageno, 115
Papini, Giovanni, 145
paranoiac, 192
paranormal information, 11
parapsychologists, 127, 157
    observations of, 239
parapsychology, 78, 270
Parnes, S. I., 249
participation mystique, 90
Pauli, Wolfgang, 91, 128
Payne, Robert, 63
pendulum swings, right versus left
    hemispheres of, 224
Penfield, Walter, 15
Penrose, R., 136
Pentateuch, 255
Perils of the Soul, 97

Pharisees, 257
Phidias, 62
Philemon, 98
phylactery, the, 83, 84
Piaget, Jean, 207
Picasso, Pablo, 106, 131-148, 171, 208, 213, 236, 275
  ambivalence of, 146
  body image of, 136, 138
  castration anxiety of, 146
  personalities, multiple, 140-142
  Rose, Blue, Cubist, and "African" periods of, 131
Piero, Ser, 62, 66
Plato, 16, 259
  "divine madness of", 53
  fable of the Charioteer, of, 241, 259, 273
Plesch, Janos, 119
Podach, Erich, 50
poetry therapy, 250
Pollock, Jackson, 147
Polonius, 105
"poltergeist", 94
polyglot, 252
Popper, Karl, 5, 51, 82, 89, 188, 241, 268
positron emission tomography, 211
Postman, N., 209
power, quest for, 39
precognition, 10, 157, 193
precognitive hunches, 53
preconscious, the Freudian, 268
Preiswerk, Helene, 92
premonitions, 43
  self-fulfilling, 159
Prescott, W. H., 175, 176, 182
Pribram, Karl, 6, 74, 218, 259
primary integration, 210
primary processes, 217
Progoff, Ira, 162, 163, 165, 170
programs, 5, 242
  linguistic, 252
Prometheus, 241, 245, 259, 275

prophecy, 193
prosody, 7, 9, 196
proto-cybernetics, 74
protolietrate period, the, 256
Proust, Marcel, 152
psi factor, 186
psi phenomena, 10, 128, 157, 169, 270, 271
  need-determined type, 239
psychical research, 78, 162
psychics, 171, 192, 243
psychoanalysis, 39, 72, 73
psychokinesis, 10, 94
psylocibin, 52
Puccini, Giacomo, 148
Puertocarrero, 179
Putnam, F., 237

Quantum Theory, 125-128
Quetzalcoatl, 176, 184, 185, 245

Rank, Otto, 4, 24, 80
Raphael, 208
Raro, 141
Rauschning, H., 193
Ravel, Maurice, 8
Reagan, Ronald, 206, 222
Reich, Charles, 249
Reich, Wilhelm, 246, 249
Rembrandt, 142
  tion, 226
right-lookers, 212, 214, 265
Reti, Ladislao, 60
reticular formation, 86
Reynal, Maurice, 136
Rhine, J. B., 92, 127, 128, 169, 270
Ribera, Diego, 141
right hemisphere, 51, 77
  dominance of, 32
  versus left hemispheric orientation, 226
right-lookers, 212, 214, 265

Rilke, Rainer Maria, 36
Roehm, 195
Rolland, Romain, 73, 80, 81
Ron D., case of, 225, 229
Rosen, C., 111
Ross, E. D., 8, 156, 165, 211, 272
Rossman, Michael, 249
Roszak, Theodore, 207, 249
Rothenberg, A., 111, 123, 124, 252
Rousseau, Jean Jacques, 245, 254, 256
Royal Touch, the, 79
Ruiz, Don Jose, 132, 133, 141
Russel, Lord John, 31

Sabartes, Jaime, 133, 140, 142
Saint Theresa of Avila, 161, 173
Salieri, Antonio, 108
Salome, 98
Samsa, Gregor, 154, 156
Sand, George, 161
Santillana, George, 56
Sapir, Edward, 253
Sartre, Jean Paul, 154
Schaffer, Peter, 113
Schenk, Laura, 67
schizophrenia, paranoid, 218
schizophrenics, 77, 219
Schnitzler, Arthur, 80
Schoenberg, Arnold, 111, 143, 147, 275
Schroedinger, Erwin, 120
Schumann, Robert, 141, 142
Schupanizigh, 32
secondary integration, 210
self-conscious mind, the, 82, 89
self-fulfilling prophecy, 47
sensation, 212
shadow, 12, 98
Shakespeare, 80, 232, 233, 234, 235, 244, 274, 275
shaman, 192, 196
Shapiro, Meyer, 54, 63

Shaw, Bernard, 183
Sheldon, 204
Siegfried, 98
Sinclair, Upton, 127, 128
sinistraversion, 111, 203-215, 270
Slochower, Harry, 151
Snow, C. P., 125, 223
Solomon, Maynard, 24, 27, 28
Sophocles, 80
Soustelle, Jacques, 176
Speer, Albert, 194
Spencer, Robert, 72
Spengler, Oswald, 216
spermatorrhea, 63
Sperry, R. W., 7, 18, 34, 211, 251
Spielrein, Sabine, 95
Spinoza, Baruch, 41, 50
Stalin, Joseph, 198, 199
   and Hitler, 199
Stein, Gertrude, 144
Steiner, Rudolf, 157
Sterba, E. and R., 24, 25, 28, 30
Sterlin, Helm, 195
Sterlin, Joseph, 191
Stern, M., 81, 119
sublimation, 35, 39, 269
   in reverse, 109, 269
Sufism, 77
Sullivan, J. W. N., 30
Summerhill, 246, 249
superego, 83, 86
   commands of, 84
   controls of, 77
   Freudian, 148, 269
Superman, 39, 41, 50
Swann, Ingo, 243
Sybil, 236

tachystoscopic stimuli, 211
Tahoteh, 164, 171
Taoist philosophies, 210
Teddy U., case of, 227, 229

telepathic messages, 79
telepathic response, 91
telepathy, 10, 157, 168, 193, 239
Thanatos, 39
Thayer, 26
Thousand Year Reich, the, 197
Three Faces of Eve, 236
three I's, 14, 18, 121, 197, 226, 232, 273
   processing of, 236
three R's, 14, 18, 172, 181, 209, 226, 232, 273
Titian, 144
Toffler, Alvin, 144
Torrance, E. P., 249
Toynbee, A. J., 175
trance states, 163
transcendental meditation, 221
Treblinka, 197
Trial, The, 153
Trismegistus, Hermes, 245
triune brain, the, 14, 222
truth, intuitive, 53
Twain, Mark, 247
"twilight learning", 238, 249

Unamuno, Miguel de, 245
unconscious, the, 73, 85
Unger, Max, 32
Untergang, 45, 51

Vaihinger, 41
Vaillant, G. C., 175, 176
Valery, Paul, 54
Van Gogh, Vincent, 141, 142
Vasari, Giorgio, 61
Velasquez, Diego, 141
Verrochio, Andrea, 56, 62, 63, 64, 65, 66

Vesalius, 60
Vico, Giambattista, 216, 217
Virtue and Envy, 67
von Ertmann, Dorothea, 27

Wada test, 6
Wagner, Cosima, 49, 51
Wagner, Elisabeth, 49
Wagner, Richard, 49, 53
Watts, Allan, 207
Weber, Aloysia, 106
Weber, Constance, 106
Weber, Frau Cecilia, 106, 115
Weingarten, C., 209
Weltschmerz, 233
Wernicke, Carl, 6, 7, 9, 197
Wertheimer, Max, 123
Whitman, Walt, 157
Whorf, B. L., 253
Wigner, E. P., 128
Wise Old Man Elijah, 98
Wittels, Fritz, 70
Worth, Patience, 132

Yezer-Ha-ra, 12, 155
Yezer-Tov, 12, 155
Yin and Yang, 207
Young, J. Z., 5, 242

Zaidel, E., 211
Zarathustra, xii, xv, 40, 41-43, 48, 49, 75, 244
Zen, 77, 221, 223
Zener cards, 128
Zionism, 123
Zoroaster, 245